# Great Rescues *of*
# WORLD WAR II

Thomas J. Craughwell

# Great Rescues *of* WORLD WAR II

## STORIES OF ADVENTURE, DARING AND SACRIFICE

PIER 9

# CONTENTS

## Part 2: THE WAR IN ASIA AND THE PACIFIC

# Introduction

No war in human history has taken more lives than World War II. The numbers are staggering: in total, 72 million dead. In the Soviet Union 23 million died, perhaps as many as 10 million perished in China, nearly 6 million in Poland, more than 7 million in Nazi Germany, and 2.7 million in Japan. And then there were the Nazi concentration camps where 6 million Jews and 8 million Gentiles were murdered. As for the Pacific theatre, we will never have an accurate count of how many prisoners of war died during forced marches or in Japan's POW camps, but the number must be in the tens of thousands.

The point of reviewing this tragic record is to put into perspective the heroism of the rescuers—those who saved people who would otherwise have swelled those dreadful numbers further. In a time of inhumane cruelty carried out on an epic scale, these men and women risked their lives—and sometimes sacrificed their lives—to save the lives of others. And bear in mind that most of the people the rescuers saved were complete strangers.

Almost everyone knows the stories of Oskar Schindler, the German industrialist who protected more than a thousand Jews who worked as forced labour in his factory, and Raoul Wallenberg, the Swedish diplomat who rescued perhaps as many as 50,000 Hungarian Jews from deportation to Nazi death camps. But there were countless others who saved lives—Serbian shepherds, Danish clerks, Chinese fishermen, French schoolteachers, Filipino farmers, Italian nuns, even headhunters in the jungles of Borneo. In most cases the names of these heroes have been lost or forgotten, but some of their stories have survived. In this volume we have collected twenty-two stories of men and women, some of them members of the armed forces, others ordinary civilians, who demonstrated not only great personal courage but also tremendous resourcefulness in order to rescue downed Allied flyers, or get Jewish children to safety, or in a few extraordinary cases liberate entire camps of POWs.

Lucie Aubrac, for example, taught geography at a girls' school in the French town of Clermont-Ferrand. After the Nazis occupied France, Lucie and her husband Raymond joined the Resistance. When the Nazis arrested Raymond, Lucie, who was six months' pregnant with their second child, planned a daring raid to free her husband from a Gestapo prison.

Then there is the incredible story of the people of Denmark, who rose up almost unanimously to help their Jewish neighbours escape the Nazis and reach safety in neutral Sweden.

In the war's Pacific theatre we learn of Chinese fishermen who saved sixty-four men of the Doolittle Raiders, and Filipino farmers who sheltered American missionary families deep in the jungle.

Especially fascinating are the stories of two diplomats—Chiune Sugihara, Japan's consul in Lithuania, and Aristides de Sousa Mendes, Portugal's consul in Bordeaux—who issued tens of thousands of visas to terrified Jewish refugees so they could travel out of Europe to some neutral country. Then there is Giorgio Perlasca, an Italian businessman who masqueraded as a Spanish diplomat and passed out thousands of safe-conducts and other protective documents to Hungarian Jews, sometimes actually pulling individuals or families out of the cattle cars that were about to carry them to the death camps.

Some readers may be surprised to see Pope Pius XII listed here among the rescuers. For forty years there has been a fierce debate regarding the pope's actions during World War II; today it is generally accepted as 'common knowledge' that Pope Pius XII did not speak out against the Nazis and did nothing to help the Jews. Yet by going back to original sources—particularly to Jewish sources—we find that the pope was outspoken in condemning the Nazis (and was cheered for doing so by the United Jewish Appeal for Refugees and Overseas Needs in Chicago, by Rome's Chief Rabbi, Israel Zolli, and by the editorial board of the *New York Times*). More importantly, Pope Pius, working with the priests, monks and nuns of Rome, saved the lives of more than 7000 Italian Jews by hiding them in monasteries, convents, church attics and basements, even in the Vatican and his summer residence, Castel Gandolfo.

By telling these stories we pay homage to the men and women in uniform as well as to the men and women civilians who, when confronted with almost unimaginable evil, found the courage to risk their own lives in order to save the lives of others. They deserve to be remembered.

# THE WAR
## IN EUROPE

# CHAPTER 1

# KINDERTRANSPORT
## Into the Arms of Strangers

///////////////////////////////////////////////////////////////

They were nearly safe. Following standard procedure, the customs officials would pass through the cars, then the train would roll on from the German town of Bentheim across the border into Holland. Once in Dutch territory, the children would be beyond the reach of the Nazis. The date was 1 December 1938; the children were 196 Jewish orphans whose orphanage in Berlin had been burned by a Nazi mob just three weeks earlier during Kristallnacht (the Night of Broken Glass). Since the orphans were the very first Kindertransport children to leave Nazi Germany for safety in Great Britain, neither the German and English organisers, nor their assistants at the port at the Hook of Holland, who would help the children transfer from the train to the boat that would carry them across the English Channel, knew what to expect on the trip.

Eight-year-old Josepha Salmon arrived at Harwich on 2 December 1938 in the first group of Kindertransport refugees to be sent to safety in England.

When the train rolled to a stop at the Bentheim railway station, it was not customs officials who boarded it but members of the *Schutzstaffel* (German for 'Protective Squadron'), more commonly known as the SS. Norbert Wollheim, twenty-five years old, a German Jew who had organised the transfer of children from Berlin, was accompanying this first train as an escort. Years later he recalled what happened at the German–Dutch border:

> [*The SS*] *got on the coaches and they behaved like animals—actually, to say that is an insult to the animal world. They did not attack the children, but they tore into the luggage. Even if you had some toothpaste, they tried to open it, looking for jewels and for foreign currency and things like that.*

As the SS men pawed through carefully packed clothes and toys, the children wept and shrieked in terror. The SS did not find any contraband among the orphans' possessions, but they took so long examining every item in every suitcase and knapsack that the railway company eventually insisted that the two cars containing the children be uncoupled from the rest of the train to allow the other passengers to make their connection with the ferry.

When the train arrived in Holland without the children, the women of the Dutch committee who were expecting them became anxious. Truus Wijsmuller-Meijer hurried to Bentheim, where she found the railway cars on a side track, filled with weeping children and the brutal SS guards. 'What's going on?' she demanded.

Sneering, the men replied, 'We are doing our duty.'

'You're not doing your duty,' Wijsmuller-Meijer shot back, 'you are behaving very badly.'

Truus Wijsmuller-Meijer's courage, combined with her authoritative and commanding tone, abruptly silenced the SS men. They immediately stopped vandalising the children's belongings and left the train. Another train bound for the ferry port arrived soon after, the two cars were coupled to it, and the children gladly caught the ferry to Harwich in England, disembarking on the morning of 2 December 1938.

Passers-by glance casually at the shattered storefronts of Jewish businesses
vandalised by Nazi mobs on Kristallnacht, the night of 9–10 November 1938.

# People without a future

There have been Jews in Germany since the days of the Roman Empire, but they did not enjoy full citizenship, with all the rights of their Gentile neighbours, until 1870. As the ghetto walls fell and they entered fully into every facet of public life, many newly liberated Jews began to identify themselves as German first and Jewish second. Anti-Semitism still ran strong in places, but by and large German Jews assimilated easily into the larger society.

Then, in 1933, Adolf Hitler and the Nazi Party rose to power. Hitler's anti-Semitic rhetoric was frightening, but many Jews tried to dismiss it as an aberration. When new legislation barred them from government jobs, from schools, and eventually from commerce and even cultural life, many began to fear that perhaps Hitler and the Nazis were not a passing phase but a genuine threat. Many of those who tried to emigrate as anti-Semitism escalated found that most countries enforced a quota system that admitted only a limited number of Jewish immigrants every year. Even if a Jewish family found a country that would admit them, the Nazis had passed a law which forbade them taking with them currency, jewellery or other valuables, thus guaranteeing they would arrive in their new homes penniless. The Jews of Germany, and then of Austria and Czechoslovakia, when those two countries came under Nazi control, were trapped, and the outside world was doing very little to help them.

Between Hitler's 1933 rise to power, and 1938, the British government had admitted only 11,000 German Jewish refugees, but Kristallnacht proved a catalyst for change. Kristallnacht was a government-organised, nationwide pogrom designed to terrorise the Jews of Germany and Austria. On the night of 9–10 November 1938, Nazi mobs rampaged through cities and towns, screaming for Jewish blood. By sunrise the rioters had killed at least 100 Jews, injured thousands more, rounded up 30,000 men and shipped them off to concentration camps, burned a thousand synagogues and religious, community and charitable institutions, and wrecked tens of thousands of homes, shops and businesses, leaving the smashed windows of ruined businesses all over the streets (hence the name 'Crystal Night'). Kristallnacht was the Nazis' clearest statement to their own citizens and to the world that the Jews had no future in the Third Reich.

Five days after Kristallnacht, some of the most prominent Jewish men in Britain met with Prime Minister Neville Chamberlain to urge him to admit more Jewish refugees into Great Britain, or at least permit children and teenagers to immigrate on a temporary basis. Among the delegation were the former High Commissioner of Palestine, Herbert Viscount Samuel; Walter Samuel, Lord Bearsted, the Chairman of Shell Transport & Trading Company; Dr J.H. Hertz, Chief Rabbi of the British Empire; and Dr Chaim Weizmann, a leader of the Zionist movement and the future first president of Israel. After this meeting the Home Office agreed to admit more Jewish immigrants, and between November 1938 and the start of World War II in September 1939 approximately 44,000 Jews from Germany, Austria and Czechoslovakia arrived in the United Kingdom. A special program was also created to rescue Jewish children and house them with British families until the situation in their homelands had altered and they could return safely to their own families.

In an appeal to Parliament, Foreign Minister Samuel Hoare said, 'Here is a chance of taking the young generation of a great people, here is a chance of mitigating to some extent the terrible suffering of their parents and their friends.' And in a radio address, former prime minister Stanley Lord Baldwin stirred the conscience of the British people, saying, 'I ask you to come to the aid of victims not of any catastrophe in the natural world, not of earthquake nor of flood nor of famine, but of the explosion of man's inhumanity to man.'

## Working around the clock

The response of the British government and the British people to the crisis was astonishing. Within days Parliament voted to accept the refugee children, but insisted that every child upon arrival must be ensured a home, either with a family, in an orphanage or in some other form of group housing. Furthermore, £50 must be set aside for each child to pay for his or her travel expenses back to their homeland once the Nazi crisis was over. On 25 November, the BBC Home Service gave Viscount Samuel air time, during which he called upon British families to open their homes to the refugee children. Samuel's appeal resulted in more than 500 offers.

Great Rescues of World War II

The first group of Kindertransport children smile and wave as their ferry arrives at the English port of Harwich.

To be candid, the screening of potential foster families was cursory at best, rarely requiring more than a clean house and a family that looked respectable. Infinitely more critical to the British organisers was getting the children out of Germany, Austria and Czechoslovakia quickly. Acting as the representative of

## What became of them?

After Jack Hellman's mother and father arrived in England in 1939, they placed their names on a waiting list to migrate to the United States. Permission to migrate came in 1941, and the family left Baron de Rothschild's estate for New York City. In 2000, Jack appeared in the documentary film, *Into the Arms of Strangers: Stories of the Kindertransport*, which won an Academy Award for Best Documentary.

Vera and Eva Diamant have both published books about their Kindertransport and wartime experiences in England. Vera's book is entitled *Pearls of Childhood*, and Eva's is called *By the Moon and the Stars*. Although the Nazis killed their mother and father and almost all of their family, after the war Vera returned to Prague to help set up house for her one surviving aunt. In 1949, she returned to England. Eva settled in New Zealand. The sisters also participated in *Into the Arms of Strangers*.

Norbert Wollheim continued his work as an escort, assisting many children to make the journey to England. But he was not able to escape Nazi Germany himself. In 1943, the Nazis deported Wollheim, his wife and their three-year-old son to Auschwitz. His wife and child, along with sixty-eight of his relatives, were killed in the Holocaust; he alone survived. Norbert Wollheim died in 1998, aged eighty-five.

Throughout the war Truus Wijsmuller-Meijer helped Jews and others who were being hunted by the Nazis to escape. After the war she devoted herself to working with people with disabilities, especially to finding jobs for the disabled. The Dutch government awarded Wijsmuller-Meijer an Officier in de Orde van Oranje-Nassau and made her an Honorary Citizen of Amsterdam, and the French government presented her with the Médaille de la Reconnaissance. Truus Wijsmuller-Meijer died in 1978, aged eighty-two.

For many years after the war, Nicholas Winton's work with the Kindertransport was forgotten, but he has at last been honoured for the efforts that saved the lives of 664 Czech children. In 1998, Vaclav Havel, President of the Czech Republic, decorated Winton with the Order of T.G. Marsaryk, and in 2002 he received a knighthood from Queen Elizabeth II. In 2008, the Czech government nominated Nicholas Winton for the Nobel Peace Prize.

several Jewish refugee agencies in Britain, Norman Bentwich travelled to Berlin, where he and the leaders of the Jewish community recruited volunteers and established a network to ease the process of transporting the children out of the country. At the top of the list were children and teenagers especially at risk: teenagers already incarcerated in concentration camps; young Poles in danger of being deported; children whose parents were already in concentration camps, or whose parents had become impoverished; and the children in Jewish orphanages.

Working around the clock, volunteers compiled lists of children, collected the necessary travel documents, advised parents what the children should take with them, and assigned each child a date of departure. The first train carrying refugee children rolled out of the Berlin railway station on 1 December; on 10 December another train left from Vienna.

To prepare for the coming flood of young people, several Jewish organisations pooled their resources and expertise with Christian charities, the Quakers, and the non-denominational Christian relief organisation, Inter-Aid, to ease the migration process; this coalition of charitable organisations called themselves the Movement for the Care of Children from Germany. Later they would rename themselves the Refugee Children's Movement, or RCM.

## 'When Jewish blood flows off the knife'

It was a fine day in March 1939, and the broad green lawn outside The Cedars was perfect for a soccer game. Within minutes of their arrival at their new home, twenty-six refugee boys were kicking a ball back and forth across the grass. A group of English boys walked over from the village and joined the game, and all played happily until it was time for dinner. As the Jewish boys headed towards the house, the English boys waved goodbye, and one called out, 'We'll see you tomorrow!' Twelve-year-old Jack Hellman ran to his housemother and exclaimed, 'Someone who's not Jewish wants to see us tomorrow!'

Jack (Hans Joachim was his German name) and his devoutly religious parents lived in Tann, a village of about 1500 people in eastern Germany. Hellman's father and mother operated a prosperous general store; most of young Jack's friends were Christians. But after Hitler came to power, Tann became a very frightening place for Jews. Lying in bed at night, Jack saw the weird shadows cast by the torchlight processions passing beneath his window, and he heard his neighbours, people who he had known all his life, singing, 'When Jewish blood flows off the knife, we feel twice as good.'

At school Jack's teacher, a fervent Nazi, beat the Jewish children mercilessly. Gentile boys and girls he had played with would no longer even speak to him. Then one day, six or seven teenage boys attacked him on the street. Screaming 'Jew bastard!', they threw him through a plate glass window. Jack's cuts were so severe he had to be hospitalised. He was only nine years old. To protect him from further attacks, Jack's parents sent him to live in a Jewish children's home in Frankfurt.

On Kristallnacht, Jack's home in Tann and his parents' store were ruined; the Nazis arrested his father and sent him to Buchenwald concentration camp. In Frankfurt, a Nazi mob shattered the windows at the children's home before breaking in and arresting every male between the ages of sixteen and sixty-five.

In the days that followed, Jack's housemother at the school wrote to Baron James de Rothschild, of the British branch of the immensely wealthy international banking family, asking if he would accept as part of the Kindertransport twenty-six boys from her school, her two daughters, herself and her husband. In January 1939 the baron wrote back that he would sponsor them all, and on 16 March Jack was among the large party from the Frankfurt school that travelled to safety in England.

Baron and Baroness de Rothschild housed the refugees on their own estate in a large and very beautiful brick house known as The Cedars. The Rothschilds were very kind to the refugees, so much so that Jack felt sufficiently at ease to ask the baron for a great favour: would he file the necessary papers so Jack's parents could come to England to work at the Rothschild estate? The baron agreed, and Jack's parents arrived in England on 1 September 1939, the day Hitler invaded Poland and World War II began. The family remained on the Rothschild estate until they received permission to migrate to the United States two years later. Years later Jack said, 'Those years in England were the happiest of my youth ... My parents, too, I never saw them as happy in the United States as they were those two years in England.'

# Troubles

While 90 to 95 per cent of the refugee children were Jewish, the Kindertransport also rescued children whose parents were Communists, or political opponents of the Nazis, or had in some other way antagonised Hitler. Settling the Jewish children, however, could be difficult. The people of the British Isles were overwhelmingly Christian, and the Jewish community in the 1930s was very small, numbering about 350,000. The largest concentration was in London, home to approximately 180,000 Jews; there were other large communities in Manchester and Leeds. Many refugee children were settled with Jewish families, but about one-third were not.

Nicholas Winton, a twenty-nine-year-old London stockbroker who was especially active in bringing children from Czechoslovakia to England, stated plainly that his interest was saving as many young lives as possible—the religious issue did not trouble him nor was it an issue on his mind at the time. It bothered some others, however—the Barbican Mission, for example, which offered to take a large group of refugee children, had its own agenda. 'I had no clue at the time that that particular organisation was there for converting Jews to Christianity,' Winton said. 'All they did was come to me and say, "We'll take so many children". I said, "Marvellous".'

The Orthodox Jewish community was especially upset that Orthodox children were not being placed exclusively in the homes of religiously observant Jews. Rabbi Solomon Schoenfeld took it upon himself to bring a thousand Orthodox children to England and find homes for them where their religious life would be fostered in an appropriate fashion; Chief Rabbi Hertz installed kosher kitchens in the holiday campgrounds that had been transformed into group homes for many others.

The concerns of the Orthodox were not unfounded. Some very young children were given new names by their foster families and raised as Christians. And there were other problems, particularly for teenage boys or girls, some of whose foster families used them as servants. Yet in the overwhelming majority of cases the children were welcomed and well cared for and kept their Jewish faith.

## 'You shall be loved'

Eleven-year-old Vera Diamant sat all alone on a wooden bench in a large empty hall at London's Liverpool Street station. Beside her were her suitcase and her knapsack; around her neck hung the tag with her identification number. All day long the refugee children from Czechoslovakia had sat in the waiting room as, one by one, their names were called and they went off with their foster family, or caught a train to a boarding school, as was the case with Vera's fifteen-year-old sister, Eva. After Eva and all the other children had gone, Vera 'was filled with incredible panic'. In an interview many years later she said, 'You can imagine: I had no address, no knowledge of English. I was so frightened what would become of me.' She wondered if perhaps her foster family had changed their minds and decided not to take her. Finally, the leader of the transport came to the little girl and explained that her foster family would be delayed for a few days, but the Kindertransport people would take care of her.

Two days later her foster mother arrived. She was a little woman, barely taller than Vera; her hat was askew, her coat was misbuttoned, but she had, as Vera put it, 'the most wonderful smile'. The woman ran to Vera, embraced her, and said, 'You shall be loved.' The woman's name was Mrs Rainford, and she and her family did love Vera, and Vera loved them in return.

In August 1939, Vera and Eva learned that two of their cousins, boys about their age, were scheduled to come to England on a transport from Czechoslovakia. They were part of a group of 250 children, the largest ever scheduled to be brought out of the country. But on 3 September, after the children had been settled in the railway coaches, word came that the train would not depart for Holland. Germany had declared war on Poland two days earlier, and the Nazis refused to permit any more trains bearing refugee children to pass through German territory. The children were taken to a concentration camp. None of them, including Vera and Eva's cousins, survived the war. Neither did the girls' mother and father.

Over a period of nine months in 1938 and 1939, approximately 10,000 Jewish and other refugee children from Germany, Austria and Czechoslovakia, and a few from Poland, found safety in Great Britain. They ranged in age from teenagers down to infants carried by their older brothers or sisters. In most cases the children never returned to their homelands because their parents were murdered in the Holocaust.

Approximately 1.5 million children fell victim to the Nazis; compared with such a number, the 10,000 saved in the Kindertransport program seems very small. Yet the Talmud teaches, 'Whoever saves a life, it is considered as if he saved an entire world.'

# CHAPTER 2

# 'THE NAVY'S HERE!'
## The Rescue of the Prisoners Aboard the *Altmark*

A British seaman pounded on the steel door of the *Altmark*, the enemy vessel in which he and his comrades were imprisoned, until a German sailor opened it and stuck his head in.

'Are you sinking our ship?' the Briton asked. The German answered with a shrug of his shoulders. 'May we go up on deck?' the seaman asked. Without saying a word the German closed and locked the door, but he returned a few moments later, threw the door wide open, and motioned for the British seamen to go up on deck.

It was night, but they could see their ship, the *Newton Beach*, a few hundred metres away. As they crowded against the rails there was a tremendous explosion, and flames erupted from the *Newton Beach*. Very quickly the ship began to sink beneath the waves. In ten minutes, it was gone. And the men, some of them teary-eyed, turned away from the railing to return to their prison below deck.

Jubilant British merchant seamen on the deck of the destroyer HMS *Cossack* after their release from imprisonment aboard the German supply ship *Altmark*.

'The Navy's here!'

## Deadly for the enemy

On 3 September 1939, two days after the forces of the Third Reich had swarmed into Poland and the day France and the British Empire declared war on Germany, Captain Heinrich Dau received a wire bearing his new orders. Henceforth the *Altmark*, the merchant tanker under his command, would be a supply ship attending the pocket-battleship *Admiral Graf Spee* as it prowled the sea lanes, hunting British and French ships to plunder and destroy. Dau was exultant as he informed his crew that they would help the *Graf Spee* 'make the high seas dangerous, uncertain, nay, deadly, for the enemy'. Allied merchant ships were to be the *Graf Spee*'s particular target.

The *Altmark* was a spacious ship, 178 metres (584 feet) long, 22 metres (72 feet) wide, capable of carrying 12,700 tonnes (14,000 tons) of cargo. Dau imagined he would transport food and diesel fuel for the *Graf Spee*, and most exciting of all, ammunition to destroy the enemies of the Third Reich. Equipped with four 9-cylinder Motorenwerke Augsburg Nürnberg (MAN) diesel engines, the *Altmark* could travel at a top speed of 21 knots per hour—reasonably fast for a ship her size.

The *Graf Spee*, the small but deadly battleship the *Altmark* would serve, was heavily armed with thirty-eight guns, eight torpedo tubes, and two Arado 196 seaplanes. The *Graf Spee* was 186 metres (610 feet) long, nearly 22 metres (72 feet) across, was propelled by eight 9-cylinder MAN diesel engines, and manned by a crew of more than 1100 men. Its captain, Hans Wilhelm Langsdorff, forty-three years old, was a gentleman who always followed his orders, but also brought a sense of compassion and generosity to the fulfilment of his duty.

## A series of surprises

The *Graf Spee* found its first victim 110 kilometres (68 miles) north-east of Recife in Brazil, on 30 September; it was the 4582 tonne (5051 ton) British tanker *Clement*, bound for Cape Town in South Africa, with a cargo of kerosene. At the sight of the German battleship, Captain Harris of the *Clement* ordered his men into lifeboats with instructions to row for the coast of Brazil; the captain remained on board with the chief engineer, Mr W. Bryant. As the crew made their escape, Harris shoved his codebook, confidential documents and a heavy weight into a cloth bag. Tying the mouth shut, he threw the weighted bag overboard.

Meanwhile, Langsdorff ordered his gunners to fire a warning shot over the *Clement*'s bow while the signalman sent Harris the message, 'Absolute radio silence! Not a sound or we shall sink you without further warning! Absolute radio silence!' But Harris had already sent off an SOS to the British Admiralty, along with a quick description of the German battleship.

As the three lifeboats carrying the forty-five crewmen of the *Clement* pulled away, a lifeboat from the *Graf Spee* pulled alongside the tanker and the prize crew climbed aboard. The German officer in charge declared that Harris and Bryant were prisoners of war, and commanded them to enter his boat. The two British officers put up no resistance. On the *Graf Spee* they were taken to Captain Langsdorff, who inquired of Captain Harris if he had sent a radio message. Harris admitted that he had.

'You have defied my orders?' Langsdorff asked.

'Indeed I have,' Harris replied.

Langsdorff shrugged his shoulders. 'I should have done the same thing.' Then he said that he would not go after the lifeboats bearing the *Clement*'s crew, nor would he order them fired upon.

Then came the surprise—Langsdorff wired the authorities in Pernambuco in Brazil that three lifeboats carrying British seamen were en route for the port, urging the Brazilians to help the shipwrecked men. Harris and Bryant expected they were on their way to a German POW camp, but later that day, when the *Graf Spee* encountered the *Papalemos*, a Greek merchant ship, Langsdorff sent a signal to its captain, ordering him to stop and take on two British officers. The Greek captain, in near panic over this encounter, replied, 'This isn't our war! We're neutral!' Langsdorff answered, 'You'll take them or I'll sink you, neutral or not.' That was enough to convince the Greek captain that discretion was the better part of valour; the *Papalemos* took the Britons on board.

Langsdorff's final duty was to sink the *Clement*. He sent a team of sappers to mine the abandoned ship, but none of the detonators worked. Irritated, he called for a torpedo to be fired at the *Clement* amidships. It blasted from its tube, cut through the water and struck the tanker—but nothing happened. Langsdorff could barely control his rage as his torpedo officer leaned in to whisper, 'Ignition failure.' Now the captain called for his gunners to sink the *Clement*. The 11-inch (279-mm) gun smashed an enormous hole in the *Clement*'s side, and the 8-inch (203-mm) guns opened up a few more—but the holes were all above the waterline; it was as if the ship had a will of its own, that it refused on principle to sink. But then a large plume of dense black smoke rose up—one of the *Graf Spee*'s shells had struck the cargo compartment, igniting the kerosene. The fire accomplished what mines, a torpedo and mortar shells had failed to do, and sank the *Clement*.

## The game changes

After the destruction of the *Clement*, between 30 September and 9 December the *Graf Spee* captured and sank seven more British merchant ships: the *Newton Beach*, carrying a cargo of corn; the *Ashlea*, carrying raw sugar; the *Huntsman*, carrying tea; the *Trevanion*, with a cargo of ore concentrates; the *Africa Shell*, which had no cargo; the *Doric Star*, which was laden with meat, dairy products and wool; and the *Tairoa*, which carried meat, wool and lead.

The generous treatment Captain Langsdorff had accorded the officers and men of the *Clement* was not extended to the crews of the other captured vessels. The message Captain Harris had been able to transmit before the German boarding party reached his ship had been passed along to the British Admiralty, and the Royal Navy had sent out hunting parties of battleships, cruisers, even aircraft carriers, all keen to find the trail of the *Graf Spee*. From Captain Langsdorff's perspective that altered the game; in the future, all British seamen he captured would be regarded as prisoners of war and transported back to Germany.

The sinking of the British merchant ships went against Langsdorff's instincts; he would have preferred to bring them back to Germany as prizes, but he could not take the time to escort them to the port at Hamburg, nor could he send them back with a German crew. The British ships did not have enough fuel for a voyage to Germany from the South Atlantic or the Indian Ocean where the *Graf Spee* had captured them, and Langsdorff did not want to waste his own ship's fuel on them. Sinking the captured ships was the only option.

From those eight captured ships Langsdorff had taken 299 officers and crewmen prisoner. There had been no casualties, not a single British seaman had been killed. The question was where to confine such a large number of POWs. Since the *Graf Spee* was a working battleship, it would have been dicey keeping so many of the enemy on board—they would look for opportunities to commit acts of sabotage. Captain Langsdorff resolved to transfer his prisoners to one of his supply ships; he chose the *Altmark*.

The *Altmark* did not have accommodation or bedding for 299 extra men, but Captain Dau made the best of the situation. His ship's carpenters built tables and chairs from packing crates and ammunition boxes; the British seamen were given carpets and bales of jute from their captured ships to use as beds and blankets. The prisoners were to remain in strict confinement except for forty-five minutes in the morning and thirty minutes in the afternoon when they were permitted on deck for exercise and fresh air. Dau gave his crew strict orders not to fraternise with the British. 'Let's treat them correctly,' he told his men, 'but no more.'

## Captain Dau's vindictive mood

The crews of the British merchant ships were not members of the Royal Navy, they were civilian employees of the companies that owned the vessels. By taking these men prisoner, Captain Langsdorff of the German Navy had stepped into a grey area regarding international law—did he have the right to treat civilians as combatants?

Captain Dau was concerned about it; he spent a night studying the relevant textbooks and legal cases, and said to a subordinate the next morning, 'There is no provision for this contingency at all—as I see it.' Ultimately he justified his actions—holding civilians on his ship as prisoners of war—by blaming the British Royal Navy which had tried to blockade German ports. Conveniently working himself up to a state of righteous indignation, Dau declared, 'They [the British] are thus making war on our women and children … the enemy's navy is responsible for untold hardships which our German people must suffer.' To the British prisoners the *Altmark*'s captain resembled a caricature of a German—bright red complexion, Kaiser-style beard, awkward, jerky gestures; now he worked himself into a tirade, and saliva sprayed uncontrollably from his mouth. 'I do not like you!' Dau cried.

Great Rescues of World War II

The *Altmark* ran aground in neutral Norway's Jossing Fjord; after being refloated at high tide and found to be little damaged, the vessel returned to Germany.

'I do not like the English! I have no reason to love the English!' Then, on the verge of hysteria, 'Britain will be crushed! Take them below!'

As they turned away from the frenzied captain, eighteen-year-old Peter Watson-Filcek, an apprentice from the *Trevanion*, muttered under his breath, 'I think the feeling's mutual.'

While he was in this vindictive mood, Dau summoned the *Altmark*'s cook and baker; when they entered his quarters the captain handed each man a sheet of paper. 'Here is a list of maximum allocations per day,' he said. He had determined that his prisoners should eat less than what was standard for civilians in Germany; the daily ration for each prisoner aboard the *Altmark* was to be:

*250 grams of bread*
*125 grams of meat*
*40 grams of fat*
*100 grams of dried peas, beans, rice, or other vegetables*
*25 grams of coffee, tea, sugar, as long as the supplies lasted*
*40 grams of margarine or other spread*
*50 grams of dried potatoes*

In making up this formula, Dau had failed to take into consideration the Indian crewmen he had taken on board, whose dietary requirements differed greatly from the English. In the first place, the Muslim Indians would not accept pork, so their meat allocation had to be mutton, and the Hindus would not eat meat, so their allocation of vegetables must be increased. In the second place, both the Muslims and the Hindus requested a very substantial ration of rice, a staple in their country, but even if rice was eliminated from the menu of the *Altmark*'s crew and the British prisoners, there would still not have been enough to satisfy the Indians.

Despite the rage he felt against the enemies of Germany, Dau was fascinated by his Indian prisoners. He came out on deck to watch the Muslims lay down frayed pieces of carpet and pray in the direction of Mecca, and he speculated that the Hindus had been reluctant to strip for a medical inspection because 'some of them worship the genital organs'.

# The Battle of the River Plate

For ten weeks the *Graf Spee* eluded all the hunting parties sent out by the British Admiralty. Then, on 13 December 1939, the heavy cruiser HMS *Exeter* and two light cruisers, HMS *Achilles* and HMS *Ajax*, found the battleship off the mouth of the River Plate, between Uruguay and Argentina. Initially Captain Langsdorff believed he had encountered a rich convoy of British merchant ships under the protection of a few cruisers. But as the ships came closer he realised that they were one of the hunting parties—and steaming straight for the *Graf Spee* at full speed.

The *Exeter* was the first to come within range of the *Graf Spee*'s guns. At Langsdorff's command his gunners fired three salvoes; all missed their target. The *Exeter* returned fire, and one of her shells made damaging contact with the *Graf Spee*. Meanwhile, the *Achilles* and the *Ajax* were coming up fast, ready to enter the fray. Langsdorff ordered his heavy guns to keep firing; finally the German gunners scored direct hits on the *Exeter*'s bridge and one of the gun turrets, killing sixty-one British sailors and wounding twenty-three. The *Exeter* suffered eleven direct hits before it withdrew from the battle, limping off in the direction of the Falkland Islands. But before retreating, the British heavy cruiser had inflicted serious damage on the German battleship, tearing great holes in the hull, penetrating a compartment just above the waterline and setting the vessel on fire.

By now the *Achilles* and the *Ajax* had moved into position and were attacking the *Graf Spee* with their smaller guns. Commodore Henry Harwood of the *Ajax* brought his cruiser close to the battleship so the *Graf Spee*'s 11-inch (279-mm) guns could not be used against him. Harwood's gunners smashed one of the German guns, killing every man in the turret, but the *Ajax* was hit, too, with its two after-turrets destroyed. However, *Ajax* and *Achilles* kept firing.

By now the *Graf Spee* was in very poor shape: the galley and the munitions elevator were destroyed, the bridge, the mast and the torpedo compartment were badly damaged. Thirty-six German sailors were dead, and sixty-one were wounded. Rather than take more punishment, Langsdorff turned his battered ship towards the coast of South America. The *Graf Spee*'s radio engineer picked up signals which gave the precise location of the *Achilles* and the *Ajax*, which Langsdorff interpreted as a call to other Royal Navy ships in the region for reinforcements.

Langsdorff set a course for the port of Montevideo, the capital of neutral Uruguay. As the *Graf Spee* passed Punta del Este, an exclusive beach resort at the entrance to the harbour, the sun-worshippers gathered along the water's edge to watch the badly damaged battleship creep slowly towards the docks.

Under international law a 'belligerent war-ship', as the Hague Convention described a vessel such as the *Graf Spee*, was permitted to dock in a neutral country for three days. Langsdorff calculated it would take at least two weeks to repair his ship, and petitioned the Uruguayan government to grant him an extension.

While Langsdorff negotiated with Uruguayan officials, the British ambassador in Montevideo, Eugen Millington-Drake, was leaking false information that a major British naval force was in international waters near the city, including the aircraft carrier HMS *Ark Royal* and the battle cruiser HMS *Renown*. (In fact, only the heavy cruiser HMS *Cumberland* was anywhere near Montevideo.) Langsdorff, frustrated by the Uruguayan government's refusal to let him remain in port longer than the three days required by international law, and anxious about the reports of a large British fleet coming to finish him off, made a difficult decision: he would scuttle his own ship rather than try to fight his way through the British blockade.

First he freed the British seamen he had taken prisoner when he captured and sank the *Tairoa*. Next he disembarked his dead; Montevideans who had emigrated from Germany or were of German descent took charge of the funerals and burials for the German sailors. Finally, he arranged for himself and his surviving officers and men to be transferred to Buenos Aires in Argentina, a nation that had friendly relations with the Third Reich.

Early in the evening of 17 December 1939, Captain Langsdorff took the *Graf Spee* on its final voyage. About 6 kilometres (4 miles) off Montevideo, Langsdorff and the demolition crew set explosive devices throughout the battleship, took to the ship's launch and sailed for Buenos Aires, about 200 kilometres (124 miles) away. At 8 pm an immense explosion rocked the *Graf Spee*, sending her to the bottom of the River Plate estuary.

Graphic evidence of the scuttling of the *Graf Spee* off
Montevideo by Captain Langsdorff and his demolition crew;
they evaded the explosion in the ship's launch.

'The Navy's here!'

## A ruckus below

Through sheer perseverance George King, the engineer of the *Doric Star*, had convinced one of the guards on the *Altmark* to let him come on deck to draw fresh water so the prisoners could wash. Since the scuttling of the *Graf Spee* two months earlier, the 299 British seamen imprisoned on the *Altmark* had suspected they were heading for Germany and a concentration camp, but they could not be certain, and for many days Captain Dau had forbidden them to come up top for exercise. King's quick errand on deck had given him a glimpse of the *Altmark*'s surroundings, and he was confident that he had recognised the coast of Norway. The news he carried back to the hold excited the men, even if it meant they were now very close to Germany.

On 14 February 1940, a Norwegian vessel signalled the *Altmark* to stop. Captain Dau expected the Norwegians were sending him pilots to see his ship safely through Norwegian waters, and the small boat that came alongside the *Altmark* did bring pilots, but it also brought a Norwegian naval officer who insisted upon detailed information regarding the *Altmark* and its cargo. Were there guns on board? Did Captain Dau carry any prisoners? Dau, adopting an indignant tone, reminded the officer, 'The *Altmark* is a tanker, not a warship.'

Just at that moment Dau heard a dull rumbling sound from the hold. In a breach of protocol he left his guest so he could give orders to his second in command to go below and quiet the prisoners.

When the *Altmark* came to a stop the British seamen had deduced that the ship was being boarded by Norwegian pilots, and had immediately begun pounding and kicking the steel door and walls of the hold, making a terrible din that they hoped would carry up from the lower decks to wherever the Norwegians were. To mask the ruckus, Dau ordered the freight winches turned on—they made enough noise to drown out any sound the prisoners could make. Then, to quiet the men entirely, the Germans killed the lights in the hold and turned the fire hoses on the prisoners. Drenched with icy water in the dark, the British settled into an angry silence. That night, Dau decided to dismiss the Norwegian pilots, saying he could find his own way through their territorial waters. It was sheer bravado, but Dau was worried that the prisoners might make another attempt to attract attention.

Outside the fortified port of Bergen the *Altmark* was stopped again, this time by a Norwegian destroyer. The officer who came aboard informed Dau that he must search his ship. The German captain could barely control his temper; this was harassment, this was an insult to Germany, and he adamantly refused to allow a search of his vessel. In that case, the Norwegian officer responded, the *Altmark* must leave the area of Bergen at once; as Captain Dau had dismissed the Norwegian pilots, the officer suggested that the ship follow the Feje Osen passage.

Dau suspected the Norwegians were making a nuisance of themselves to please the British, and he wasn't entirely wrong. The Norwegians were aware that the Royal Navy had been searching for the *Altmark* for weeks, and now the boat and its cargo of prisoners was inching its way through unfamiliar waters. A coastwatcher at Bergen wired the British Admiralty:

ALTMARK *STEAMING TWO MILES OFF*
*NORWEGIAN COAST NORTH OF BERGEN.*

The Admiralty wired Captain Philip Vian aboard the *Cossack* in the North Sea to proceed at once to Bergen and intercept the *Altmark*.

On 16 February, with a violent shudder that threw the prisoners into a tangled heap on the floor of the hold, the *Altmark* ran aground at the entrance to the Jossing Fjord. The British seamen cheered, Dau cursed, and the crew of the *Altmark* strapped on their life vests, grabbed their sea-bags, and hurried from bow to stern and back again, waiting for the order to abandon ship. Above them soared the snow-covered sides of the fjord, below them large floating slabs of ice were piling up around the *Altmark*, and a few hundred metres away were two Norwegian gunboats and two British destroyers, guaranteeing that the German ship would not escape.

When Vian and the *Cossack* joined the blockade, the situation altered slightly. The Norwegian government was of two minds: it wanted to help recover the prisoners on the *Altmark*, but it also wanted to maintain its neutrality; if Norway permitted the *Altmark* to pass through its territorial waters, it was sending 299 men to a concentration camp, but if Norway permitted the British to board a German vessel in Norwegian waters, this would provoke Germany. What should Norway do?

Captain Vian had instructions from the Admiralty to board the *Altmark* and liberate its British prisoners. If the Norwegians fired upon the *Cossack*, Vian was authorised to defend himself, but using the least force necessary. About 10 pm on 16 February, Captain Vian gave his crew the order 'prepare for boarding'. The crew removed the side rails, and put in place the fenders that would shield the *Cossack* when it bumped up against the *Altmark*. As the *Cossack* pulled alongside the German ship, the British leaped onto the *Altmark*'s deck; the Norwegian gunboats stood by and did not interfere.

In spite of Captain Dau's protests to the contrary, there were some weapons on the *Altmark*—as the first British sailors landed on deck, two German crewmen raised their rifles and fired. The British responded with a volley of their own that killed four men and wounded five others. In fifteen minutes, the *Altmark* was entirely in British hands. Dau had no choice but to surrender.

Down in the hold the prisoners could hear noises on deck, but couldn't tell what was happening. When they heard the hatch door open, they feared the Germans were coming to kill them. Then a voice called down, 'Any Englishmen down there?'

All the men shouted, 'Yes!'

'Come up, then,' the man at the hatch cried. 'Come up! The Navy's here!'

## After the rescue

The *Cossack*, escorted by four British destroyers, carried the 299 prisoners to Leith in Scotland, where they were greeted by jubilant crowds.

Two days after he scuttled the *Graf Spee*, from his room in the Naval Hotel in Buenos Aires Captain Hans Langsdorff wrote to his superiors:

> *I can now only prove by my death that the fighting services of the Third Reich*
> *are ready to die for the honour of the flag. I alone bear the responsibility for*
> *scuttling the pocket-battleship* Admiral Graf Spee. *I am happy to pay with my*
> *life for any possible reflection on the honour of the flag. I shall face my fate*
> *with firm faith in the cause and the future of the nation and of my Führer.*

Then he wrapped himself in the *Graf Spee*'s battle ensign, and shot himself in the head.

After the 'Altmark Incident', as the episode came to be known, the German navy renamed the *Altmark* the *Uckermark*. It continued to serve as a supply vessel, and in 1942 was sent to Japan to supply the cruiser *Michal*. On 30 November 1942, while the crew was in the mess eating lunch, a massive explosion tore apart the *Uckermark*, sinking her and the two ships anchored beside her. The cause of the explosion, which killed fifty-three men, has never been determined.

On 7 May 1945, the day Germany surrendered to the Allies, Captain Heinrich Dau killed himself.

Captain Philip Vian fought the German navy in the North Atlantic and the Mediterranean. In 1944 he was promoted to vice admiral and was sent to the Pacific as commander in charge of the British fleet's air operations. After the war he achieved the rank of admiral and was named Knight Grand Cross of the order of the Bath. Vian died in 1968; he lies buried in St Paul's Cathedral in London.

HMS *Cossack* berthing at Leith, Scotland, where the merchant seamen rescued from the *Altmark* disembarked to a rousing welcome.

# CHAPTER 3

# THE MIRACLE OF THE LITTLE SHIPS
## The Evacuation at Dunkirk

Charles Lightoller did not object to the British Admiralty requisitioning his 17.5 metre (57½ foot) motor yacht, *Sundowner*, but he insisted that no one would man the boat but himself, his thirty-four-year-old son Roger, and their friend Gerald Ashcroft, a seventeen-year-old Sea Scout. Lightoller was sixty-six years old but, the Admiralty conceded, given his extensive experience as a seaman, he would be master of his own vessel.

Lightoller went to sea when he was only thirteen, the beginning of an adventurous life that took him to the South Atlantic, West Africa, India and Australia. What appeared at the time to be the pinnacle of his career came in 1912 when he was named Second Officer of the White Star Line's magnificent new *Titanic*. The tragic night the liner struck the iceberg and began to sink, Lightoller took command of the lifeboats on the port side of the ship, where he adhered to a strict policy

Endless lines of Allied troops snaking along the 14 kilometre (9 mile) beach and through the shallow offshore waters awaiting evacuation from Dunkirk.

Great Rescues of World War II

A pall of thick black smoke rises from the bombed port of Dunkirk. The smoke was so dense it largely thwarted the Luftwaffe's attacks on the British vessels evacuating troops from the beach.

The Miracle of the Little Ships

of women and children first. When all the lifeboats were full and away, at the last possible moment Lightoller dived into the sea and swam for an overturned collapsible lifeboat. With about thirty other survivors he clambered aboard and took command, calming the others and teaching them how to distribute their weight so they would not be pitched back into the frigid water. In this precarious position they drifted for hours, until at last, about dawn, rescue came. Lightoller was the last survivor of the *Titanic* tragedy to climb aboard the rescue ship *Carpathia*.

On 1 June 1940, the two Lightoller men and Ashcroft sailed the *Sundowner*, accompanied by five other ships, to Dunkirk. The rescue mission was personal for them—Charles Lightoller's second son, Trevor, was with the British Expeditionary Force; if he was still alive, he would be pinned down by the Germans on the beaches of Dunkirk. What the crew of the *Sundowner* did not know was that Trevor had been safely evacuated two days earlier.

As they approached Dunkirk, the three on the *Sundowner* saw soldiers standing in orderly lines in the sea, waiting to be hauled into a rescue boat—any rescue boat. They pulled 130 men onto the yacht, packing them in like sardines. It was too many passengers for a boat that size, but until the *Sundowner* was filled to capacity they could not bring themselves to turn anyone away.

Riding low in the water because of the great weight it carried, the *Sundowner* began the slow journey back to England. German aircraft strafed the rescue ships, but by employing evasive manoeuvres, Charles Lightoller saved his yacht and the men on board. Equally dangerous, unfortunately, were the swift-moving British destroyers—the wake from such a ship could swamp a yacht, and several times Lightoller's seamanship was tested. As the *Sundowner* entered Ramsgate Harbour, the soldiers in their eagerness to get ashore surged to one side, nearly causing it to capsize. Roger Lightoller ordered them to lie flat on the deck and not move until he said so. The *Sundowner* docked unscathed, with none of the evacuees harmed.

## The destruction of Rotterdam

Germany's sudden invasion of the Netherlands, Belgium and France on 10 May 1940 took the Allies by surprise, not least because the Netherlands and Belgium were neutral nations. The Netherlands had an army, but it was so ill-equipped and

Some of the evacuees lost items of uniform as they waded out to board the small boats that took them to the destroyers standing in deep water offshore.

poorly trained that Hitler expected to conquer the country in twenty-four hours; for four days, however, the Dutch fought valiantly, holding off the invaders. It was the vicious destruction of Rotterdam that convinced them to surrender. On 14 May, Colonel P.W. Scharroo, commander of the garrison of Rotterdam, rejected German General Hans Schmidt's proposal that he surrender the city. Schmidt responded that he would give Scharroo three hours to rethink his position before he bombed the city. In fact, the bombing had begun at almost the moment Scharroo received Schmidt's message. Ninety Heinkel He-111 bombers flew low over the heart of Rotterdam, releasing 97 tonnes (107) tons of high explosives in just fifteen minutes, and setting off a firestorm in the medieval Old Town. The bombing and the subsequent fires took the lives of approximately 900 civilians, injured thousands more, left 80,000 people homeless, and levelled 2.5 square kilometres (1 square mile) of Rotterdam. While the Dutch were still reeling in shock over the devastation, the Germans threatened to do the same to Amsterdam, The Hague and Utrecht.

Colonel Scharroo surrendered Rotterdam to the Germans while it was still in flames. The next day, the entire Dutch army surrendered. By this time the Dutch royal family and the government had fled to England, where they set up a government-in-exile. A portion of the French Seventh Army, which had come to the Netherlands' aid, was trapped in the southern province of Zeeland and had become prisoners of the Germans.

In Belgium meanwhile, King Leopold III had faith that his army of 500,000 men could keep the Germans in check until help arrived from Britain and France. In particular he put his confidence in Fort Eben Emael, a triangular-shaped complex of concrete and steel blockhouses that in 1940 was regarded as the strongest fortification in the world. It covered a vast area—600 metres (1969 feet) long and nearly as wide—and in some places its defensive walls stood 40 metres (131 feet) high. The fort was ringed by trenchworks, and defended by massive revolving cannon, machine guns and anti-tank weapons. There was an extensive underground tunnel complex furnished with an air-filtration system to protect the defenders against poisonous gas attacks. Eben Emael stood on the Belgian–German border, directly in the path of the German invasion force, and Leopold expected that its garrison would be able to pin down the Germans until Allied reinforcements arrived to drive them back.

But the Nazis did not roll up outside the fort like medieval knights preparing to storm a castle. On 10 May, ten glider planes swooped down and landed on the roofs of the blockhouses where they disgorged seventy-seven German paratroopers armed with hollow-charge weapons. This new technology had the force to penetrate concrete and steel, and once it did so, released molten metal that incinerated anything or anyone in its path. Within thirty minutes the invaders had broken through most of the blockhouses of Eben Emael, destroyed gun emplacements and killed approximately 650 Belgian defenders. The next day, the commander of the fort surrendered.

There were 390,000 British troops on the Continent at this time, and their commanders rushed to respond to Leopold's appeals for help. Sadly, there had been no prior coordination between the British and Belgian armies, and with Nazi forces swarming over Belgium there was no time to develop a workable combined strategy. The two armies operated as separate commands, pursuing different objectives. At the same time, the French First Army, also responding to Leopold's call, found itself in full retreat from the advancing panzer divisions, while the French Ninth Army had been destroyed. Fearful that the British might also be destroyed, on 16 May Lord Gort, commander of the British Expeditionary Force on the Continent, gave the order to pull back. As they retreated, the British troops marched through towns and villages where only days earlier they had been welcomed as heroes; now those same towns and villages were deserted.

The Belgians had earlier established another line of defence along the Albert Canal, a man-made waterway that stretches for about 130 kilometres (81 miles) between Antwerp and Liege. These troops were defending not only a main approach into Belgium, but also the north-eastern arrondissements, or districts, of France. The line did not hold: on 11 May the Belgians retreated from the canal, and German panzer tanks rolled into the country that King Leopold had hoped would be another Switzerland, its neutrality universally respected.

The Belgians nonetheless put up a courageous resistance to the invasion, blowing up the bridges that led to Maastricht in the north of the Netherlands, as well as bridges and main roads in the Ardennes Forest in the southern part of their country. These efforts halted the Germans temporarily, but by 17 May they had overrun eastern Belgium. By 20 May they had penetrated into northern France as far as the North Sea coast, at a point between Abbeville and Calais. On 23 May the northern French port of Boulogne surrendered, followed on 27 May by the port of Calais. The Germans were now in control of all Belgium, and every northern French port except Dunkirk. To avoid further bloodshed and destruction, on 28 May, without consulting France and Britain, King Leopold surrendered to the Third Reich.

## The retreat to Dunkirk

By the thousands, citizens of northern France and Belgium abandoned their homes and took to the roads, hoping to find safety in the south. Occupying the middle of the roads were the tanks and trucks and troop carriers of the British Army—all overflowing with men, who clung even to the sides of the vehicles. The civilians crowded the pavements on either side of the military. The lucky ones rode in automobiles—middle-class families crowded into Renaults and Citroëns, well-to-do families in the comfort of a Delahaye or a Chrysler, some driven by their chauffeurs. Tradesmen filled their trucks and vans with family members, friends and neighbours. Large farmers' carts, drawn by massive Belgian draughthorses—handsome light chestnut animals with flaxen manes and tails—could hold a dozen people and their luggage. The less fortunate pushed their children, the elderly and infirm, and their belongings in charrettes, two-wheeled handcarts that resemble a wheelbarrow but are larger, sturdier and more stable.

From time to time the immense crowd would hear a shrieking whistle warning that German Stukas were bearing down on them. As the panicked refugees fled for cover in the ditches on either side of the road, the Stuka pilots initiated their terrifying nosedives, dropping out of the sky at a seventy-degree angle at 495 kilometres per hour (308 miles per hour), strafing the crowd with fire from the two machine guns mounted on the wings.

Covering the retreat was the responsibility of Lieutenant General Alan Brooke. The son of an Anglo-Irish family with a long tradition of service in the British military, Brooke enjoyed the additional advantage of being fluent in French, the result of spending most of his childhood and youth in France. The surrender en masse of the Belgian army had opened a gap 50 kilometres (31 miles) wide on the northern flank of the British and French forces. Eager to exploit this opening and capture a quarter of a million Allied troops, the Germans had sent their panzer divisions racing to trap them in a pincer manoeuvre. Foreign Minister Joachim von Ribbentrop had assured the Führer, 'The French Army will be destroyed and the English on the Continent will be made prisoners of war.' It appeared that von Ribbentrop's promise was about to be fulfilled.

Brooke stretched out his Second Corps, comprising five divisions, across the 50 kilometre (31 mile) gap, and although the Germans threw seventeen divisions against his five, the line held. Covered by Brooke's perimeter of defence, the Allied troops retreated to Dunkirk, while the civilians kept travelling south where, it was said, there was no fighting.

## A reprieve

On 14 May 1940, the BBC announced, 'The Admiralty have made an Order requesting all owners of self-propelled pleasure craft between 30 and 100 feet [9 and 30 metres] in length to send all particulars to the Admiralty within 14 days from today if they have not already been offered or requisitioned.' Considering the grim situation in Holland, Belgium and northern France, the British military was already planning an evacuation of the British Expeditionary Force and any Allied troops. Code-named Operation Dynamo, the evacuation began on 26 May; by this time more than 300,000 British and Allied troops were stranded at Dunkirk, spread out along 14 kilometres (9 miles) of beach.

On the first day of the evacuation, the British Navy and the little ships manned by civilians rescued 7000 men. That same day Operation Dynamo and the men trapped on the beaches received an unexpected reprieve. The German panzer tanks that had been rolling across Holland, Belgium and northern France at 50 kilometres per hour (31 miles per hour) had appeared unstoppable, but on 26 May General Karl Rudolf Gerd von Runstedt concluded that his divisions were stretched too thinly over too much territory. He informed Berlin, and Hitler, after reviewing General von Runstedt's assessment, ordered the panzer divisions to remain where they were for three days, long enough for the infantry to catch up with them.

Those three days would give the men at Dunkirk a bit of breathing space from attack by ground forces, but Herman Goring, Marshal of the Luftwaffe, persuaded Hitler to send in dive-bombers to destroy them. Several factors conspired against the success of this tactic, however: the soft sand absorbed the impact of the bombs, while the dense clouds of black smoke resulting from their explosions obscured the pilots' vision. Nor did the Luftwaffe go unchallenged—Royal Air Force fighter planes from bases in south-east England, providing cover for the evacuation, attacked in force. The loss of aircraft on both sides was immense. Nonetheless, German combat aircraft succeeded in sinking or incapacitating six British and three French destroyers.

## 'The most tragic thing I ever have seen'

As dusk fell on 26 May, the men captaining the flotilla of ships caught their first sight of Dunkirk—the town behind the beach was burning, and the Luftwaffe's 250 and 500 pound (113 kilogram and 227 kilogram) bombs plunging deep into the dunes of grey sand were erupting in immense pillars of fire. But while the explosions looked hellish, most of them were harmless—few men on the beach were killed or wounded. The pall of thick black smoke hanging over the scene helped the British as much as it hindered the Luftwaffe, screening the small boats as they came into shore and hiding the exhausted soldiers who waded out to them. Arthur D. Divine, who manned one of the small rescue ships, described the scene:

> The foremost ranks were shoulder deep, moving forward under the
> command of young subalterns, themselves with their heads just
> above the little waves that rode in to the sand. As the front ranks
> were dragged aboard the boats, the rear ranks moved up, from ankle
> deep to knee deep, from knee deep to waist deep, until they, too,
> came to shoulder depth and their turn.

The rescue went on against the deafening sounds of anti-aircraft shells exploding overhead, the sickening whine of stricken planes falling into the sea, the fierce staccato of machine-gun fire. Rescuers and the men they were intent upon rescuing shouted themselves hoarse as they tried to communicate with one another. Some of the small ships ferried their cargoes of men to the destroyers, while others, once they had reached capacity, turned around to carry the soldiers to safety across the English Channel.

Divine was about to turn back for home when he heard the roar of aircraft overhead. German planes burst out of the plume of black smoke, heading straight for an English troopship tied up alongside the only pier at Dunkirk, where a crowd of 1000 French soldiers stood waiting to go aboard. The German bombers released their payloads over the troopship, struck the boiler-room, and the vessel exploded into flames. The Frenchmen who survived the attack staggered back to the beach. 'It was quite the most tragic thing I ever have seen in my life,' Divine said; he never learned what became of those men.

## 'A miracle of deliverance'

On 4 June 1940, the last ships brought the last of the soldiers from Dunkirk to England. That same day Prime Minister Winston Churchill rose in the House of Commons to deliver a remarkable oration, part news report of the events at Dunkirk, part reassertion of Britain's determination to fight on against the Nazi war machine, part prophecy that awaited the day when 'the New World, with all its power and might, steps forth to the rescue and the liberation of the old'.

The greater part of Churchill's speech, however, concentrated on Dunkirk. 'A miracle of deliverance, achieved by valour, by perseverance, by perfect discipline, by faultless service, by resource, by skill, by unconquerable fidelity, is manifest to us all,' he said. But he cautioned his audience against excessive jubilation. 'We must be very careful not to assign to this deliverance the attributes of a victory,' he said. 'Wars are not won by evacuations. But there was a victory inside this deliverance.'

# The numbers

THE RESCUED

198,229 British troops rescued

139,997 French, Belgian and Dutch
troops rescued

THE SHIPS INVOLVED

**British**

38 destroyers

32 personnel ships

693 private yachts, fishing boats,
and other small ships

**French**

8 destroyers

6 sloops

4 personnel ships

**Dutch**

30 scoots [schuyts]; small wooden
sailing boats

THE CASUALTIES

**British**

11,014 killed

14,074 wounded

41,338 missing, presumed
captured

**French**

approx. 90,000 killed

approx. 200,000 wounded

approx. 35,000 missing,
presumed captured

**Germans**

27,074 killed

111,034 wounded

18,384 missing

**Belgians and Dutch**

23,350 Belgians killed, wounded
or missing

9779 Dutch killed, wounded or
missing

AIRCRAFT AND SHIPS LOST

145 RAF planes

132 Luftwaffe planes

6 Royal Navy destroyers

3 French Navy destroyers

226 small ships

ABANDONED ON THE BEACHES AT DUNKIRK

2472 field guns

63,879 vehicles

454,000 tonnes (500,000 tons) of
supplies

Weary Allied troops line the deck of a rescue vessel as it leaves
Dunkirk and heads for the British coastline and safety.

# CHAPTER 4

# THE MAN WHO SIGNED 30,000 VISAS

### Aristides de Sousa Mendes, Portugal's Consul in Bordeaux

Pedro Nuno de Sousa Mendes arrived home from lectures at the University of Bordeaux on a day in mid-June 1940 to find hundreds of people spilling off the footpath into the street in front of his home, clogging the main entrance to the house, jamming the staircase that led up to the offices of the Portuguese consulate. Taking a deep breath he plunged into the crowd. 'Let me through, please,' he said, but the panicky refugees, thinking he was trying to get ahead of them, jostled him and shoved him back. 'I live here,' Pedro Nuno explained. 'I'm the consul's son.' Still, the crowd was suspicious; only by forgetting his good breeding and elbowing people out of his way did the boy manage to get through the doorway and up the stairs to his father's office.

The misery of their unwanted status is reflected in the faces of the children as a Jewish family trudges past a jeering group of uniformed Nazis.

The Man Who Signed 30,000 Visas

The crowd was better controlled here, standing in relatively tidy lines before a table where the consul, Aristides de Sousa Mendes, was signing visas and his secretary, José Seabra, was stamping them. Pedro Nuno's sister Isabel and her husband Jules d'Aout were assisting—keeping a steady stream of passports flowing across the table. Also seated at the table was Rabbi Chaim Kruger, a refugee from Poland and a houseguest of the Mendes family—he was issuing visas under Mendes' authority.

Technically, Seabra, as consular secretary, should have recorded the name of each visa recipient in the official register, but given the size of the crowd and the urgency of getting them to Portugal before the Nazis arrived in Bordeaux in south-west France, he had abandoned such formalities. Isabel and Jules, who had fretted that Aristides was ruining his diplomatic career and the future of his family, had been won over in the end and were working feverishly. Even the consul had adopted a shortcut—to save time he had stopped signing each visa with his full name, settling instead for the abbreviated 'Mendes'. As Pedro Nuno watched, his father scrawled his name quickly across another visa and called out politely, 'Next person, please.'

The refugees filled the formal drawing room and the dining room of the Mendes family's apartment; only the kitchen and the bedrooms were declared off-limits. Many of these frightened strangers were Jews, some from as far away as Warsaw and Prague. Others were members of the armed forces of the defeated nations of Poland, Belgium and France, who could expect to be sent to slave labour camps if the Nazis found them. Others, some of whom were German, were outspoken critics of the Third Reich—leaders of labour unions, Catholic priests and Protestant ministers, university professors, journalists, Communists. The visa-seekers came in droves to the Portuguese consulate because Mendes had declared, 'From now on I'm giving everyone visas. There will be no more nationalities, races, or religions.'

## 'Common sense will prevail'

Aristides de Sousa Mendes came from a devoutly Catholic, politically conservative family that had always supported the kings of Portugal and longed for their restoration to the throne after the Revolution of 1910 drove the royal family into exile. For centuries the Mendes family had been well-to-do landowners in northern Portugal, but in the twentieth century its members followed new career paths: Aristides' father was a judge, and Aristides and his twin brother César entered the diplomatic service. Aristides had a taste for exotic locales, and delighted in being posted to British Guiana and Zanzibar. His wife Angelina (they married in 1909 when he was twenty-four and she was twenty-one) enjoyed travel, too, and remained with him through all his posts, bringing along their children as well as their servants. In imitation of their parents the fourteen Mendes children learned to feel at ease wherever they were living—Brazil, San Francisco, Belgium. They were a close-knit, loving, unpretentious family—so much so that one visitor mistook their servants for Mendes relatives.

In September 1938, Mendes was posted to the consulate in Bordeaux. The family's new home, which also housed the consular offices, stood in the middle of the city on the Quai Louis XVIII; from its windows the family enjoyed a lovely view of the Garonne River. The consulate secretary, José Seabra, welcomed them to Bordeaux. Seabra was a small, fastidious man, exceedingly polite, and unyielding when it came to government regulations and the necessity of filling out and filing all the proper paperwork.

With the spectre of war hanging over Europe, appointment to the consulship in Bordeaux might have alarmed some men, but Mendes was optimistic. 'The war won't take place,' he assured his family. 'Common sense will prevail.' Angelina did not take such a bright view of the situation. Hitler's re-armament of Germany, his annexation of Austria in March 1939, his persecution of the Jews, the physically and mentally disabled, and of anyone else who fitted his description as undesirable convinced Angelina that the Führer was ready to plunge the world into war once again. Two weeks after the Mendes family moved into the house on Quai Louis XVIII, the Nazis occupied the Sudetenland in Czechoslovakia, and three weeks after that launched Kristallnacht, a nationwide pogrom against the Jews of Germany and Austria which saw anti-Semitic mobs rampage through the streets of German and Austrian cities and towns, destroying Jewish-owned businesses, burning synagogues, wrecking countless homes, killing. The SS rounded up thousands of Jewish men and shipped them to concentration camps. On 1 September 1939, German tanks

Great Rescues of World War II

A group of German soldiers pass through
a small village in the depths of winter, 1939,
as the inhabitants keep out of sight.

The Man Who Signed 30,000 Visas

rolled across the border into Poland and World War II began. Antonio Salazar, prime minister and dictator of Portugal, declared that his country would remain neutral. Neighbouring Spain also remained neutral.

## The Portuguese Stalin

Early in February 1940, the Spanish doctor Eduardo Neira Laporte visited Mendes at the consulate to request visas for himself and his family. The government of Bolivia had agreed to permit the Laportes to migrate there, but to reach their new home they were obliged to travel through Portugal and sail from Lisbon. Laporte was a distinguished man—a physician, a former professor at the university in Barcelona, but he was also a Communist. If he remained in what would soon be Nazi-occupied France, Laporte would be arrested and shipped to a concentration camp. Portugal, however, did not want Communists on their soil either, even if only for a brief time.

The procedure at the time required Mendes to receive approval from the Foreign Ministry for each individual who requested a visa. Mendes wrote to the ministry for authorisation, but after four weeks of waiting he still had received no reply. On 1 March, Laporte returned to the consulate nervous, almost frantic. The ship to South America would sail from Lisbon on 12 March, it was imperative that he and his family be aboard. At once, Mendes signed the necessary visas.

On 11 March, Mendes at last received an answer from the Foreign Ministry—the Laporte family's request was denied. It was too late; the next day the Laportes arrived at the Lisbon dock, where they presented immigration officials with the visas signed by Mendes. The immigration men permitted them to embark, but the story of their irregular visas trickled up to Count Pedro Lemos Tovar, Secretary General of the Foreign Ministry. Count Tovar was not impressed and sent Mendes a formal reprimand.

Writing to his brother César about the Laporte situation, Mendes said, 'The ministry is giving me a lot of trouble … the Portuguese Stalin [Tovar] decided to pounce on me like a wild beast. I hope that will be the end of the matter, but I can't rule out another attack. I've no problems with my conscience.'

In following his conscience, formed by his Catholic faith, Mendes was rejecting the declared policy of his government. In November 1939, Portugal's Foreign Ministry sent its diplomats a document that became known as Circular 14, listing the types of persons who were to be denied Portuguese passports and visas:

> *Russians*
>
> *Jews*
>
> *Persons who were denied citizenship in the country where they lived, such as Gypsies*
>
> *Holders of 'Nansen Passports', identity documents issued to stateless persons by the Society of Nations (a forerunner of the United Nations)*
>
> *Individuals who could not provide a sound reason for entering Portugal, or whose passport suggested that they would not be able to return to their homeland.*

Furthermore, the Foreign Ministry insisted, no visa could be issued without its authorisation. Even in ordinary times the procedure was slow. In a time of crisis, the Foreign Ministry's regulations were intolerable—at least in Mendes' opinion.

The visas Mendes had issued to the Laporte family constituted his first act of rebellion against a government policy he considered unjust, inhuman and immoral. He committed further small-scale acts of rebellion: when a thirty-five-year-old Portuguese woman requested a visa for her travelling companion, a nineteen-year-old boy who was a native of Luxembourg, Mendes registered the young man as the woman's brother.

After the Nazis invaded the Netherlands, Luxembourg, Belgium and France on 10 May 1940, thousands of refugees poured into Bordeaux, hoping to catch a ship to safety, or escape overland into Spain. Women, children and the elderly camped in the train stations; other refugees slept in their cars, on park benches, in subway tunnels. Cafés, restaurants and bakeries could not meet the demands of the throngs of hungry people. Pont de Pierre, the main bridge across the Garonne, was one immense traffic jam of cars, trucks, buses, even horse-drawn carts crammed with passengers and piled high with personal possessions.

In a scene re-enacted across Europe, bread is distributed to a crowd of starving Polish Jews brought to Berlin at war's end. Homeless and stateless, they depended on other countries to offer them a home.

Great Rescues of World War II

# No questions asked

Many refugees made the port of Lisbon in Portugal their goal—from there they could travel by ship to anywhere in the world. Consequently, the consulate in Bordeaux was swamped by huge crowds begging for visas. On 21 May, Mendes sent a telegram to Prime Minister Salazar asking him for advice on how to proceed. Salazar answered that Mendes should follow the directives of Circular 14.

About this time Mendes by chance met Chaim Kruger, a Polish rabbi, who had fled with his family first to Antwerp, then to Bordeaux, and now was looking for a way out of France. On impulse Mendes invited Rabbi Kruger and his family to live with his family. It was no hardship—the apartment had fourteen rooms, and only two of the Mendes children were living at home. The Krugers moved in, and Mendes began the paperwork to get them visas. Predictably, the Foreign Ministry rejected the Krugers' applications. Mendes promised the rabbi that he would do everything in his power to help him get out of France. 'It's not just me that needs help,' Rabbi Kruger replied, 'but all my fellow Jews who are in danger of their lives.'

Pedro Nuno Mendes, who was part of this conversation, recalled that at that moment his father's shoulders sagged, and his face took on an expression of profound exhaustion. He excused himself, and went to bed.

For three days Mendes did not leave his room. He groaned as he tossed on his bed, he suffered bouts of heavy sweating, but he refused to see a doctor. The family had no idea what was troubling him. On the fourth day, he got up, bathed, shaved, dressed, and rejoined his family. In a loud and cheerful voice he declared, 'From now on I'm giving everyone visas.' For those three days he had been tormented by the conflicting demands of obeying the law and obeying his conscience. Now that he had resolved the matter, that he had committed himself to saving as many lives as he could, his peace of mind had returned. That day, 16 June 1940, Mendes sat down at his desk in the consular office and issued visas to every person who came before him—no questions asked.

To move the process along, Rabbi Kruger waded into the crowd in the office and on the stairs, collecting their passports and bringing them back to Mendes, who signed each one, then passed them to Seabra who stamped them.

Seabra, who had a deeply rooted respect for rules and regulations, had tried to dissuade Mendes. 'For the sake of your wife and children, please stop!' he had pleaded. 'You're ruining your life and that of your family.' When Mendes rejected his arguments, Seabra agreed to cooperate, although within limits. Initially he insisted on recording the name of every individual who received a visa in the official register, collecting the customary fee for each visa issued, and tried to enforce regular consular office hours. But soon Seabra was converted, too. For the sake of the refugees whose lives depended on these Portuguese visas, he gave up the time-consuming procedure of entering the name of each visa recipient in the register, he stopped asking for the fee from people who had no spare cash, and he kept the consulate doors open until Mendes admitted that he was exhausted and called a halt for the day.

One night the family was eating a late supper in the kitchen when an eight-year-old girl walked into the apartment. '[She] asked us what she should do to escape,' Pedro Nuno recalled years later. 'She said her parents had been machine-gunned.' Angelina sat her down and served her supper while Mendes promised the child she could spend the night with his family, and he would help her in the morning. When she had finished eating, the little girl took out an envelope; inside was a diamond, which she tried to give to Aristides and Angelina. Of course, they would not accept it. 'Quick,' Aristides said, 'hide that in your pocket!' The next morning he issued visas for the little girl and a refugee family who agreed to take care of her.

## The Habsburgs escape

Some very prominent individuals turned to Mendes for help in escaping the Nazis, including Albert de Vleeschauer, the minister for Belgium's colonies in Africa, who was trying to get to the Congo where a Belgian colonial government-in-exile was being set up. Robert Montgomery, a Hollywood actor who was stranded in France, received a visa from Mendes; so did three members of the fabulously wealthy Rothschild family—Edouard, Henri and Robert.

Undoubtedly the most distinguished persons to apply to Mendes for visas were the Habsburgs. The Empress Zita, last empress of the Austro-Hungarian Empire, and her son Archduke Otto were eager to leave France. They were not afraid that

Hitler would kill them—that would have caused an international uproar—but they did worry that the Nazis might try to use them for propaganda purposes.

On 19 June three cars and two trucks drove out of Bordeaux, heading for the Spanish border. Their passengers were the Habsburgs, de Vleeschauer and his family, Mendes' daughter Isabel, her husband Jules d'Aout, and their young son Manuel; in all, there were twenty-two children in the convoy. Two Belgian refugees joined the convoy at the last minute: Rosa Delerue, the first woman admitted to Louvain University, and Father Edouard Van Rooy, a Dominican priest and theologian who had been outspoken in his scorn for the Nazis' murderous racial policies.

That night the Luftwaffe bombed Bordeaux, killing over eighty people, injuring more than 100, inflicting heavy damage on the city, and terrifying the thousands of refugees. In bombing Bordeaux, the Nazis gave Marshal Philippe Pétain and the French Vichy government a demonstration of what they could expect right across France if they continued to delay making an armistice with the Third Reich and failed to collaborate with the German occupation of the country.

## The unworthy and undesirable masses

Eighteen-year-old Tereska Fzwarc and her Polish Jewish mother and grandparents were living in Paris when the family received a surprise visit in June 1940 from a cousin newly arrived from Poland. He came with terrible news of what the Nazis were doing to Poland's Jews, and urged the family to get out of France. Like thousands of others, Tereska and her family fled south, to St-Jean-de-Luz, a coastal town south of Biarritz, right on the western French–Spanish border. They wanted to get to Lisbon where they hoped they could take a ship to England to join Tereska's father. One of her uncles had heard that the Portuguese consul in Bayonne was issuing visas to anyone who asked; he collected all the family's passports and took a train to Bayonne. Tereska and her relatives waited anxiously in St-Jean.

A few days later the uncle returned triumphant—he had the visas. Packing quickly, they hurried to the border town of Irun. 'As we crossed the border with Spain at Irun,' Tereska recalled years later, 'the Germans were just beginning to arrive.' As the family passed through, a French customs officer watched the advancing German troops and said, 'They won't be staying long, the bastards!'

After the bombardment of Bordeaux there were far fewer refugees in the city; everyone who could travel headed for the Spanish border in a last-minute effort to cross before the German occupation extended over all of France. Mendes had travelled south, too, to Bayonne, where once again thousands of frightened people were clamouring for Portuguese visas.

Portugal's consul in Bayonne, Faria Machado, and the vice-consul, Vieira Braga, were career diplomats who followed their government's directives in Circular 14 scrupulously. The day Mendes arrived at the consulate he found a familiar scene— an immense crowd that blocked the streets, the foyer, the staircase, the consular offices. Forcing his way through the crowd, Mendes confronted Braga first. 'Why don't you help these poor refugees?' he asked. 'How would you like to find yourself, your wife and children in the same circumstances as the refugees? You say you are here to carry out the instructions of your superiors. Very well, I am still the consul at Bordeaux and, consequently, your superior. I therefore order you to pass out as many visas as may be needed.' That was how Tereska Fzwarc's uncle got the visas.

For three days and two nights an assembly line set up by Mendes processed thousands of visas. A young man assisting the consul collected passports from the crowd outside, carried them to the office for the necessary signature and stamp, then returned with two large sacks of visas and called out the names of the fortunate individuals who now had the documents necessary to enter Portugal. Mendes said later that in spite of their misgivings, Machado, Braga and Ambassador Francisco de Calheiros e Menses, Portugal's representative in Belgium, who had fled the country after the German invasion and happened to be in Bayonne in June 1940, all signed visas; but in later years all three denied that they ever helped him.

It is certain that Machado wired his superiors at the Foreign Ministry telling them of the vast number of irregular visas Mendes was issuing and asking for further instructions. About the same time Ambassador Pedro Teotonio Pereira, Portugal's representative in Madrid, wrote to Salazar that Generalissimo Francisco Franco was displeased with the thousands of Jews and opponents of the Nazi regime bearing Portuguese visas who were passing through Spanish territory. Franco was a fascist, but not a Nazi, yet he believed the only way to secure Spain's neutrality was to stay friends with Hitler. He could not afford to play host, however briefly, to people the Third Reich considered its deadly enemies.

Salazar was furious. Like Franco, he wanted to remain in Hitler's good graces, and he wanted Franco's friendship and political support. Consul Mendes' flagrant disobedience was jeopardising Portugal's relationship with both Spain and Germany.

The Secretary General of the Foreign Ministry sent one of his aides, Armando Lopo Simeao, to Bayonne to investigate the situation. Pereira, perhaps on his own initiative, perhaps under orders from Salazar, also travelled to Bayonne. There the ambassador and the bureaucrat discovered that things were as bad as Machado had described. Determined to shut down Mendes' visas-for-all operation, Pereira and Simeao wrote a new policy defining what types of people were eligible for a Portuguese visa: Americans, British, French Christians, Belgian Christians if they were 'personalities'—meaning noteworthy individuals—and individuals who already possessed a boat ticket which proved they were catching a ship in Lisbon for a destination outside Europe. In a report to his superiors at the Foreign Ministry, Simeao explained why he and Ambassador Pereira had written these new criteria for a visa: 'We wanted to keep out the mass of unworthy and socially undesirable people.'

## 'Orders must be obeyed'

When the telegram from Prime Minister Salazar addressed to Consul Mendes arrived at the Bayonne consulate, Mendes was not there to receive it. He had gone to nearby Hendaye to issue visas to refugees stranded there. Pereira, Simeao and Machado—who knew that Salazar had relieved Mendes of his duties as consul and stripped him of the authority to grant visas—piled into a car and drove to Hendaye, where they confronted him. As he read the message from the prime minister, Pereira said, 'Orders must be obeyed.' Mendes replied, 'Not if those orders are incompatible with any human feeling.' But with no authority to issue more visas, Mendes returned to Bayonne to decide his next move.

The next morning Pereira ordered Mendes to return to Bordeaux; the ex-consul refused, and went instead to the Spanish border. Salazar wanted Mendes to return to Lisbon; he refused that order, too. With no consular powers there was little Mendes could do at the border, but he could not stay away—the possibility, however remote, that he could help a few more refugees drew him. It was 28 June, three days after France signed an armistice with Germany that placed the nation firmly under the control of the Nazis, and two days after the first German troops entered Bordeaux.

At every major border crossing into Spain there were scenes of pandemonium. Sometimes the Spanish guards let a crowd of refugees through, sometimes they were selective in who they permitted to cross, and sometimes they closed the crossing point entirely, refusing even to glance at travel documents and standing impassive as statues, unmoved by appeals for pity.

Mendes had his car; he drove out to the crossing at Irun, where there was an enormous traffic jam—the guards were not letting anyone cross. He remembered an obscure crossing point he had used before the war to avoid just such traffic snarls. He waved over several cars full of refugees and instructed them to follow him.

Mendes led them to this out-of-the-way border crossing. There were no hordes of frantic refugees here—there was no activity at all. And the station was so primitive it did not even have a telephone; the guards would not be able to call anyone for instructions. Mendes introduced himself. 'I'm the Portuguese consul,' he said. 'These people are with me. They all have regular visas, as you can check for yourselves, so would you be so kind as to let them through?'

The guards raised the barrier and the convoy of refugees entered Spain.

After escorting the group to safety, Mendes returned to the apartment in Bordeaux where he and Angelina packed their personal possessions. On 8 July, they loaded their suitcases into a red Dodge convertible for the two-day drive to their home in northern Portugal. Mendes left France knowing his diplomatic career was in ruins, but consoled by the thought he had helped many people escape the Nazis. He probably did not have any clear idea of the exact number of visas he had signed, but it has been estimated that he saved the lives of 30,000 men, women and children, 10,000 of whom were Jews.

## Mendes after the war

Salazar would not tolerate disobedience, no matter what the motive. Aristides de Sousa Mendes' flagrant defiance of his government's policy regarding visas had enraged the dictator. By issuing tens of thousands of visas without authorisation, Mendes had brought dishonour on Portugal, and made Salazar appear ridiculous in the eyes of Spain and Germany. Portugal's Foreign Minister called for a hearing to examine Mendes' conduct in France.

In a letter to the government, Mendes stated that his primary reason for issuing thousands of visas in defiance of Circular 14 was the profound compassion he felt for the people who came to the consulate begging for his help. 'Their suffering cannot be expressed in words,' he wrote. 'Some had lost their wives, others had no news of their children, and others again had seen their loved ones die during German bombing raids.' But compassion was not his sole motivation, as he explained further on. 'There was something else that could not be ignored: the fate that awaited all those people should they fall into the hands of the enemy.'

The men on the tribunal that reviewed Mendes' case must have felt some sympathy for him; although they found that he had wilfully violated government policy, they recommended a relatively mild punishment—demotion to a rank below consul. But that was not good enough for Salazar. Acting on his authority as dictator, he demanded that Mendes 'retire' from the diplomatic corps.

Mendes never worked again. Salazar's displeasure killed any chance he might have had to move on to a different career. No one would hire the disgraced diplomat. With no other source of income, he and Angelina survived by mortgaging their property, but of course they had no means to repay the debt. By the time Aristides de Sousa Mendes died in 1954, he was destitute.

It was Mendes' children who began the campaign to make their father's heroic work known. His daughter Joana wrote to David Ben-Gurion, Prime Minister of Israel, telling him how her father rescued 10,000 Jews. Ben-Gurion forwarded the letter to the Yad Vashem Centre in Jerusalem, which studies the cases of Gentiles said to have saved Jewish lives during the Holocaust. In 1967, after examining the evidence, the authorities at Yad Vashem declared Aristides de Sousa Mendes a Righteous Gentile, and struck in his honour a commemorative medal which read: 'To Aristides de Sousa Mendes, from the grateful Jewish people'. A ceremony to honour Mendes was organised at the Israeli consulate in New York; five of his children—including Joana—attended. Also present was Rabbi Chaim Kruger.

In 1988, forty-eight years after Salazar had forced Mendes from office and into a life of disgrace and poverty, the Portuguese government rehabilitated him.

CHAPTER 5

# THE PATH ACROSS THE PYRENEES

Andrée de Jongh and the Comet Line

There had been strong winds the day before, so Belgian farmer Marcel Fauconnier went out to the woods to collect fallen branches for fuel. His household coal supply was exhausted, and the German-occupation force had laid claim to all stocks of coal in the country. As he walked through the woods, picking up branches, he saw a black boot and a few centimetres of khaki trouser sticking out from a tangle of wild raspberry bushes. 'Oh my God!' Fauconnier exclaimed in Flemish. 'Here's English!'

Under the bushes a panicky voice cried, 'Oh, Jesus Christ, we're caught!'

At that, Marcel Fauconnier switched to English: 'No you're not.'

'Who the hell are you?' the voice demanded.

'Well, I live here,' Fauconnier replied. 'And I lived in Canada, and I can speak English. You guys come. How many are you here?'

Andrée Dumont OBE, code-named Nadine, was one of Dédée's original Comet Line couriers. Captured in August 1942, Nadine, like Dédée, was sent to Ravensbrück and Mauthausen concentration camps, and survived the war.

A moment later four scruffy soldiers climbed out of the raspberry patch—twenty-three-year-old Corporal Enoch Bettley, twenty-eight-year-old Sergeant Allan Cowan, twenty-year-old Private Duncan Grieg and twenty-one-year-old Private Samuel Slavin, all of them Cameron Highlanders from Scotland. They were members of the 51st Highland Division, which had been captured by the Nazis, and until a few days ago had been marching to Germany and a forced labour camp. But on 4 July 1940, when none of the guards was looking, the four men had leaped into a wheat field, staying low until the Germans had moved on.

The four escapees were hiding near the farming village of Parike when Fauconnier came across them. They were hungry, thirsty and, what was far worse, still in uniform. At nightfall Fauconnier returned to their hiding place with baskets full of sandwiches and fresh cherries, several bottles of excellent Belgian beer and a bundle of civilian clothes.

The crucial problem was a way to keep the four men safe from the Germans. Initially, with Fauconnier's assistance, they created a dugout in a secluded part of the forest, but it was wretched living in the damp and the dirt, and finally Fauconnier's mother insisted that the only solution was to bring them into the family farmhouse. They remained with the Fauconniers for a time, but it was a crowded living arrangement. When a friend of Marcel's in a neighbouring village offered to shelter two of them, it was a great relief.

With the entire country under Nazi occupation, the four Britons could not stay with their hosts indefinitely. But how could Belgian farmers arrange for four escaped POWs to return to Britain?

## Long-term guests

The near-miraculous evacuation of the British Expeditionary Force (BEF) from Dunkirk in early June 1940 had not rescued every British soldier in France. The men of the 51st Highland Division, sent to defend the Maginot Line when the German offensive began in May 1940, had tried to rendezvous with the BEF, but the advancing German forces had cut them off near Abbeville. Outnumbered, outgunned, and with supplies dangerously low, the 51st retreated to St Valery-en-Caux, a small port town about 30 kilometres (18½ miles) west of Dieppe.

By the time they reached the coast, they were out of food and ammunition. On 12 June, eight days after the last small ship took the last soldier from the beaches of Dunkirk, the 51st's commander, Major General Sir Victor Fortune, surrendered himself and his 9000 men to Field Marshal Erwin Rommel.

The Germans marched their prisoners north towards the Fatherland, forcing them to cover at least 30 kilometres (18½ miles) each day on nothing but a single slice of bread and a cup of thin soup. Any man who broke ranks to snatch sugar beets or potatoes from the fields beside the roads was beaten or shot. Despite the brutality, the POWs were only lightly guarded, and dozens of them seized any opportunity that presented itself to dash into the woods, or hide among the grain fields. To the soldiers' great relief, the people of Belgium were overwhelmingly pro-Allies. Villagers and farmers took the escapees into their homes, gave them a bed to sleep in and civilian clothes to wear, fed them, even taught them French or Flemish to help them blend in. Many such soldiers remained with their hosts for months; it was a dangerous situation, but necessary—for at the time, no one had any idea how to get them safely to neutral Switzerland or Spain, let alone back to Britain.

Understandably, young men tended to become restless sitting around a farmhouse all day with nothing to occupy them. Boredom eventually drove Samuel Slavin, for one, to run the risk of leaving the security of the Fauconniers' home to spend his Saturday evenings in a local café.

Bettley, Cowan, Grieg and Slavin lived with the Belgians for six months, but as the Nazis tightened their grip on daily life, it became apparent to everyone involved that the four escapees needed to move to a location where they would be less conspicuous. Everyone in the neighbourhood knew who they were and where they were staying, and although no one had yet betrayed the soldiers or their hosts, there could be no guarantee that so many people could keep the secret forever, particularly if they or members of their families were arrested by the GFP (the Geheime Feldpolizei). These plainclothes military police had moved into Belgium to investigate espionage, sabotage and anti-German activities, and to hunt down escaped POWs and anyone who assisted them. To take the pressure off, the four Cameron Highlanders decided to relocate to Brussels where, they hoped, they would pass unnoticed. It was here that they heard of the Comet Line.

Post-war ruins of the Krupp munitions factory and surrounding factories in Essen, Germany. The Krupp plant was the subject of numerous Allied air raids.

# From Brussels to Gibraltar

RAF bomber pilot Sergeant Bob Frost, only nineteen years old, had to run two more bombing missions and his tour of duty would be complete. He had just completed a successful mission, bombing the Krupps munitions factory in the German city of Essen, but as he turned away his plane was hit by anti-aircraft fire. As the plane started to go down, Frost bailed out. Falling through cold, wet cloud, he pulled the cord on his parachute and landed with a sharp jolt in a farmer's field outside the Belgian village of Kapellen.

Freeing himself from the tangle of his parachute, Frost slogged across the field to the farmhouse, hoping some sweet old lady would take him in, serve him a hearty meal and let him spend the night in a cosy featherbed—but a burly young farmer answered his knock. He addressed Frost in Flemish, Frost replied in what he described later as 'schoolboy German'. On hearing the language of the despised Nazis, the farmer slammed the door in the pilot's face. It took some shouting through the door before Frost managed to convince the farmer that he was not a Nazi but a downed RAF pilot who needed help.

The family, who eventually took him in, were the Vangilbergens. They did feed him, and they gave him a place to sleep in the attic. More importantly, they got in touch with their contacts in the newly organised Comet Line who would help Frost return to England.

First he was taken to Brussels, to the home of a stockbroker who gave him false identity papers: Sergeant Bob Frost became Richard Simonis, a Belgian sailor living in Bordeaux. His backstory was that he had come to visit his sick mother.

One day a visitor came to the stockbroker's apartment, a petite young woman a little over 150 centimetres (5 feet) tall, with fluffy dark hair, and eyes that were ever alert. She was introduced to Frost as 'Dédée', but her real name was Andrée de Jongh, she was twenty-six years old—and the founder of the Comet Line. She explained the escape route: first by train from Brussels to Paris, then another train from Paris to Bayonne in south-west France, followed by an arduous trek through the Pyrenees into Spain. From a safe house in Spain she would call the British consulate in Bilbao to send a car to take Frost to Madrid, where the staff of the British Embassy would arrange for him to travel to the British colony of Gibraltar, and then home.

It seemed somewhat far-fetched to Frost that a young woman could pull off such an escapade, but then he looked into Dédée's eyes. 'They were absolutely burning and there was an air of supreme confidence about her,' he recalled later, adding, 'I fell in love.'

And the plan worked exactly as she laid it out. With Dédée and four other downed Allied pilots, Frost went by train to Bayonne, where forty-four-year-old Basque mountaineer, Florentino Goikoetxea, a giant of a man who knew every goat track between France and Spain, was waiting to accompany them through the Pyrenees. At nightfall they set off—Goikoetxea, Dédée and the five airmen. It was a punishing eight-hour trek of hard climbing and stumbling over rocks in the dark. The pilots were all young men who considered themselves in prime physical condition, but they panted for breath as they forced their aching bodies along the high mountain paths. Dédée, on the other hand, moved effortlessly, conditioned by more than two dozen such hikes through the rugged mountains.

Early in the morning they reached the safe house in Spain; Dédée left her charges to rest while she hurried to the nearest telephone to alert the British consulate that her five escapees were safe. Shortly afterwards, a luxurious diplomatic car pulled up, Frost and his fellow pilots climbed in and the car raced them off to Madrid. A day or two later they were back in England, enjoying leave in London.

## A vast escape network

The Nazi invasion, followed by the surrender of King Leopold III, had shocked the Belgians. Andrée de Jongh's father, Frédéric, had wept with shame, but the invasion made Andrée furious, and she vowed to do something to resist the Germans. She was a commercial artist, but once the war started she trained with the Red Cross to become a nurse. She had no military training, and certainly no experience in espionage, but as stories spread via word of mouth of Belgian, French and British prisoners of war who had escaped their captors and were looking for a way to reach England, Andrée began planning a rescue operation. There were already farmers as well as people in the cities hiding Allied troops—she could build on that. In only a few months she was directing a network that stretched for nearly 1000 kilometres (621 miles) and involved hundreds of Belgians, French and Spaniards.

Trying to get the escapees out by boat across the English Channel was too risky, so Andrée had designed something more elaborate—escape across Nazi-occupied Belgium and France, through the Pyrenees to Spain and then on to the British-held outpost of Gibraltar. She needed three centres of operation—Brussels, Paris and the Pyrenees. Jean Greindl, who adopted 'Nemo' as his alias, assumed responsibility for the operation in Brussels. Andrée's father moved to Paris, where he organised that stage of the route, which included finding people willing to let their homes and apartments be used as safe houses. Andrée, who took 'Dédée' as her alias, recruited French and Spanish Basques, including Florentino Goikoetxea, to help her get her soldiers across the mountains.

Every step of the journey was dangerous, and even in the Pyrenees Andrée and her charges were not safe. On the French side, the Nazis patrolled all the major highways and many of the side roads. On the nominally neutral Spanish side, the Guardia Civil, most of whose members had been trained by the Gestapo and nursed strong pro-Nazi sympathies, were keen to capture Allied soldiers and their escorts and turn them over to the Germans. Without Goikoetxea's intimate knowledge of the mountains, Dédée would never have been able to get her men to Spain.

In late autumn 1941 she made her first trip 'down the line', escorting two British escapees, Bobby Conville of the Glasgow Highlanders, and Allan Cowan of the 51st Highlanders, one of the Fauconniers' 'houseguests'. She took them directly to the British consulate in Bilbao. Vice consul Arthur Dean received them, but he was secretly very doubtful of Dédée's story, and of her offer to bring other escapees to safety. How could he be expected to believe that a diminutive twenty-five-year-old Belgian woman with no experience in clandestine affairs had successfully brought two British soldiers from Brussels to Bilbao? Dean suspected she was working for the Germans, and that she would try to use him to hunt down other Allied troops hiding in Nazi-occupied Europe. He told her to come back in two weeks for an answer; by then he would have had time to consult with his colleagues at the British Embassy in Madrid.

Michael Creswell, the political secretary in Madrid, was intrigued by what he heard about Dédée and drove to Bilbao two weeks later to meet her. She explained her plan in detail, and said candidly that she needed money—lots of

Great Rescues of World War II

Cavalrymen of the US 11th Armored Division are cheered by the prisoners liberated from the Mauthausen concentration camp on 6 May 1945. Dédée was among the survivors.

## Andrée de Jongh's life after the war

It took many months for Andrée de Jongh to recover her health after her liberation from the Mauthausen concentration camp. Once she was strong again, she was deluged with invitations. In 1946 King George VI and Queen Elizabeth invited de Jongh to Buckingham Palace, where she received the George Medal for bravery, the highest award Great Britain can bestow on an individual who is not a British subject. Following the ceremony, the RAF Escaping Society held a dinner in de Jongh's honour, with Air Chief Marshal Sir Basil Embry acting as host. The United States presented her with the Medal of Freedom; France named her a Chevalier of the Légion d'Honneur; and Belgium, her native land, appointed her a Chevalier of the Order of Leopold, awarding her the Croix de Guerre with palm.

Once the awards ceremonies were over, de Jongh left her homeland to continue her humanitarian work. As a child she had listened as her father told stories of the Belgian missionary priest, Father Damien de Veuster, who spent his life on the Hawaiian island of Molokai treating lepers who had been abandoned there. Inspired by the selflessness of this heroic priest, de Jongh travelled to the Congo (a Belgian colony at the time), where she worked in a leper hospital. She spent many years nursing lepers in Africa, until she became too weak to continue her work. De Jongh returned home to Belgium, where she died on 13 October 2007, at the age of ninety.

it—for civilian clothing, food, forged documents, train tickets and bribes. Since she was rescuing British servicemen, she quite reasonably expected the British government to fund her missions. Creswell agreed to help; he convinced MI9, British military intelligence, to supply funds for the Comet Line, the code name for the escape route. By the time all the arrangements had been confirmed, the Comet Line was bringing not only escaped POWs across the mountains, but also Allied pilots who had been shot down during bombing missions over Germany and German-occupied Europe.

## The man with the missing finger

The Germans and the Guardia Civil were not Dédée's only enemies. Operating in Brussels was the Belgian traitor Prosper de Zitter, who lured Allied troops into supposed safe houses only to hand them over to the waiting Gestapo.

De Zitter was a small man, less than 170 centimetres (5½ feet) in height, with a dark complexion and dark hair, and one physical feature no one who met him ever forgot—he was missing the first two joints of the little finger on his right hand. De Zitter was an unsavoury character: in 1913 he had fled to Canada after raping a woman in Ypres. In 1929 he returned to Belgium and became an automobile salesman, but again got into trouble with the law, this time for embezzlement and bigamy.

In 1940, when the Germans invaded Belgium, de Zitter offered the Gestapo his services as a collaborator. Since he was fluent in English, which he spoke with a strong Canadian accent, he was assigned to infiltrate groups that were rescuing escaped British POWs. Passing himself off as a member of the Resistance, he rented homes and apartments in Brussels that he said were safe houses, invented a false escape line, and made a point of cultivating the friendship of a network of Catholic parish priests who risked their lives to hide Allied servicemen and help them reach the English consulate in Spain.

De Zitter varied his methods of betrayal: sometimes his charges were seized in a Nazi raid on a safe house; at other times he put the escapees he was 'helping' on a Brussels-to-Paris train, the well-known first stage of the journey to Spain; when the men stepped off the train in Paris, the Gestapo would be waiting for them.

Over the course of three years de Zitter betrayed hundreds of fugitive Allied POWs, downed pilots, true members of the Resistance and ordinary Belgians—including those unsuspecting parish priests—who had tried to help the servicemen. In 1945, as the Third Reich began to collapse, de Zitter fled to Germany. After Germany's surrender, the Allies arrested him in Wurzburg and sent him back to Belgium, where he was tried and convicted. In 1948, in an enclosed courtyard of the police barracks in Ixelles, de Zitter was executed by firing squad.

## The arrest

It was January 1943, and Dédée was making her thirty-third trip down the line with three British airmen. From the railway station at Bayonne in southern France it had taken two hours of slogging along muddy roads in heavy rain to reach the whitewashed farmhouse that was home to one of the most dependable helpers along the Comet Line, a Basque widow named Frantxia, who lived there with her three school-aged sons. Here the little group's Basque guide, Florentino Goikoetxea, was waiting for them with bad news. The storm had flooded the Bidassoa River at the foot of the Pyrenees, making it impossible to wade across. The nearest bridge was a five-hour hike from the farmhouse, and could only be reached by a road that was patrolled by the Nazis. Even if they managed, somehow, to get across the river, the rocky trails through the mountains were slick with ice. They must break their journey for a few days until the water level fell and the trails cleared.

Goikoetxea had barely finished speaking when outside the dogs began to bark. The children ran to the window to see who was coming. 'Donato is here,' one of the little boys cried. Donato had worked for Frantxia as a farmhand, and had once been hired by Dédée as a guide. Instinctively, Dédée had not trusted the man; she had not used him again. Donato brought news that it was too risky to take the pilots to the nearest village—everyone would know who they were. It would be best if everyone remained at Frantxia's house until the weather improved.

Early the next morning Goikoetxea went out to inspect the river and the trails, and Frantxia sent the children to school. The pilots stayed in an upstairs bedroom, in case anyone came to the house. Late in the morning, German troops appeared and surrounded the farmhouse; ten of them burst into the house, seized the three pilots and the two women, and forced them out in the yard. 'Where is the other one?' the German officer demanded—a question which confirmed Dédée's suspicions about Donato, who was in fact an informer working with de Zitter.

As the Germans marched their prisoners to Bayonne, friends carried word of the raid to Goikoetxea. The news broke his heart, for he was deeply attached to Dédée. At the same time as news of the arrest spread up the line, Goikoetxea made the perilous trek across the mountains to bring word to the British consulate in Bilbao and to Michael Creswell in Madrid.

The Germans took their five captives to the Villa Chagrin Prison in Bayonne. They beat the British pilots until one of them cracked, telling his interrogators everything he could remember about the Comet Line and the people who had assisted them along the way. Dédée was next. She endured twenty interrogations with beatings and torture before she admitted to being the mastermind behind the line. The Gestapo scoffed—it was ludicrous to imagine that a tiny young woman could be the architect of such an elaborate escape plan. They believed she was trying to protect her father, whom they already had in custody in Paris.

The Nazis sent Dédée and Frantxia to Ravensbrück, a concentration camp for women in northern Germany. Later, Dédée was transferred to Mauthausen, a slave labour camp outside Linz in Austria which had a large sub-camp for women and children. On 6 May 1945, the men of the 11th Armored Division of the United States Army liberated Mauthausen. Dédée was sick and emaciated, and could barely walk, but she was alive. Frantxia had died only three weeks earlier in Ravensbrück. Dédée's father was dead, too, shot by the Gestapo in the Paris prison where he had been incarcerated. After Donato's betrayal dozens, perhaps hundreds of Dédée's co-workers along the Comet Line were arrested, tortured and shipped off to concentration camps. No one knows precisely how many were killed.

But one statistic is certain: of the approximately 800 Allied POWs and pilots the Comet Line escorted to safety, 118 were guided personally by Andrée de Jongh.

# CHAPTER 6

# THE LIST
## Oskar Schindler and the Jews of Plaszow

Twenty-year-old Anna Duklauer believed she did not have much longer to live. No matter how hard she worked in the laundry of the Plaszow slave labour camp in Poland, vicious black-uniformed Ukrainian guards beat her regularly. Every day the camp commandant, Amon Goeth, murdered inmates who displeased him—even children. Nothing could have prepared Anna for life in such a place. She had grown up with her brother and sister in Zakopane, a popular ski resort. Her parents were well off and had assimilated into Polish society, although they had not abandoned their Jewish faith. Now, four years after the Nazis invaded Poland, Anna's mother Sofia and her fourteen-year-old brother Morris were dead, killed in the gas chambers; her father Julius and sister Erna were also in Plaszow, clinging to life.

During his visit to Israel in 1962, Oskar Schindler received a rousing airport welcome from some of those he saved from the Holocaust.

One day in spring 1943, as Anna was working as usual in the laundry, a small Jewish man unobtrusively approached her and offered her a job in Oskar Schindler's enamelware factory outside the camp. Every inmate of Plaszow knew that at the Schindler factory no worker was beaten or starved or killed. Schindler would not permit the SS or the Ukrainian guards inside his factory, nor would he permit any of his skilled workers to be deported to the death camps. Nonetheless, Anna was not certain that she should go—it would mean leaving her father and sister behind. Erna made the decision for her. 'Go!' she said. 'With Schindler, there is life. You must go.'

And so Anna went to work in the enamelware factory. Her twelve-hour workday was divided between making pots and pans on the factory floor, and preparing meals in the factory kitchen. The Nazis killed her sister, her father, all her relatives and friends, but as a Schindler Jew, as they came to be called, Anna survived.

## A land of opportunity

Oskar Schindler was born in 1908 in the town of Zwittau, then part of the Austro-Hungarian Empire, now in the Czech Republic. His parents were German Catholics who identified strongly with their German culture—no language but German could be spoken in their home. Oskar's father, Hans, made a good living manufacturing and selling farm machinery, despite being both a chronic alcoholic and a shameless womaniser. Emilie Schindler, Oskar's wife, claimed in her memoirs that on one occasion Hans became so drunk that he raped his own sister-in-law.

As a boy Oskar had no interest in school. At the age of sixteen his grades were so poor that he forged a report card; when school officials discovered the deception they expelled him. The next year Oskar's father accused of him stealing insurance premiums. (Hans had expanded his business interests to include selling insurance policies.) Oskar, it seemed, might turn out to be even worse than his father.

Then Oskar met Emilie Pelzl. Just a few months older than himself Emilie was lovely, with large eyes and a dazzling smile. Oskar was tall, slender, blond-haired and blue-eyed, and even at the youthful age of nineteen he possessed charisma. The couple married in 1928. In the decade that followed Oskar Schindler followed his father's example, not only establishing himself as a successful businessman, but also indulging in bouts of heavy drinking and in chasing women. He became increasingly self-assured and strong-willed, watchful of money-making opportunities and not in the least concerned whether his business activities were strictly legal. And Emilie forgave his indiscretions again and again.

In October 1939, a few weeks after the German army swept over Poland, Schindler arrived in the Polish city of Krakow with the idea of getting involved in the black market. He already had connections in the Nazi Party—which he had joined in 1935—and had served the Third Reich by filing intelligence reports on Czechoslovakia in the years leading up to the German takeover of that country. Within weeks of his arrival Schindler had established ties with the black marketeers of Krakow, but he had also realised that a new kind of business opportunity was presenting itself. The Germans were seizing the property of Polish Christians and Jews—everything from jewellery and bank accounts, to private homes, automobiles and business enterprises. An enamelware factory called Rekord, Ltd, which had been taken over from its Jewish owner, appealed to Schindler's business instincts. He leased it from the German-run Court of Commercial Claims, which administered all expropriated property in Poland, and began soliciting army contracts for the manufacture of enamel-covered pots and pans. He renamed the company Deutsche Emalwarenfabrik Oskar Schindler—the German Enamelware Factory Oskar Schindler, or Emalia for short. He purchased the existing equipment for US$8750 and paid the court US$750 in rent each quarter. It was a genuine bargain, particularly when one considers how much money he made from the business between 1940—the year he began operations—and 1944, when he shut down the enamelworks to produce armaments; during those years Schindler earned more than US$6 million.

## A booming business

In the winter of 1939–40, Oskar Schindler's Emalia went into operation. The factory floor covered over 1200 square metres (3197 square feet) and he had 100 workers, seven of whom were Jews. The Nazis regarded all Poles, whether Christian or Jewish, as sub-human, suitable only for slave labour or extermination. As a result, Schindler paid his Christian workers very little, and his Jewish workers he paid nothing at all—their salaries he sent directly to the SS, as the law required.

To ingratiate himself with the officers who could help him secure army contracts, Schindler sent them expensive gifts such as caviar, cognac and silk shirts. To acquire these items he worked his contacts in the black market, including Poldek Pfefferberg, a twenty-six-year-old Jewish physical education teacher, veteran of the Polish army and, at the time he met Schindler in 1939, with no other way of earning a living, operating as a black marketeer. From their first meeting Pfefferberg and Schindler liked each other, and their ties remained strong for the rest of their lives—Schindler put Poldek and his wife Ludmila to work in his factory, and placed their names on the famous life-saving List; and it was Poldek who brought Oskar Schindler's story to the world, first through the novelist Thomas Keneally, and then through the film director Steven Spielberg.

Schindler's business boomed in 1940: he hired 300 workers, half of whom were Jews. In 1942 he expanded the size of the Emalia factory to well over 13,000 square metres (4265 square feet) and increased his labour force to 800— men, women and children. Among his labourers were 370 Jews, all of them drawn from the Krakow ghetto, just a short walk from the factory gates. Initially Schindler rarely appeared on the factory floor, and hardly ever spoke with his workers, Christian or Jewish. The Jews especially, who had learned from bitter experience to keep a safe distance from Germans, did not view their boss as anything more than just another Nazi profiteering from the conquest of Poland. But over time it occurred to the Jewish workers that they were spending half of each day in a kind of protected paradise. In Schindler's factory there were no SS men to humiliate them, beat them or shoot them. The more daring among them got the nerve to knock on Schindler's office door and petition the Herr Direktor to permit members of their family or close friends to join the Emalia workforce. Often enough, Schindler agreed.

What the Jewish workers on the factory floor did not know was that Schindler had begun to falsify paperwork for some of them. Jewish lawyers, doctors and engineers, whom the Nazis did not consider essential workers, were listed in his files as metalworkers, mechanics and draughtsmen, because these trades were considered essential to the war effort. Furthermore, Schindler listed child labourers as adults; and the paperwork for older men and women stated they were twenty years younger than their actual age. Perhaps this began as a self-serving attempt to hang on to the best workers; in the end, sympathy intervened.

## The liquidation of the ghetto

Outside Emalia, however, Schindler's Jewish workers were at the mercy of the Nazis. They were crowded together with 20,000 fellow Jews in the ghetto—a neighbourhood newly walled in by the occupying Germans, that formerly housed only 3000 people. Inside the ghetto food was scarce; so were fuel and medicine; and sanitation was minimal. One day in June 1942 the Gestapo, assisted by pro-Nazi Polish police, swept through, driving 5000 people into an open square where they were stripped of their valuables—watches, jewellery, even wedding rings—then marched 3 kilometres (2 miles) to the train station. Those who were weak or moved too slowly—the elderly, the sick, the children—the Gestapo shot; the bodies were left where they fell. At the railway station the survivors were forced into freight cars and taken 110 kilometres (68 miles) away to the Belzec concentration camp, where all of them were murdered.

Among the people taken that day were fourteen of Schindler's male workers, including Abraham Bankier, his accountant and office manager. Edith Kerner, one of his secretaries, alerted Schindler that the men were about to be deported to a death camp. By the time he got to the station the freight cars had been sealed and the train was ready to pull out. Furious, Schindler demanded that the SS guards open the doors and release his workers. Protesting all the while that their tally of deported Jews would not be correct, the guards did as Schindler ordered, and he returned to Krakow with Bankier and the rest of the group.

The Krakow Aktion, as the Nazis called it, was followed by an even more brutal round-up on 28 October, the first stage in the complete clearing of the ghetto. German troops and fanatically anti-Semitic Latvian and Lithuanian guards entered the ghetto at six in the morning. They shot the children in the orphanage and the patients in the hospital. By five in the afternoon, when the officers in charge declared the Aktion completed, 600 Polish Jews lay dead, and between 6000 and 7000 had been shipped to Belzec for extermination.

Great Rescues of World War II

Forty years after the war, barbed wire, basic barracks buildings and bleak conditions can only begin to suggest the horrors prisoners endured in the Auschwitz concentration camp.

The final liquidation of the Krakow ghetto took place on 13 and 14 March the next year. The Nazis and their collaborators killed 2000 Jews outright, sent another 2000 to the gas chambers at Auschwitz, and marched the remaining 4000—those who were considered fit for work—to the newly constructed forced labour camp at Plaszow, built on the site of a Jewish cemetery in the southern suburbs of Krakow. The camp's commandant was SS Captain Amon Goeth.

## The sadist

Early one summer morning a tall Nazi officer stepped onto the balcony outside the bedroom of his villa. He was wearing his uniform trousers, but no shirt, and his stomach, soft and flabby from good living, spilled over the top of his pants. In his hands he held a new high-powered rifle, equipped with a scope. Raising the rifle and taking careful aim, he fired—just one shot. Many hundreds of metres away, in the playground of the Kinderheim, the Children's Home, of the Plaszow concentration camp, a Jewish child fell dead.

Amon Goeth and Oskar Schindler were the same age; both were the sons of successful businessmen (Goeth's father operated a publishing company in Vienna), and neither had shown much interest in academic studies. While Schindler had joined the Nazi Party because it was the best way to advance his business career, Goeth was a true believer in everything preached by Adolf Hitler: the superiority of the Aryan race, the destiny of the German people to rule the world and the absolute necessity of exterminating all sub-human races—first and foremost the Jews. At the age of seventeen he joined the Styrian Home Protection Organisation in Vienna, the most ardently fascist and anti-Semitic group in Austria. Four years later Goeth joined the SS and became active in undermining the government of Austria in preparation for the Anschluss, or takeover, of the country by Nazi Germany.

After Germany conquered Poland in 1939, Goeth learned how to administer slave labour camps from Albrecht Schmeldt, a fellow SS officer who managed a slave labour force of 50,000 Polish Jews and Christians in numerous camps. In February 1943 Goeth was made commandant of Plaszow.

Violent, unpredictable and sadistic, Goeth seemed less interested in profiting from the labour of Plaszow's inmates than in terrorising them. He kept two Great

Danes that he trained as attack dogs—at his command they ripped apart any inmate who displeased him. He shot his private chef because the soup the man had served was too hot. He had a work crew of sixty men executed because three workers had been found with food hidden in their coat pockets. Goeth's two Jewish housekeepers, Helen Hirsch and Helen Sternlicht, lived in terror of this man, who beat them on the slightest pretext. He nearly tore out a hank of Helen Sternlicht's hair because he did not like the way she was ironing a shirt. He struck the side of Helen Hirsch's head so violently that he punctured her eardrum, causing her to go deaf in that ear—his reason: he did not care for the way she had set the table. One of Goeth's worst crimes was packing onto trucks 294 children from the camp's Kinderheim and sending them to Auschwitz, where they were all murdered in the gas chambers. It is estimated that Amon Goeth was responsible, personally or through his guards, for the deaths of 8000 men, women and children at Plaszow.

## Life after the war

Oskar and Emilie Schindler reached the safety of the American zone in Germany. From there they migrated to Argentina where they tried their hands at farming, but had little success. By 1957 they were bankrupt, and Oskar announced that he would travel to Europe to look for a new business opportunity. He never returned to Argentina, and he and Emilie never saw each other again.

Back in Germany, Schindler opened a cement factory. It failed in 1961. He began another business in partnership, but the partner backed out after Schindler was honoured by Israel as a Righteous Gentile. 'Now it is clear that you are a friend of Jews,' said the man, 'and I will not work together with you any more.' This businessman was not the only German who hated Schindler—it was not uncommon for strangers to curse him as he walked down the street.

Oskar Schindler never managed to support himself again; in the last years of his life, he was subsidised almost entirely by the Schindler Jews. Yet even as the recipient of such generosity, Schindler was a hopeless spendthrift; at one point, when he was short of cash, he even pawned the gold ring his workers gave him the night he left Brunnlitz.

On 9 October 1974, Oskar Schindler died of liver failure. He was sixty-six years old. At his request, his body was taken to Jerusalem and buried in the Catholic cemetery on Mount Zion. Hundreds of Schindler Jews stood weeping as his coffin was lowered into the grave.

## Feigning friendship

From Schindler's perspective, the clearance of the Krakow ghetto was bad for business. His workforce was no longer within walking distance of the factory and, given Goeth's predilection for summary executions, on any given day Schindler could lose a skilled metalworker in Plaszow. If Emalia were to remain operating, Schindler had to become Goeth's friend.

The two men had things other than their background in common. They had been athletes when they were young. They were advancing rapidly in their careers. They shared a taste for women and alcohol and easy money. But they differed in one important aspect: Goeth was always a brute, but Schindler could adapt to any situation, and appear to enjoy himself with anyone. To keep his business running, and to keep his best workers, Schindler was willing to appear to become Goeth's best friend.

Goeth hosted many lavish parties at his villa above the labour camp, and Schindler often supplied the liquor and the women for these occasions. Sometimes he even spent the night there with one of the commandant's female guests. Schindler's true opinion of Goeth is not recorded, but by at least feigning friendship he got what he wanted from the commandant—and what he wanted was his own sub-camp where he could relocate his factory and where all his workers would live.

With Goeth's assistance, and through the generous distribution of bribes, Schindler received permission from the SS and the German Armaments Inspectorate to build and operate his own sub-camp. To make his proposal more attractive, he said he planned to expand his operation to include the manufacture of armaments, but in truth Schindler's munitions generated only a minuscule part of his income—only US$200,000 compared to the US$6 million he made from the sales of enamelware.

Compared to Plaszow, the Emalia camp was almost luxurious. True, it was surrounded by a 2.8 metre (9 feet) fence, and armed guards kept an eye on the inmates from watchtowers, but Schindler also built a bathhouse, a delousing facility, a medical and dental clinic that was supervised by Emilie Schindler, and a laundry. At Plaszow, inmates had clung to life on 3–3.5 kilojoules (700–800 calories) a day—at the Emalia camp, daily rations were raised to 8.5 kilojoules (2000 calories).

Since the SS would not supply so much food, Schindler used his own money to buy the extra requirements on the black market. There were guards in the camp, but they were under strict orders not to come onto the factory floor or in any way mistreat the workers. When SS inspectors arrived, Schindler won their goodwill by serving them extravagant meals washed down with bottle after bottle of fine wine.

Schindler also continued to indulge Goeth with elaborate parties, but these he hosted at his house in Krakow rather than at the Emalia camp. When Goeth was drunk, he tended to be violent, and Schindler did not want to risk the lives of any his workers.

## The List

In February 1944, the Soviet Red Army recaptured the city of Novgorod in Ukraine and drove the Nazis out of Estonia and back to the pre-war borders of Poland. With the Third Reich's war machine calling up more and more German males to fight, fewer men were available to work in the munitions factories. In the summer of 1944, to make up for the shortage of citizen workers, commandants of the labour camps were ordered to ship their healthiest inmates west to Germany and to send all those who could not work to death camps for liquidation. Initially Schindler had no success in keeping his workers; in August that year, 400 Schindler Jews were included among the nearly 5000 Plaszow inmates who were sent to the Mauthausen labour camp outside Vienna.

The loss of the 400 may have impelled Schindler to try a scheme more daring than the establishment of his own sub-camp. Falling back on his talent for bribery and cajolery, he petitioned Berlin to permit him to dismantle the factory outside Plaszow and take it—along with his remaining skilled workers—to Brunnlitz in the Sudetenland, in what is now the Czech Republic, to concentrate on munitions. One of Schindler's closest friends in the Nazi hierarchy, Erich Lange of the Army High Command's Ordnance Department, visited the necessary officials in Berlin to persuade them that Schindler's factory was vital to the war effort, and that his labour force comprised essential workers. Schindler did not rely entirely on Lange's powers of persuasion; he later estimated that he had paid out US$40,000 in bribes to move the factory and his workers to Brunnlitz.

The famous Schindler's List was drawn up between 21 October and 12 November in 1944. It held the names of 700 men and boys, and 300 women, all of whom were to be transferred to Brunnlitz to work in the reassembled factory. A famous scene in Steven Spielberg's film, *Schindler's List*, shows Schindler and his Jewish accountant Itzhak Stern compiling the list together, but it probably did not happen that way. Exactly who drew up the list is a point of contention among historians; it appears most likely that it was put together by Emalia office staff, and that Schindler was not involved.

Further complicating the story, two versions of the List survived the war—the first compiled in Plaszow in autumn 1944, and the final list dated 8 May 1945. Not all the names that appear on the first list appear on the second. Perhaps these missing individuals died or were killed before Schindler could move them; perhaps he did not succeed in getting them out. It is also possible that whoever put together the first list showed too much overt favouritism for family and friends, and the list was later amended for this reason.

## Detours to the death camps

As with the origins of the List, the journey to Brunnlitz is also a complicated tale. The train carrying the 700 Schindler men and boys did not go to Brunnlitz, but to Gross-Rosen, a concentration camp over 300 kilometres (186 miles) away. To get his men released and sent on to Brunnlitz, Schindler offered generous 'gifts' of coffee, tea, schnapps, even expensive porcelain, to the Gross-Rosen commandant, Johannes Hassebroek. After two alarming days in Gross-Rosen, the camp guards hurried the Schindler men and boys onto a train to Brunnlitz.

The 300 Schindler women and girls suffered a detour even more harrowing. For reasons that have never been adequately explained, their train was directed to Auschwitz. When they arrived at the death camp and jumped down from the freight cars, they found themselves standing in a swirl of soft white flakes falling from the sky—but this was not snow, it was ash from Auschwitz's crematoria.

Screaming obscenities, female SS guards struck the Schindler women with whips and rifle butts as they drove them at a run to the sanitation facility. Here they were shaved of all body hair, subjected to a humiliating body-cavity inspection, given a delousing treatment that burned their skin, then forced into a massive shower room. As the iron doors clanged shut, the women became hysterical. They were certain they were about to be gassed, but it was water, not the lethal fumes of Zyklon B, that flowed from the shower heads.

The Schindler women's stay in Auschwitz dragged on for four nerve-wracking weeks—long enough to lead them to believe they would never be released. Exactly how they were delivered to safety in Brunnlitz is difficult to ascertain, although Emilie Schindler and Itzhak Stern tell essentially the same story. When Schindler learned that his female workers were in Auschwitz he promised his beautiful secretary, Hilde Albrecht, a magnificent diamond ring if she would travel to Auschwitz and convince the commandant to release them. In her memoirs, Emilie describes Hilde as 'strikingly beautiful, slender, and graceful'. She came from a wealthy and prominent German family, she had worked for the Wehrmacht, and she had contacts at the highest levels of the Nazi bureaucracy. Several days after she arrived at Auschwitz, the Schindler women reached Brunnlitz. Emilie Schindler, who met the train, said they arrived 'in disastrous condition—fragile, emaciated, weak'. But soup had been prepared for them, and warm water for washing, and doctors were standing by to tend the sick and the injured.

## Unfortunate and difficult times

The tea-table was full of delicacies, and Frau von Daubek insisted that Emilie Schindler taste each one. Everything was delicious; she had not enjoyed food like this since leaving Poland. Only after she had sampled each one did Emilie get down to business. Her hostess was a prosperous landowner who also operated a large grain mill. Food in the Sudetenland was scarce, and what could be had on the black market cost a fortune—much more than in Poland. It was becoming increasingly difficult for the Schindlers to find the 10,000 kilograms (22,000 pounds) of food each month to feed their workers; by necessity, the daily ration was decreasing, and the workers were getting thinner and weaker.

'What I need,' Emilie said, 'is grain from your mill. And it is urgent. I only want to help our Jews … so that they will not starve to death.'

Frau von Daubek folded her napkin as she listened, and sat in silence for a few moments. 'I understand your situation perfectly,' she said, 'and I realise we are going through unfortunate and difficult times. Anyway, I would like to help you if I can. Please go to the mill and speak to the manager. Tell him from me that he is to give you whatever you need for your people.'

Late that afternoon, Emilie returned to the factory with a wagon piled high with sacks of grain and flour.

## Rising expenses

It cost Oskar Schindler a fortune to keep his Jewish workers safe, fed and alive during the last seven months of the war. Because all the people on his List were registered as skilled labourers, he had to pay each one a salary. Or rather, he paid their salaries directly to the SS—and this sum was enormous, about US$2000 per day. Costs increased when he accepted another ninety-eight Jews into the Brunnlitz factory.

To relocate the factory equipment from Plaszow to Brunnlitz had cost US$40,000. To build the new camp at Brunnlitz had cost US$80,000. But these were one-off costs. The ongoing expenses, aside from buying extra food for more than a thousand people on the black market, included handing out a steady stream of bribes in both cash and such rare commodities as liquor and tobacco to the SS guards inside the factory camp and to local Nazi officials. After the war, Schindler estimated that during his short time at Brunnlitz he paid out nearly US$18,000 in bribes.

Then there were the unexpected expenses. Josef Leipold, the SS commandant of the Brunnlitz factory camp, made it a rule that no more than eighteen workers at a time could be excused from work because of illness. The figure was arbitrary, and as food became scarcer, more of the Schindler Jews became too weak and ill to work. Schindler assuaged Leipold's ire by promising, 'I am also going to pay for the sick workers. I'll give you the money, don't worry about it.'

Meanwhile, the von Daubeks turned a blind eye as Schindler Jews helped themselves to grain from the mill. And Schindler found another ally in Johannes Kompan, an old classmate who operated a wholesale grocery business. Kompan funnelled as much fresh vegetables, cheese and bread to Brunnlitz as he could manage.

# The runaways

In April 1945, everyone in the Brunnlitz factory camp—the Schindlers, the Jews, the SS guards—knew that the Russians were closing in, that the Nazis' days in the Sudetenland were numbered. Now began one of the most delicate negotiations of Schindler's life. At any moment Commandant Leipold would receive orders from Berlin to liquidate the Brunnlitz camp, and he might fulfil that order by taking the inmates on a forced march westward, or by murdering them. Even before such orders could arrive, Leipold told Schindler he was going to order the guards to take the sickest and weakest Jews into the woods and shoot them. Schindler promptly threatened to tell the army High Command that Leipold's men were malingerers who ought to be sent immediately to the front. But on 30 April Hitler committed suicide, an event followed shortly afterwards by Alfred Jodl's surrender to the Allies on 7 May, and any further discussion about the fate of the Jews in Brunnlitz was rendered immaterial. Russian forces poured into the Sudetenland.

The Schindler Jews were free, but Oskar and Emilie would have to run away. As a member of the Nazi Party and a war profiteer, Oskar was an obvious target for Russian revenge. The Schindlers resolved to travel as quickly as possible to the American lines—where they might be detained, but at least they would not suffer summary execution. Shortly after midnight on 9 May, as they prepared to leave, his Jewish workers presented Oskar Schindler with a gold ring, along with a signed statement declaring that from 1942 onward he had done everything in his power 'to save the lives of the largest number of Jews possible', and that they owed their lives 'exclusively to Dir. Schindler's efforts and humane treatment'. After hasty, emotional farewells, Oskar and Emilie drove off into the night. The Schindler Jews remained in the Brunnlitz camp, wondering what would happen next.

The unanswered question in the story of Oskar Schindler is why a crass opportunist became the saviour of 1098 Jews. Twenty years after the war, Moshe Bejski, one of the Schindler Jews, who went on to become a justice of Israel's Supreme Court, asked Oskar why he did what he did. 'I knew the people who worked for me,' Schindler replied. 'When you know people, you have to behave towards them like human beings.'

# CHAPTER 7

# POPE PIUS XII
## A Righteous Gentile

It was still dark when twenty-two-year-old Michael Tagliacozzo woke with a start to the sound of fists pounding on his apartment door. The date was 16 October 1943, and the Nazi round-up of the Jews of Rome had begun. Panic-stricken, still in his pyjamas, Tagliacozzo climbed out the window onto the balcony of another apartment where he begged his frightened neighbours, an Italian Catholic family with whom he was barely acquainted, to hide him. They did.

Uneasy about remaining so close to his home, the young man next sought refuge with one of his former teachers, Maria Amendola, also a Catholic. She sheltered him while her parish priest, Don Vincenzo Fagiolo, arranged for him to be given refuge in the one place the Nazis would not enter—Vatican territory.

Pope Pius XII blesses news correspondents, military and civilian, in his apartments in the Vatican shortly after the Allied liberation of Rome in 1944.

A few days after the round-up, Don Fagiolo escorted Tagliacozzo to the Seminario Romano, the Roman Seminary, a vast religious complex that includes the Basilica of St John Lateran, Rome's cathedral church. The Lateran complex is one of several properties scattered in and around Rome that form part of Vatican State. Under the law of nations, which even the Nazis tended to respect, no hostile force could enter Vatican territory without creating an international incident. Here at last Michael Tagliacozzo was safe.

His host, the vice rector of the seminary, Don Pietro Palazzini (later Cardinal Palazzini), asked if he were hungry. When Tagliacozzo admitted that he had had nothing to eat for two days, Don Palazzini hurried off to the kitchen and returned with a tray of food which he served to Tagliacozzo personally. 'Father Palazzini gave me a meal with God's goods,' Tagliacozzo recalled later. 'A bowl of vegetable soup, bread, cheese, fruit. I had never eaten so well.'

Safe within the seminary were approximately 200 refugees hiding from the Nazis, fifty-five of whom were Jews. To Tagliacozzo's surprise, Don Palazzini installed a kosher kitchen, and the seminary faculty encouraged their Jewish guests to maintain their daily prayer, including services on the Sabbath. Upon learning that Tagliacozzo was especially devout, Don Palazzini presented him with a copy of the Hebrew Bible. 'That inspired me,' said Tagliacozzo, 'with faith and hope in the future.'

## Impure blood

In 1938, Italy's fascist government conducted a nationwide census which categorised citizens and residents by race. The census-takers found 46,656 Jews in the country, including 9415 foreign Jews who had taken up residence. Most of this group were refugees from Germany, Austria and Poland who hoped to escape Nazi persecution. Italian dictator Benito Mussolini (Il Duce) was a fascist, but his government had not targeted the Jews in any way that resembled the ferocity of the Nazi approach.

On the whole Italian Jews tended to be better educated and better off than their Gentile neighbours. A 1901 survey had found that 50.1 per cent of the Italian population could read and write, but among Italy's Jews the literacy rate was 94.3 per cent. Furthermore, while at least 50 per cent of all Italians were involved

Rudolf Hess, deputy to Adolf Hitler, inspects a Guard of Honour on a visit to Rome in October 1939 that signalled the two countries' increasingly close relationship.

in agriculture, 70 per cent of the Jewish population made their living in commerce, working in offices, or practising in one of the professions such as law, medicine, science, engineering and education.

When Benito Mussolini took power in 1922, his government proclaimed, 'All religious faiths will be respected, with special regard for the dominant one, which is Catholicism.' Italian Jews, like Italian Protestants, were to have equal rights under the law, but because of the special status Catholicism enjoyed in the country, both Protestants and Jews, in particular, would have to put up with some irritations. For example, in factories, offices, schools, courts and government buildings crucifixes were displayed prominently; all members of the armed forces, whether Catholic or not, were obliged to attend a Catholic sermon every week; and the law which had granted non-Catholics the right to divorce was repealed. Furthermore, the Catholic religion was to be taught in all primary and secondary public schools.

The Jews chafed under these policies, but they could live with them. Extreme Italian fascists, however, were outraged that Mussolini had not adopted a more aggressive policy. On the night of 1–2 November 1926, a rogue band of such extremists broke into the principal synagogue of Padua, vandalised the sanctuary, and damaged sacred objects. But the extremists attacked no Jews, they spilled no blood. And over the next decade, such anti-Semitic flare-ups remained rare.

By 1936 Mussolini was working hard to effect closer ties between Italy and Germany; he knew a simple way to win the good opinion of the Nazis was to adopt a harder line against the Italian Jews. In July 1936 Mussolini published his 'Manifesto of the Race', which proclaimed that, like the Germans, the Italian people were 'a pure Aryan race'. The Manifesto asserted that 'Jews do not belong to the Italian race', that they were an alien people who could never assimilate into the Italian nation. In 1939, in the interest of safeguarding the country's 'racial purity', Mussolini issued an order expelling Jews from the civil service, the armed forces, and schools and universities. Jewish children would be tolerated in primary schools, but no Jewish student would be admitted to an Italian secondary school, college or university. And there were other restrictions, including: a Jew could not employ a Christian in his or her home; marriage between Jews and Christians was forbidden; books written by Jewish authors were to be removed from university libraries.

# The displaced professors

The dismissal of Jewish staff members from the universities was as much a blow to the universities as to those who lost their livelihood. At the time, about 8 per cent of university professors in Italy were Jewish. One of the foremost displaced scholars was Professor Roberto Almagia, one of Italy's most prominent geographers and cartographers. He held an endowed chair at the University of Rome, where he had taught since 1915, and was a member of the Italian Royal Academy.

If Mussolini hoped to shame illustrious scholars such as Professor Almagia, his efforts were frustrated by the pope. After Almagia's dismissal from both the university and the academy, Pope Pius XII named him director of the Vatican Library's geography division.

Almagia was soon joined at the Vatican by several Jewish colleagues, including Professor Giorgio del Vecchio, the dismissed dean of the University of Rome's law school; Professor Giorgio Levi della Vida, a world-renowned expert on Islam; and Professor Tullio Levi-Civita, the foremost physicist in Italy. The pope also helped the mathematician Vito Volterra emigrate to the United States.

Another displaced professional was Dr Guido Mendes, a renowned lung specialist—he and Pius XII had known each other since they were boys. In a 1965 interview with the *Jerusalem Post*, Mendes recalled those days when he and his family were frightened and uncertain what to do. Then he received an invitation from the pope to visit him at the Vatican. 'Pope Pius XII … offered to help me leave Italy and gain admittance to any country I chose,' Mendes told the *Post*'s reporter. 'When I mentioned Palestine, the pope promised to intervene with the British authorities and secure a certificate of immigration. [Monsignor] Montini [later Pope Paul VI] dealt with the matter, and as a result my entire family arrived in Palestine in 1939.'

# 'The Jewish God and his vicar'

As a young priest in Milan, Achille Ratti was bookish, and interested in ancient languages. To improve his command of Hebrew, he studied with a local rabbi. When he became director of Milan's Ambrosian Library, Ratti often consulted with the city's scholarly chief rabbi regarding the Ambrosian's collection of Hebrew manuscripts.

Ratti had his first experience of anti-Semitism in 1918 when he travelled to Warsaw as the papal nuncio, or ambassador, to Poland. Soon after he arrived, Polish Christians in Kielce, Lviv and Lemberg rioted against their Jewish neighbours, killing dozens, wounding hundreds, and destroying thousands of Jewish homes, businesses and synagogues. Such violence was a new experience for Ratti, and he was horrified. He had brought with him funds from the Vatican treasury to help Poles rebuild their lives in the wake of World War I: now he distributed these funds to Polish Christians who had suffered losses during the war, and to Polish Jews who had suffered losses in the recent pogroms.

In 1922 Ratti was elected pope, taking the name Pius XI. During the early years of his papacy Pius XI saw the influence of the Nazi Party and its attendant anti-Semitism spread throughout Germany. In his 1928 Christmas message he declared, 'Just as [the Holy See] reprobates all rancour and conflicts between peoples, it particularly condemns unreservedly hatred against the people once chosen by God; the hatred that commonly goes by the name of anti-Semitism.' He labelled Adolf Hitler 'the greatest enemy of Christ and of the Church in modern times' and, speaking to the College of Cardinals, denounced the Nazi swastika as 'a cross hostile to the cross of Christ'.

Pius XI found a strong supporter of his anti-Nazi policy in his secretary of state, Cardinal Eugenio Pacelli, a Vatican diplomat who had been the papal nuncio in Germany throughout the 1920s and harboured no illusions about Hitler and the Nazis. In April 1935, before a crowd of 250,000 pilgrims at the shrine of Lourdes in France, Cardinal Pacelli denounced the Nazis as:

> ... *miserable plagiarists who dress up old errors with new tinsel. It does not make any difference whether they flock to the banners of the social revolution, whether they are guided by a false conception of the world and of life, or whether they are possessed by the superstition of a race and blood cult.*

In 1937, Pius XI and Cardinal Pacelli collaborated on an encyclical that was a direct attack on Nazism. It was published in German rather than the traditional Latin, and sent to every German bishop with instructions that every parish priest in the country must read it aloud from the pulpit of his church on Palm Sunday, 21 March 1937. Entitled 'Mit Brennender Sorge' ('With Deep Anxiety'), the document denounced Nazism as a form of neo-paganism and urged the Catholic citizens of Germany to resist all appeals to abandon their faith for Hitler's newly invented German National Church. 'Whoever follows this so-called pre-Christian Germanic conception,' Pius XI wrote, 'of substituting a dark and impersonal destiny for the personal God, denies thereby the Wisdom and Providence of God.'

The pope also attacked the racism that was a fundamental part of National Socialism: 'The peak of the revelation as reached in the Gospel of Christ is final and permanent. It knows no retouches by human hand; it admits no substitutes or arbitrary alternatives such as certain leaders pretend to draw from the so-called myth of race and blood.'

The Nazis never forgave Pius XI and Cardinal Pacelli for their condemnation of National Socialism. The very next day the Nazi newspaper *Volkischer Beobachter* published a vicious denunciation of the 'Jewish God and his vicar in Rome'. Two years later when Pius XI died, but before Pacelli had been elected Pope Pius XII, the Nazi organ *Das Reich* smeared the two men with the term they considered most vile: 'Pius XI was a half-Jew, for his mother was a Dutch Jewess; but Cardinal Pacelli is a full Jew'.

## The high price of heroism

Even before the war broke out on 1 September 1939, Pius XII was helping Jews escape from Europe. Using their diplomatic contacts around the globe, Vatican officials initiated an impressive migration program. Between 1939 and 1941, the Vatican helped 3000 refugees—religious Jews and Christians of Jewish descent—reach safety in South America. By 1944, the Vatican under Pius XII had supplied passports, money, tickets and letters of recommendation to foreign governments that enabled approximately 5000 more Jewish refugees to emigrate.

Word of the Holy See's work to rescue European Jews found its way to the United States. On 2 January 1940, the Chicago-based United Jewish Appeal for Refugees and Overseas Needs sent a contribution of US$125,000 towards the Vatican's efforts to save 'all those persecuted because of religion or race'.

Following the Nazi invasion of Poland and the outbreak of war, countless Catholic priests, nuns and laypeople, inspired by the actions of Pope Pius XII, risked their lives in hiding Jewish refugees or trying to get them to the safety of neutral Spain, Portugal and Switzerland. Such heroism often came at a very high price, as the bishops of the Nazi-occupied Holland learned. On 19 April 1942, the Dutch Catholic bishops published a letter denouncing 'the unmerciful and unjust treatment meted out to Jews by those in power in our country'. In response, the Nazis made a special effort to round up every Dutch monk, nun and priest who had even a drop of Jewish blood. Some 300 religious members were deported to Auschwitz, where all were dispatched immediately to the gas chambers. Among the victims was Edith Stein, a Carmelite nun, philosopher and mystic. In 1998, Pope John Paul II declared Edith Stein a saint.

The Nazis followed up this massacre by murdering 110,000 Jewish men, women and children—79 per cent of the Jewish population of the Netherlands, the highest percentage in any Nazi-occupied nation of western Europe. It was a bitter and agonising lesson for the Dutch bishops and for Pius XII. Writing to Konrad von Preysing, Bishop of Berlin, shortly afterwards, the pope referred to the tragic events:

*We leave it to the [local] bishops to weigh the circumstances in deciding whether or not to exercise restraint, ad maiora mala vitanda [to avoid greater evil]. This would be advisable if the danger of retaliatory and coercive measures would be imminent in cases of public statements of the bishop. Here lies one of the reasons We Ourselves restrict Our public statements. The experience We had in 1942 with documents which We released for distribution to the faithful gives justification, as far as We can see, for our attitude.*

The pope was not the only one who learned to exercise restraint. The International Red Cross and the World Council of Churches in Geneva avoided making any statement that would antagonise the Nazis and so obstruct their work to save or at least ease the conditions of Jews, Slavs, Christian clergy, gypsies, homosexuals, Communists and other victims of Nazi persecution.

But in his Christmas address of 1942, Pius XII broke his own rule as he appealed to the world to take a vow never to let Nazism or any system like it afflict humankind again. 'Mankind owes that vow to the hundreds of thousands of persons,' he said, 'who, without any fault on their part, sometimes only because of their nationality or race, have been consigned to death or slow extermination.'

Although he did not use the words 'Jews' or 'Slavs' or 'gypsies', both the Allies and the Axis understood perfectly what Pope Pius XII was saying. On Christmas Day 1942, the *New York Times* published an editorial praising the pope's message:

> *When a leader bound impartially to nations on both sides condemns as heresy the new form of national state which subordinates everything to itself: when he declares that whoever wants peace must protect against 'arbitrary attacks' the 'juridical safety of individuals:' when he assails violent occupation of territory, the exile and persecution of human beings for no reason other than race or political opinion: when he says that people must fight for a just and decent peace, a 'total peace'—the 'impartial judgment' is like a verdict in a high court of justice.*

Reinhard Heydrich, chief of the Reich Central Security Office, which directed the activities of the Gestapo, had the pope's Christmas message carefully analysed so that no nuance of anti-Nazi sentiment would be missed. The final report declared:

> *In a manner never known before the pope has repudiated the National Socialist New European Order. His radio allocution was a masterpiece of clerical falsification of the National Socialist Weltanschauung. It is true, the Pope does not refer to the National Socialists in Germany by name, but his speech is one long attack on everything we stand for ... God, he says, regards all peoples and races as worthy of the same consideration. Here he is clearly speaking on behalf of the Jews ... virtually accusing the German people of injustice towards the Jews, and makes himself the mouthpiece of the Jewish war criminals.*

Based on this report, Nazi Foreign Minister Joachim von Ribbentrop instructed Germany's ambassador to the Holy See, Diego von Bergen, to advise the pope that 'Germany does not lack physical means of retaliation'. Two days later, after von Bergen had his audience with Pius XII, he reported back to von Ribbentrop, 'Pacelli is no more sensible to threats than we are.'

## 'The Germans are coming!'

Fifty years later, the memory of the round-up of the Jews of Rome was still vivid for Olga di Veroli. 'It rained all night,' she remembered, 'and sometime after midnight there was the sound of gunshots.' Once the shooting stopped and there were no more disturbances, Olga and her family felt secure enough to drift off to sleep. About five in the morning they woke again, this time to the insistent ringing of their doorbell. A little girl, a neighbour's daughter, stood at the threshold. 'Hurry!' she cried. 'The Germans are coming!'

The di Verolis were members of a Jewish family that had lived in Rome for centuries. Their neighbourhood beside the Tiber River had been the heart of Rome's Jewish community for 2000 years, and they knew every street, every alley. Now they used this intimate knowledge to their advantage as Olga's father, Umberto, led his family out the back door of their apartment building. Following dark, unfrequented side-streets, they made their way to the Church of San Paolo, where Don Gregorini, a good friend of Umberto di Veroli, was the parish priest. Afraid of attracting unwanted attention, Umberto tapped lightly on his friend's door. Don Gregorini threw it open and hustled the family inside. 'Come in, come in,' he whispered. 'We know everything.'

Olga and her immediate family were safe.

Eyewitnesses to the Nazis' pre-dawn raid on Rome's Jewish ghetto said they saw whole families leaping from windows in an effort to get away. One woman tossed her baby to a stranger, moments before the Nazis seized her. Nazi troops rolled an elderly woman, half paralysed and dying, out of her home and lifted her, wheelchair and all, into the back of a truck for deportation to Auschwitz.

By the end of the day the SS had rounded up 1259 Jews, of whom 896 were women and children. Among those taken away were forty-one of Olga di Veroli's relatives.

In its report to Berlin, the Gestapo in Rome deplored the interference of Italian Christians: 'The behaviour of the Italian people … in many individual cases amounted to active resistance … As the German police were breaking into some homes, attempts to hide Jews in nearby apartments were observed, and it is believed that in many cases they were successful.'

In fact, the 'active resistance' of the Italian people, particularly the priests, monks and nuns, and Pope Pius himself, was extremely successful. The fate of the 1259 taken from the ghetto by the Nazis was tragic, but there were nearly 8000 other Roman Jews that the Nazis did not find. Where were they?

According to Michael Tagliacozzo, who has become the foremost authority on the Nazi occupation of Rome, at the beginning of the war Pope Pius had urged the city's Catholic clergy and religious members to hide Jews and other refugees in their churches, monasteries and convents. On the night the Nazis swept through the ghetto, 4258 Jewish people were concealed in 155 Catholic buildings across Rome. The Vatican itself was home to 477, and at least 3000 were hidden in Castel Gandolfo, the pope's summer residence. The Jews of Rome remained safe in these sanctuaries for eight long months until, on 5 June 1944, they were able to surge into the streets with their fellow Romans to welcome the Allied troops who liberated the Eternal City.

At the end of the war, as Jewish survivors of the occupation of Italy told how they had been saved, expressions of gratitude from chief rabbis, community leaders and Jewish organisations throughout the world poured into the Vatican. One of the simplest and most direct was that of Dr Raffael Cantoni, who led the Italian Jewish Assistance Committee during the war. 'Six million of my co-religionists have been murdered by the Nazis,' Dr Cantori said, 'but there could have been many more victims had it not been for the efficacious intervention of Pius XII.'

On 31 July 1944, Rabbi Israel Zolli presided over the broadcast of
a service from the Grand Synagogue in Rome, newly liberated by the
US Fifth Army represented by Rabbi Aaron Paperman.

## The Chief Rabbi and the Pope

One Sunday evening in September 1943, Lieutenant Colonel Herbert Kappler, head of the Gestapo in Rome, demanded from the city's Jews 50 kilograms (110 pounds) of gold. If the gold was not delivered to his office within twenty-four hours, 200 Jews would be deported forthwith to Auschwitz.

Working feverishly, the Jewish community surrendered family heirlooms, wedding rings and ornaments from the synagogue, but by midday on Monday the collection amounted to only 35 kilograms (77 pounds)—and the clock was ticking. A leader of the synagogue of Rome suggested to the chief rabbi, Israel Zolli, that he go to the Vatican and ask for a loan of the necessary 15 kilograms (33 pounds). Zolli was eager to go, but worried about his appearance. 'I am dressed like a beggar,' he said.

But the rabbi's shabby clothes were used to his advantage: the leaders of the synagogue arranged with a contact at the Vatican to admit Zolli through a service entrance used by workmen. In this way he could avoid the Gestapo agents who guarded the main entrances to Vatican City and would have demanded to see his identification papers. Once they saw the stamp denoting 'Hebrew Race', Zolli would not have been permitted into Vatican territory.

A driver took Rabbi Zolli to a service entrance, where he was introduced as an engineer called in to consult on a construction problem. Zolli let the work crew talk, approved their suggestion for fixing the problem, then followed his escort to the office of the Vatican treasurer, to whom he explained the dire situation. 'The New Testament does not abandon the Old,' Rabbi Zolli said. 'Please help me.'

The treasurer excused himself, returning just a few minutes later. As soon as Pope Pius had heard the story, he had authorised a gift, or a loan if the rabbi preferred, of the 15 kilograms (33 pounds) of gold.

A few weeks later, during the Nazis' sweep through the Jewish ghetto, Roman Christians opened their homes and saved the lives of Rabbi Zolli, his wife and their children.

But Rabbi Zolli's story does not end there, or even with Rome's liberation by the Allies. On 13 February 1945, in the Basilica of Santa Maria degli Angeli, Israel Zolli, Chief Rabbi of Rome, and his wife Emma Majonica were baptised into the Roman Catholic Church. At the font, Zolli took the name Eugenio—the given name of Pius XII.

# CHAPTER 8

# A WRONGED WOMAN

## Lucie Aubrac Rescues Her Husband

Lucie Aubrac's tears were genuine, even if her story wasn't. Between sobs she pleaded for the release of her lover from the Fort Montluc prison. 'I must marry quickly before my parents notice I'm expecting a child,' she said. 'It's terrible. He promised to marry me. I don't want to be an unwed mother.'

Klaus Barbie, chief of the Gestapo in Lyon, remained impassive as he spelled out the plain facts of the case: 'He has been arrested as a Gaullist. It is out of the question that we release him, he's a terrorist.' Then he added, 'He's a terrorist; he will have to pay.'

At the age of thirty, Klaus Barbie was a handsome man, slender, with a strong chin and a long, fine nose. He had been attracted to Nazism while still in his teens, when he joined the Hitler Youth. Then he enlisted in the SS, the elite military unit often referred to as Hitler's Praetorian Guard. The SS were men without conscience, without pity, who carried out the most horrific atrocities against Jews, gypsies, Communists, homosexuals, Slavs—anyone identified as an enemy of the Third Reich. It was in the Netherlands that Barbie

French Resistance heroes Lucie and Raymond Aubrac pictured early in their marriage, and before they experienced first-hand the horrors of the Nazi occupation of France.

made a name for himself, hunting down Jews and anti-Hitler Germans who thought they would be safe among the Dutch. As a reward for his thoroughness, in 1942 he was named chief of the Gestapo in Lyon, where once again he hunted for Jews as well as for members of the French Resistance.

Lucie's appeal to Barbie was futile, and now that she had received her answer he wanted her gone. Barbie's assistant, a tall young German woman, shoved Lucie towards the door, saying, 'Go away, miss, we can't do anything for you.'

Lucie stumbled down the stairs and across the street, where she collapsed on a bench. To vent her grief and frustration, she tore off her earrings—little daisies made of white glass—and hurled them to the pavement where they shattered. But this petty, destructive gesture did no good; the tears kept coming.

Then she heard footsteps. Looking up, Lucie saw a woman in an apron approaching, a glass of water in her hand. 'I'm the superintendent of the house behind you,' the woman said, by way of an introduction. 'Drink some water and stop crying.' Obediently, Lucie accepted the glass and sipped the water until her sobs subsided.

## Ordinary people

Lucie Bernard was born in 1912 in Burgundy to a Catholic family who owned a small vineyard. Her parents worked hard, saving their money so Lucie could have an education and enter one of the professions. She studied at the University of Strasbourg, and became a teacher of history and geography.

In December 1939 Lucie married Raymond Samuel, a twenty-five-year-old Jewish engineer who had joined the French army when Nazi Germany invaded Poland. In June 1940, after little more than six weeks of fighting, France surrendered to Germany, Raymond was taken prisoner with many others and interned in a POW camp in Strasbourg. Fearful of what would happen if the Nazis discovered he was Jewish, and also a Communist, Lucie put together a desperate plan to get him out of the camp.

During a visit, Lucie was able to slip Raymond a box of Pinatra (dinitrophenol) tablets, a substance often used at the time as weight-loss medication. Taken in large doses, it also caused high fevers. After Lucie left him, Raymond swallowed the tablets; the next morning he was suffering from a dangerously high fever. Uncertain of the cause and unwilling to risk an epidemic that would reduce the number of slave labourers the camp could ship to Germany, the camp officials had Raymond transferred to a hospital. Once again Lucie received permission to visit her husband, and this time she smuggled in *bleus*, traditional French workman's overalls.

Whispering together, husband and wife plotted his escape: Lucie would drive her car to a quiet street that ran alongside the hospital wall. Raymond, wearing the *bleus*, would scale the wall, then they would drive straight to Lyon in the then unoccupied zone of France.

The plan worked flawlessly. No one saw Raymond leave his bed or climb over the hospital wall. Driving non-stop, they reached the border of unoccupied France before the authorities in Strasbourg had time to list Raymond as an escaped prisoner of war.

They eased effortlessly into a new life in Lyon, where they adopted the surname Aubrac to conceal Raymond's Jewish identity. He found work as an engineer, and Lucie took a teaching job at a secondary school in nearby Clermont-Ferrand. In 1941 their son Jean-Pierre was born. With a small group of friends also opposed to the Nazi occupation of France, the Aubracs published an underground newspaper called *Libération*. Soon they were using the name Libération-Sud for their fledgling paramilitary resistance organisation.

The Aubracs' cell within the Resistance was small and its early missions were modest. Lucie's first experience with the group was an act of simple sabotage. The Nazis and their Vichy collaborators were confiscating meat, sugar, dairy products, even flour, to feed the Third Reich's war machine. When Libération-Sud learned that a train loaded with sugar would arrive during the night at a local railway station before continuing its journey to Germany, Lucie and her comrades slipped into the railyard, broke open the freight car doors and soaked the sugar with fuel oil. 'I suppose it was infantile,' she said later in an interview with journalist David Schoenbrun, 'but it made us feel good to be taking direct action and it showed us what we were capable of doing. We discovered a will, a courage and daring that we did not know we possessed. We were after all just middle-class people, teachers, journalists, shopkeepers, quite ordinary people.'

# Desperate resistance

The Resistance in France comprised a variety of groups. In the countryside there were the *maquis*, bands of armed guerrillas who attacked the Germans and French collaborators. Small groups published underground newspapers that exposed Nazi atrocities. In cities and towns there were saboteurs who targeted railway lines, communications networks, fuel depots—any part of the infrastructure. And there was an underground 'government', the National Council of the Resistance, led by Jean Moulin and directed from England by the exiled French general, Charles de Gaulle.

Since the Resistance was a clandestine organisation, it is impossible to arrive at an accurate estimate of how many men and women participated, but certainly tens of thousands were involved. Resistance members included Jews who had escaped the round-ups, Catholic priests and nuns, shopkeepers, housewives, farmers, intellectuals and activists of both the far right and the far left, and professional military men such as General Charles Delestraint.

Delestraint and Charles de Gaulle were long-time friends—both had been career officers in the army, both had feared that France was woefully unprepared to resist a German invasion. When the Nazi army steamrolled its way across France, de Gaulle fled to England; Delestraint remained behind and became involved in the Resistance.

A Resistance group that called itself the Secret Army was planning a major uprising against the Nazis. They set about organising it in methodical fashion, acquiring maps on which they marked off every police station, town hall, railway line and bridge they would have to seize and hold. These men and women were courageous and utterly committed, but they lacked leadership. From London, de Gaulle sent a message to Delestraint asking him to take command of the Secret Army, unify its various cells and work in conjunction with other segments of the Resistance, including the National Council of the Resistance, to obstruct the Nazis and undermine the Vichy government. Delestraint accepted, and so the Resistance had a professional military man to lead them.

Unlike the Secret Army, Moulin's National Council was not a combat force but a coalition of eight Resistance organisations, six political parties and two trade unions, which also coordinated the activities of the *maquis*. The National Council declared that Charles de Gaulle was the sole representative of the interests of France and refused to recognise the authority of the Vichy regime.

The members of the Resistance blew up bridges and railway lines to disrupt the movement of troops and supplies. They attacked small German military units. They rescued downed Allied pilots and helped them escape to England or at least to safety in neutral Spain.

Nazi reprisals for such activities were brutal: during the five years the Germans occupied France, under a policy known as 'collective punishment' they executed at least 30,000 civilian hostages. A particularly notorious example of collective punishment occurred on 10 June 1944, in the village of Oradour-sur-Glane. To retaliate against a *maquis* group that had seized a German officer, an SS battalion cordoned off Oradour-sur-Glane and ordered all the inhabitants, about 650 people, into the town square. The women and children were marched to the village church and locked in. The men were taken to several large barns where they were machine-gunned; as the wounded and the dying lay groaning on the floor, the Nazis set fire to the barns. Then they fired a gas bomb into the church; when it failed to asphyxiate the women and children inside, they tossed hand-grenades and fired machine guns into the crowd, then set fire to the church, incinerating dead and wounded alike. Only six men and one woman escaped the massacre; 190 men died in the barns, 245 women and 207 children died inside the church.

## 'Are you Max?'

On 21 June 1943, Raymond Aubrac was scheduled to rendezvous with six other leading members of the Resistance, including Jean Moulin.

When the Nazis first occupied northern France, Moulin, an ardent leftist and prefect of Eure-et-Loir, had refused to cooperate. To 'teach him a lesson', the Nazis had arrested him and hauled him off to prison, where he was severely beaten before being released. Moulin went south to unoccupied France, where he became involved in one of the first Resistance organisations. In October 1941 he managed to get to London, where he met with de Gaulle. An immediate rapport sprang up between the two men, and de Gaulle sent Moulin back to France as his envoy with authority to coordinate the various anti-Nazi organisations that were emerging.

For their conference that June day Moulin and his comrades had arranged to meet in Caliure, a suburb of Lyon, at the office of a medical man sympathetic to the Resistance, Dr Frederic Dugoujon. The men had just entered when the Gestapo burst through the door. They seized everyone in the waiting room—the doctor's patients as well as the Resistance members—slapping and punching them, throwing them against the walls. The Gestapo were handcuffing their prisoners when Dr Dugoujon entered the room. One of the Gestapo kicked the doctor in the stomach, then shoved him against the wall, too.

In this single round-up, Barbie knew he had captured the most important men of the Resistance, including Jean Moulin, but ironically the Nazis knew Moulin only by his code name, 'Max'; they did not know what he looked like. Dr Dugoujon recalled that at Gestapo headquarters in Lyon, Barbie paced slowly back and forth before his prisoners, asking each man, 'Are you Max?' When no one would answer, Barbie sent Raymond Aubrac, Dr Dugoujon, the still-unidentified Moulin, and two other Resistance leaders to the Fort Montluc prison. He kept three other prisoners—Henri Aubry, Bruno Larat and André Lassagne—at Gestapo headquarters.

At Montluc, Barbie supervised Raymond's interrogation personally. His thugs beat Raymond repeatedly with whips and clubs, then Barbie joined in, pounding Raymond with his fists.

Back at Gestapo headquarters, Henri Aubry was enduring savage physical and psychological torture. The Gestapo beat his chest, arms and shoulders until they were black and swollen. Three times he lapsed into unconsciousness from the pain, but each time the Gestapo revived him for a fresh round of beatings. Between torture sessions Aubry was dragged out to the courtyard, where a firing squad stood ready. He was propped against the wall; the Nazis raised their rifles; their officer gave the command 'Fire!' But there was only the clicking sound of unloaded rifles. The Nazis played this cruel game four times. After two days, Aubry broke down and identified Moulin.

Even after Aubry identified him, Moulin asserted that Barbie had the wrong man, that he was an artist named Jean Martel. Barbie gave him a sheet of paper and a pencil, and ordered him to prove it by drawing something. Moulin drew a caricature of his interrogator.

## Who was the traitor?

Who betrayed Jean Moulin, Raymond Aubrac and the other leaders of the Resistance? This is a question that can still stir up old animosities and set off complicated conspiracy theories. Deep political divisions in France have made it even more difficult to establish the facts about the person or persons involved in the betrayal of Moulin and his comrades. Leftists insist that during the war they fought with the Resistance, while their opponents on the political right collaborated with the Nazis. The right maintains that while they were fighting as members of the Resistance to liberate France, the leftists were collaborating with the Nazis. It is an argument that has been raging in France for more than sixty years, and has spilled over into the memoirs and oral histories of the Nazi occupation. That said, many historians of the Resistance movement suspect that the traitor was one of Moulin's close associates, René Hardy.

On the night of 7–8 June 1943, en route to a meeting with General Charles Delestraint, Hardy was arrested by the Gestapo and dragged off to Barbie's notorious torture chamber. The next day the Gestapo arrested Delestraint and released Hardy, who had emerged from his brief confinement without a scratch.

On the day of the round-up at Dr Dugoujon's office, Hardy was the only person who was not handcuffed. He was also the only person to escape, bursting out the door and through the cordon of Gestapo guards. The captives inside heard the Gestapo open fire, but only later did they learn that Hardy got away with only a minor wound to his upper arm.

All this suggested to the Resistance that Hardy was the man who had betrayed their leaders. While he recuperated in a hospital, senior members of the Resistance ordered Lucie Aubrac to have Hardy killed, or to kill him herself. She mixed cyanide with jam, and sent a small jar of the toxic concoction as a gift to the wounded man. Hardy, who suspected the Resistance would try to kill him, refused to taste it.

These facts, taken together, point to Hardy as the traitor who handed Jean Moulin to Klaus Barbie, but the truth will never be known with absolute certainty: at the end of the war, Barbie destroyed the records of Gestapo activity in Lyon, and ordered the deaths of scores of Frenchmen, including twenty double agents, who had worked for him.

In 1947 Hardy was brought to trial on charges of collaborating with the Nazis. Both the prosecutor and Hardy's defence attorney wanted Barbie to testify at Hardy's trial; for this to happen Barbie would have to be extradited from the American zone in Germany, where he was under the protection of the US Counter-Intelligence Corps then using him to infiltrate Communist cells in Bavaria. The Americans refused to allow Barbie out of Germany, and the trial ended with Hardy's acquittal.

For days Moulin endured horrible beatings, but he revealed nothing of value to the Gestapo. Before shipping him off to a death camp, Barbie sent his prize prisoner to Paris to his superiors. Moulin was barely alive: his face was battered, swollen and discoloured; his back was lacerated from beatings with a bullwhip; he had numerous broken bones, and very likely a fractured skull. He could not stand, he could barely speak. In Paris, General Delestraint and André Lassagne, both of whom Barbie had had transferred to the capital, were brought in to see Moulin and confirm that he was indeed 'Max'. The general drew himself up and said, 'Military honour forbids me to recognise Max in the pitiful man you have presented to me.'

In the first days of July the Gestapo placed Jean Moulin on a train bound for Berlin and execution, but he died somewhere outside Frankfurt. The Germans removed the body and sent it back to Paris, where it was cremated at the Père-Lachaise Cemetery.

## A promise honoured

The cruel death of Jean Moulin, which provided the certainty that Barbie was torturing his prisoners, gave Lucie the courage to try a second time to see Raymond, still held in Fort Montluc. In September 1943 she returned to Gestapo headquarters in Lyon, but this time she approached a different officer, someone she had never seen before, and altered her tactics somewhat.

She conceded that her fiancé would be executed, she did not plead for his life, but she begged for the privilege granted under French law of marriage *in extremis*, a marriage performed for a convicted criminal before his or her execution. 'I'm not here begging for mercy for this man,' she said. 'But I'm expecting his child. For my family's sake and for society's, I absolutely cannot be an unwed mother. And this child is entitled to have a father.' By this time Lucie was five months pregnant.

To her surprise, the German lieutenant appeared moved. 'Come back on Tuesday at the same time,' he told her. 'I will have time to think over your problem.'

Eleven days later, the lieutenant permitted Lucie to see Raymond, in his office and in his presence. As Lucie and the young lieutenant made small talk, the door opened and Raymond entered, escorted by two prison guards. The guards removed their prisoner's handcuffs, and left the room.

In December 1964, the ashes of the revered French Resistance leader Jean Moulin were brought to lie with the remains of other national heroes in the Panthéon, the Paris church reserved as the burial place of the famous.

A Wronged Woman

Raymond was gaunt and dirty. He had lost so much weight his clothes no longer fitted him. And he was unsteady on his feet. 'Where can he sit down?' Lucie asked. At this, the lieutenant became a member of the Gestapo once again. In a harsh, clipped voice he replied, 'That is not allowed for prisoners!'

Unable to speak privately, husband and wife recited the lines the Gestapo lieutenant expected to hear.

'I've come to ask you to keep your promise and to confirm in front of this lieutenant your desire to marry me,' Lucie said. 'I'm expecting your child.'

'Of course I stand by my word,' Raymond replied. 'I'm really sorry to have put you through such a difficult situation.'

The lieutenant put an end to the little farce. 'That's enough. You've got your promise, miss. Get your papers together and apply at the Office of Vital Statistics for permission to register your marriage in my office.' He opened the door and the two guards returned. They snapped the handcuffs on Raymond's wrists and led him back to the truck that would return him to Montluc.

## The rescue

The German lieutenant's promise that Lucie could 'marry' Raymond inspired her to take an enormous risk: on their 'wedding day' she would rescue him. It took nearly a month to plan the escape, and Lucie required the assistance of more than a dozen relatives, neighbours and friends, who variously promised to watch two-year-old Jean-Pierre, let her use their apartment to change her clothes, and offered the couple a safe place to stay after the rescue.

Most importantly, she needed two cars and experienced Resistance members who were good shots. She recruited 'Christophe' and 'Daniel', whose actual names have not come down to us. As was the case with everyone in the Resistance, they used aliases or code names to conceal their identities and protect their families. Jean Moulin used 'Rex' and sometimes 'Regis' as well as 'Max'; Raymond used 'Claude' and 'François'. Lucie was known as 'Catherine'.

Although she was meticulous in planning every detail of the rescue, there was no way to get word to Raymond of what she was doing, or of warning him to be alert and ready to run.

The afternoon of 21 October 1943 was clear and sunny, and the last time that Lucie Aubrac would play the role of the wronged woman. At Gestapo headquarters, in the office of the sympathetic German lieutenant, she and Raymond would be married, then the Gestapo guards would take Raymond back to his cell in Montluc prison to await execution in the prison yard, or deportation to a Nazi death camp.

When Lucie arrived at the lieutenant's office, Raymond was already there, waiting for her; there was no sign of the guards who had escorted him. The Gestapo lieutenant did not waste any time; the couple were not permitted to exchange pleasantries, or even a kiss. In a civil ceremony that lasted only two or three minutes, Lucie, six months pregnant, and Raymond were married. The lieutenant dismissed Lucie and called for the guards.

From Gestapo headquarters Lucie hurried to the apartment of a friend where she changed out of her wedding clothes—a fine suit—and washed off her make-up. In casual attire she set off for the place where she would rendezvous with her comrades. It was five-thirty in the afternoon when they drove a Citroën back to Gestapo headquarters and parked outside the main gates, hoping against hope that the regular time for moving captives to Montluc had not been arbitrarily changed. Christophe was the driver. Daniel, with a sub-machine gun equipped with a silencer on his lap, sat on the passenger side. Lucie, clutching a pistol, sat in the rear. They worried also that someone would notice them parked so near the building, but they did not have to worry for long—the gates swung open at the usual time, and two German soldiers stepped into the street to stop traffic as the truck bearing Raymond and another prisoner drove out. Christophe immediately pulled the Citroën into traffic behind it.

On a broad boulevard Christophe accelerated, bringing the Citroën abreast of the truck. With the swift, precise moves of a marksman, Daniel took aim and fired off a short burst from the sub-machine gun, killing the German driver and the guard in the passenger seat instantly. The driver's foot must have slid onto the brake, because unexpectedly the truck came slowly to a stop beside the kerb. As the guards in the back leaped out, Christophe, Daniel and Lucie opened fire. By the time they had emptied their clips, all the Germans were dead.

A second Citroën, the getaway car for Raymond and anyone with him, pulled up. Handcuffed together, Raymond and the other man jumped out of the prison truck and ran for it. The Citroën bearing them raced off in one direction, the other Citroën bearing Lucie, headed off in another.

It was dark when Lucie arrived at the apartment of the Nicolas family where Raymond was being hidden. Madame Nicolas had supplied her guest with soap and hot water so he could scrub himself. He had just finished when Lucie entered the room. The man she saw standing beside the washbasin was almost naked, painfully thin, his skin the unhealthy pasty white of someone who has spent too much time indoors. On his back she could see signs of the beatings he had endured. And on his face was a bandage—in the shootout, a small-calibre bullet had pierced his cheek.

Madame Nicolas brought in a tray of food, but Raymond's wound made chewing painful. While Lucie sat on the bed and ate, he smoked the pipe and drank the rum Lucie had brought him, pacing the room all the while and talking ceaselessly. Eventually, as Raymond talked and talked, the pregnant Lucie, exhausted from the strain of planning and executing the rescue, fell asleep. Later that night she awoke: the room was dark and silent, and lying asleep beside her was her husband.

## After the war

The Resistance arranged for a plane to take Lucie, Raymond and Jean-Pierre to London. They arrived there in February 1944, and a few days later Lucie gave birth to a baby girl. After the war, the Aubracs returned to France—Raymond became a government administrator and Lucie went back to teaching. She died on 14 March 2007, at ninety-four years of age. At the time of writing, Raymond was still alive.

Raymond's mother and father were deported to Auschwitz where they were killed. General Charles Delestraint was sent to the Dachau concentration camp. In spring 1945, just days before the Americans liberated Dachau, camp guards acting on orders from Berlin shot and killed him. He was sixty-six years old.

It is estimated that as chief of the Gestapo in Lyon, Klaus Barbie was personally responsible for the torture and death of at least 4000 individuals. Among his other crimes, he ordered the deportation of forty-four Jewish children, aged four to seventeen, to Auschwitz, where they were all murdered.

In spite of his reputation as a war criminal, after the Allied victory in 1945, British intelligence and then American intelligence recruited Barbie to help them infiltrate the Communist Party in Germany. In 1950, Barbie, with his wife and children, moved to Bolivia. The Nazi hunters Beate and Serge Klarsfeld found him there in 1971, but it would take twelve years of intense negotiation before the Bolivian government would agree to extradite him to France for trial.

Given the historic nature of the trial, the judge permitted it to be filmed. Barbie astonished the court and the world when he declared, 'When I stand before the throne of God I shall be judged innocent.' The court, however, found him guilty of crimes against humanity and sentenced him to life in prison. In 1987, in a prison hospital, seventy-seven-year-old Klaus Barbie died of leukaemia.

In 1964, in a solemn ceremony, the French government transferred Jean Moulin's ashes from the Père-Lachaise Cemetery to the Panthéon, the Paris church where France's national heroes are buried.

# CHAPTER 9

# A GRASSROOTS RESCUE

The Evacuation of the Jews of Denmark

At three in the morning on 8 August 1943, thirteen-year-old Leo Goldberger woke to the sound of rifle butts hammering against his family's apartment door. It was the SS, come to arrest his father, the cantor of Copenhagen's Great Synagogue. As the pounding went on and on, Leo's father went into Leo's bedroom to reassure him—under no circumstances was he going to open that door. 'This was the most terror-filled moment I had ever experienced,' Leo later recalled.

Abruptly, almost shockingly, the pounding stopped, and the Goldbergers heard their upstairs neighbour shouting that the SS were wasting their time, the Goldbergers had gone away for the summer. For good measure, the irate neighbour added that three in the morning was no time to cause a disturbance. Convinced by this performance, the Nazis left—but they posted guards outside, around the clock, to wait for the Goldbergers' return. The next day the frightened family cautiously left the building by the back entrance—which, oddly, was not guarded—and hastened to the railway station, where they caught a train

Despite the non-aggression pact between their two countries, German troops, shown here taking possession of a street in Copenhagen, invaded neutral but strategically important Denmark in 1940.

to Elsinore, the nearby seafront town where they rented a summer house every year. For the time being they were safe.

In early September, information from a sympathetic German diplomat led to the spreading of the word through the Jewish community that the Nazis planned the mass arrest of every Jew in occupied Denmark on 1–2 October, Jewish New Year. Shortly afterwards, a wealthy Jewish family also hiding out in Elsinore chartered a swift Cris Craft motorboat to carry them to safety in Sweden, and offered to take the Goldbergers too—but only if they contributed to the expense. Leo's father did not have the money for such a venture. The uncharitable family left them behind, and Leo's father decided to go back to Copenhagen, in the hope of finding someone to loan him enough money to hire a fishing boat to take his family to Sweden.

As the train drew closer to the city, Cantor Goldberger could no longer conceal his distress. By sheer chance a Christian acquaintance, Fanny Arnskov, was sharing the compartment. She moved to sit beside him and asked why he was so troubled. In a few minutes the cantor poured out his story. Arnskov was deeply moved; she promised that she would find the money and make all the necessary arrangements for the family to get out of the country. Goldberger could scarcely believe what he was hearing. When the train arrived in Copenhagen, Fanny Arnskov set out on her mission of mercy, asking the cantor to meet her back at the station a few hours later. Goldberg wandered around the city, killing time, praying that his friend would succeed. At the appointed time he returned, and found her waiting for him. She had borrowed 20,000 kroner—about US$3500 at the time—from a Lutheran pastor, Henry Rasmussen, and she had hired a fishing boat to take the family to Sweden the very next night. Such kindness from Arnskov and Pastor Rasmussen—who was a perfect stranger—left Cantor Goldberger speechless but profoundly grateful.

The next night the Goldberger family—mother, father and four sons—huddled together on the appointed beach in the dark, waiting for the flashing light from the sea that was their signal. Everyone was perfectly still; to keep the youngest child, a three-year-old, quiet his mother had given him a sleeping pill. At last the light appeared and the family hurried down the beach, wading into the icy water to the fishing boat waiting 30 metres (98½ feet) offshore. The fishermen hauled the soaking-wet refugees into the boat, led them down to the cargo area and instructed them to lie down on the floor. Unwilling to take any chances that their passengers might be seen, the fishermen covered them with a large canvas tarpaulin that stank of fish. As the captain turned his boat around and headed for Sweden, Cantor Goldberger softly chanted one of the Psalms. A few hours later, the family disembarked in Sweden.

After two happy, peaceful, secure years in Sweden, at war's end they returned home to Copenhagen. To their amazement they found their apartment in excellent condition, with all their furnishings and belongings in place—their neighbours had cared for their home during their absence. And when Cantor Goldberger called on Pastor Rasmussen to repay him the 20,000 kroner, the minister refused to accept a penny.

## Special status

The Jewish community in Denmark was tiny, only 7800 out of a population of approximately 4 million. Considering that over the previous three centuries the country had shown a steadily increasing acceptance of its Jewish population, one might have imagined that more Jews would have migrated there. In 1814 Denmark became one of the first European nations to grant civil rights to Jews; since then, many Jews had assimilated thoroughly into Danish society, becoming indistinguishable from their Lutheran friends and neighbours. At the time of the threatened Nazi crackdown in 1943, many Danes were surprised to discover that old friends and long-time neighbours were Jewish.

In the 1930s Denmark's two greatest trading partners were Great Britain and Germany, but as the Third Reich began to absorb its neighbours—Austria and Czechoslovakia—the relationship with Germany dominated the government's attention. In 1939, hoping to preserve the country's neutrality during the war everyone knew was coming, Denmark signed a ten-year non-aggression pact with Germany.

In spite of the treaty, on 9 April 1940, German troops invaded Denmark. The little country had become strategically important, both for Germany's planned invasion of Norway and as a defensive bulwark if the British attempted to invade Germany. But unlike Holland, Belgium, France, Poland and the other European nations that fell under Nazi occupation, Denmark did not experience waves of random murder, terror and destruction. There are several reasons why the country

Christian X, King of Denmark, remained in Copenhagen throughout the occupation of his country, riding daily through the city unaccompanied and becoming a beloved national symbol.

was spared: the Danish government was willing to cooperate with the Germans—up to a point—in exchange for some autonomy; the Danes were Germanic, part of the same Nordic Aryan race the Nazis extolled as the finest on Earth; and Adolf Hitler had decided to make Denmark a 'model protectorate', to show the world how the Germans would administer Europe after they won the war.

There were pro-Nazi and anti-Semitic elements in Denmark, but they were a minority who found no support from the government, which refused to pass any legislation or publish any decrees that would limit the civil rights of Jews or leave them open to persecution. And the authorities meant it. On the night of 20 December 1941, a Dane smashed a window of Copenhagen's Great Synagogue, poured a flammable liquid inside and set it alight. Neighbours saw the flames and called the fire department, which was able to extinguish the small blaze before it did much damage. Six weeks later the arsonist was tried in a Danish court, found guilty, and sentenced to a prison term of three years and twenty days. Such an outcome would have been unthinkable in any other Nazi-occupied country, but it reveals the 'special status' Germany was willing to grant Denmark for the time being.

## The underground

During the Nazi occupation there was an underground movement comprised largely of teenage boys who committed acts of sabotage such as blowing up railway lines. Among most ordinary Danes resistance tended to be passive, often indicated by no more than wearing a red, white and blue lapel pin—the colours of the Allies. Sometimes children stood in the streets and public squares passing out anti-Nazi newspapers, or the more daring poured sugar into the petrol tanks of Nazi vehicles. When Herbert Pundik's parents learned that he was distributing an anti-Nazi paper, they asked the Chief Rabbi, Max Friediger, to speak to him. The rabbi was stern with the boy. 'If you continue your illegal activities,' he said, 'you may jeopardise the entire Jewish community.'

Rabbi Friediger's concerns were shared by most of the Jewish population. The Danish authorities were almost desperate to maintain law and order in the country, to give the Nazis no excuse to seize control of the government. The Jews shared this anxiety—if a Jew committed some act of sabotage and were caught, the entire community would suffer. In fact, rabbis and other community leaders even discouraged Danish Jews from leaving the country because that might provoke the Nazis to acts of retribution. And so the Jews of Denmark did not resist, did not flee, and went about their lives as if there had never been a Nazi invasion. But early in 1943, the news began to spread across Denmark that the Nazis were exterminating the Jews of Poland.

## The crisis

In the summer of 1943 the Germans decided the time had come to abolish the Danish government, dissolve the Rigsdag, the parliament, and strip King Christian X of all political power and influence. At the same time as they planned to seize power, they would round up the Danish Jews. On 11 September, in a conversation with Dr Werner Best, Germany's chief representative in Denmark, Georg Ferdinand Duckwitz, a German diplomat, learned that the Nazis were planning a mass arrest of all of Denmark's Jews. Best revealed that the SS planned to strike on the evening of 1–2 October, which was both Rosh Hashanah and the beginning of the Sabbath, when all Jewish families would be at home celebrating the New Year. Best had no idea that Duckwitz worked with the Resistance in Germany.

Best remains a bewildering player in this story. The Holocaust Research Project has described him as 'ambitious, a cool amoral technician of power, [who] used his academic and legal skills to justify the totalitarian practice of the Nazi regime'. Early in the 1930s, during Hitler's rise to power, Best went on record as endorsing the execution of the Nazis' political opponents. In Poland in 1939 he was complicit in the murder of thousands of Jews as well as Polish Christian intellectuals. In Nazi-occupied France in 1940 and 1941, he worked to crush the Resistance while deporting thousands of French Jews to death camps.

In November 1942 Hitler sent Best to Denmark as his Reich Plenipotentiary, or ambassador with full powers to act on behalf and in the interests of the Third Reich. Some historians believe that when he received the order to supervise the deportation of Denmark's Jews, Best purposely undermined the scheme by leaking it to Duckwitz and perhaps others as well. But that would suggest that Best knew Duckwitz was a clandestine opponent of the Nazis, and there is no evidence that would lead to that conclusion.

Enthusiastic crowds of Danes welcome British airborne troops to Copenhagen in 1945. The Danish pledge of solidarity with their fellow Jewish citizens was the main reason for the rescue of the majority of Jews from the Nazis.

The debate has raged since 1948, when a Danish court convicted Best of war crimes and sentenced him to death, then commuted the sentence to five years' prison, and in the end granted him clemency and released him after serving three years.

## Spreading the word

Following his conversation with Best, Duckwitz met secretly with leaders of Denmark's Social Democratic party to warn them of the Nazi threat. Through these party leaders, word of the planned deportation spread throughout the Danish government, to the trade unions, to the newspapers, to the bishops and clergy of the Lutheran Church, and to countless ordinary Danish citizens.

Members of the underground went from one Jewish home to the next, warning the inhabitants to find a hiding place and prepare to leave for Sweden. In fact, some Danish Jews had already begun arranging the details of their escape, thanks to Werner David Melchior, son of Rabbi Marcus Melchior and a leader of the Zionist youth organisation in Denmark. Five days earlier, after one of Werner Melchior's contacts in the government had told him that the Germans were determined to round up all the Jews, the young man called his friends with the coded message '*Lekh lekha*', a Hebrew term from the Book of Genesis which means 'Rise and go'.

### The king and the yellow star

One of the most popular tales to emerge from World War II tells of what happened when the Nazis insisted that the Jews of Denmark wear a yellow Star of David on their clothing. One version of the story says that King Christian X declared that he would be the first to wear it. Another, more dramatic version has him actually wearing the Star of David on his daily horseback ride through Copenhagen. These are wonderful stories, and given the tolerant atmosphere of Denmark they sound plausible. But alas, they are urban legends.

As part of their hands-off policy in Denmark, the Nazis never required Danish Jews to wear the yellow star, so there was no reason for King Christian to engage in any act of defiance.

Nonetheless, we can track down the source of the story, and it appears to have been a cartoon published in a Swedish newspaper in 1943. The cartoon shows Denmark's former prime minister asking King Christian, 'What are you going to do, Your Majesty, if Scavenius makes all the Jews wear yellow stars?' (Erik Scavenius was the prime minister appointed by the Nazis.) The king replies, 'We'll all have to wear yellow stars.'

All across Denmark, wherever there were Jews, Gentiles opened their homes to hide them. Lutheran pastors concealed whole families in their rectories and dozens more in their churches. In cooperation with the underground, hospitals sent out their fleets of ambulances to pick up Jews and register them in the hospitals as patients under common Christian names—Jansen, Hansen, Petersen.

Among the first to heed the warnings were the few hundred Jews from Germany and eastern Europe who had come to Denmark to escape persecution and who knew from experience what the Nazis were capable of. Tragically, some Danish Jews, especially among those who were most assimilated, dismissed the warnings as melodramatic—and they were among the 500 who were taken by the Nazis and sent to a concentration camp.

Danish Christians not only helped their Jewish friends escape, they helped safeguard their property while they were away. To frustrate Nazi efforts to loot their homes and businesses, Jews transferred title or gave power of attorney to their Gentile friends, who operated the businesses, arranged for the storage of furniture and personal belongings, and rented out the vacant houses or apartments. After the war, like Cantor Goldberger, the Danish Jews returned to find their businesses running, their homes in good repair, and their personal property intact.

## The costs of escaping

From Denmark the closest place of refuge was neutral Sweden, so almost every Jew in Denmark headed for the fishing villages along the coast. Fifteen-year-old Herbert Pundik and his family were among the thousands who hired fishermen to carry them across the narrow Oresund to the Swedish ports of Helsingborg or Malmo. They left at night, but even in the darkness there was danger—Pundik remembered the searchlights from German patrol boats sweeping the area. From the fishing boat Pundik looked back to the shore—there he saw the friend of his father's who had arranged their escape, and the fisherman's wife, both kneeling, praying for the safety of Herbert and his family

Some of the early escape attempts were very poorly planned. Among the first to go was Walter Berendson, a professor of Scandinavian literature. He and two other Jews hired an experienced seaman to take them to Sweden in a rowboat no one had bothered to inspect. Not far out into the Oresund one of the oarlocks broke;

the passengers lashed it down with rope. Then the boat began to take on water; the passengers used a coat to plug the hole. The bailing bucket had been left on shore, so the passengers took turns bailing with Professor Berendson's hat. Meanwhile, the 'captain' had to do all the rowing himself—Berendson was sixty-seven years old, and the other two passengers were also too weak to row. A strong wind and rough seas prevented them from reaching the Swedish mainland; after nine hours, the boat came ashore on the Swedish island of Ven.

The cost of hiring a fishing boat from Denmark to Sweden ranged from as little as 500 kroner per person to as much as 10,000 kroner. The highest fees were paid during the first days of the evacuation when well-to-do families were willing to pay any price to get away. But very few could afford such exorbitant sums. The members of the underground and other Danish refugee organisations negotiated with many fishermen on behalf of the refugees to arrive at a reasonable fare. On average, it cost 2125 kroner per person to escape to Sweden, about US$120 by 1943 standards.

Even without the unpredictability of the wind and the waves, escape across the Oresund was dangerous. German ships patrolled the waters, which were peppered with mines. The fishermen and seamen were indispensable because they knew where the mines were and how to avoid them, and the escapees were also assisted in Danish waters by the coastguard. Anchored just within Sweden's territorial waters were Swedish ships, ready to help any boat that got into trouble.

The rescue of 7300 Danish Jews was not a well-organised operation, but a spontaneous, grassroots movement involving thousands of non-Jewish Danes who risked their lives to save the lives of friends and neighbours, even complete strangers. Motivated by conscience and a loathing for Nazism, these Danes hid Jews, gave them or loaned them the money for the passage to Sweden and looked after their property while they were gone. Of Denmark's 7800 Jews, about 500 were captured by the Nazis and sent to the Theresienstadt concentration camp in occupied Czechoslovakia, but even there they were not forgotten by their countrymen.

The Danish government insisted that its representatives, or members of the Red Cross, be permitted to visit their citizens in Theresienstadt and to send them packages of food, clothing and other necessities. Adolf Eichmann agreed, and used these visits and deliveries as a propaganda tool to show the world that Jews were not being liquidated, but were living in their own city where they were safe from the ravages of the war. This combination of Danish compassion and Nazi opportunism saved lives—approximately 450 of the 500 Danish Jews survived their incarceration in Theresienstadt.

But the real heroes were the citizens of Denmark who quietly, without any fuss, saved the lives of 7300 men, women and children for the simple reason that they were their fellow Danes and no one had the right to persecute them.

# CHAPTER 10

# OPERATION HALYARD

## Serbian Peasants, Guerrillas and American Secret Agents Rescue More Than 500 US Airmen

At their first glimpse of the man on horseback, the two downed American flyers were ready to leap into the brush at the side of the dirt track that passed for a road here—but the Yugoslav guerrillas who were acting as their guides and protectors through the mountains showed no signs of alarm, so they got hold of their nerves again. One thing was certain—the horseman was not a Nazi: he was dressed in the same rough clothes as every peasant in the region, and he sported a big, dark, bushy beard like a Serbian Orthodox monk. But he appeared bigger, more robust than the peasants—broad shoulders, thick chest, heavy arms. Here was a man whose diet was more substantial than the stale bread and goat cheese the airmen had been offered in every cottage and hut along the way.

The Allied defeat of the Nazis in Yugoslavia in October 1944 brings a guerrilla group out into the streets to celebrate openly.

As the Americans and the guerrillas drew closer, the man on horseback greeted them: 'Hi boys! Welcome to Pranjane.' The airmen could scarcely believe it—not only did this guy speak English, but he had a New York accent. He must be an American! He was. After more than two weeks of not knowing where they were, or where they were going, or who their escorts were, they were about to get some answers.

The rider introduced himself as George Musulin, a member of the Office of Strategic Services, or OSS (the forerunner of the CIA). He had been trained as part of an elite force to blend in with the people of Yugoslavia in order to rescue downed American flight crews. Musulin spoke, looked and acted like a Serb. If a Nazi patrol ever ran across him, they would not have been able to tell him from any Serb farmer or shepherd in these mountains.

The astonished Americans had lots of questions. Where were they? Who were these guerrillas? Was there any way they could get back to their base in Italy?

Musulin assured them that there was going to be a rescue. Not far away were about 200 other American airmen who had been shot down by the Nazis, and all of them were going to be flown out on C-47 cargo planes. But first, they had to build a landing strip—in these mountains.

## Operation Punishment

By late winter–early spring of 1941 it was obvious to everyone in Yugoslavia that their country would be Adolf Hitler's next target. Hoping to avoid a devastating invasion, on 25 March the regent of Yugoslavia, Prince Paul, signed what became known as the Tripartite Pact, aligning the country with Germany, Italy and Japan against the Allies. The prince genuinely believed he was acting in the best interests of his people; by siding with the Axis he hoped Yugoslavia would be spared the destruction, bloodshed and terror that Poland, Belgium, the Netherlands and France were still suffering—but most of the citizens of Yugoslavia objected vehemently to this virtual surrender. In Belgrade, the capital, crowds marched through the streets chanting, 'War rather than the pact! Death rather than slavery!'

Two days after Prince Paul signed the Tripartite Pact, high-ranking members of the government declared his seventeen-year-old nephew, the Crown Prince, to be of age, and recognised him as Peter II, King of Yugoslavia. Backed by pro-Allied elements, King Peter staged a *coup d'état* that pushed out Prince Paul and his pro-appeasement government. The young king's actions did not go unnoticed in Berlin.

At dawn just a week later, on 6 April, the inhabitants of Belgrade were thrown from their beds by a massive air raid that the Germans code-named Operation Punishment. The defiance of King Peter and his people had enraged Hitler; he ordered the Luftwaffe to bomb the Yugoslav capital 'with unmerciful harshness'. Drawing on 135 fighter planes based at airfields in Romania and 355 bombers based in Bulgaria, the Luftwaffe punished Belgrade for three days. When the last plane returned to base the capital of Yugoslavia was in flames, 17,000 men, women and children lay dead in the rubble, and many thousands more were injured. King Peter and his government fled to exile in England by way of Greece, Jerusalem and Cairo. Prince Paul fled to South Africa, where the British kept him under house arrest until the end of the war.

Even as Belgrade was being bombed, Nazi troops crossed the border, crushing the valiant but futile resistance of the Yugoslav army. On 17 April they marched into the shattered capital, and formal resistance to the occupation of Yugoslavia ceased.

## The war hero

*Time* magazine of 25 May 1942 featured a portrait of General Draza Mihailovich on its cover, with a story inside that hailed him as 'the eagle of Yugoslavia', the leader of 'the greatest guerrilla operation in history'. Mihailovich, who was forty-nine at the time the story was written, was a Serb, a lifelong soldier who had begun his military training at the age of fifteen. During World War I he was recognised as a war hero, and had received Yugoslavia's highest military award, the Kara George Star with crossed swords. After the war he served as military attaché in Sofia in Bulgaria in 1934, and in Prague in Czechoslovakia in 1936, and in both capitals there had been widespread rumours that he was working closely with underground elements against pro-Nazi forces.

In 1939 Mihailovich was appointed commander of the defence of Yugoslavia against a possible German invasion. His superiors wanted him to erect in-place fortifications along the line of Belgium's Eben Emael fortress. Mihailovich argued that such fortifications were obsolete, an opinion justified by what happened at

Eben Emael in May 1940 (see chapter 3), and that Yugoslavia should train its armed forces to be mobile, adaptable and innovative. For these insubordinate opinions, his superiors had Mihailovich reassigned to military inspections. Even in this innocuous position he got into trouble through circulating a memorandum warning that pro-Nazi forces were already at work in Yugoslavia, undermining the unity of the nation and the people's will to defend their independence. Minister of War Milan Neditch ordered Mihailovich to withdraw the memo; Mihailovich refused. Neditch charged him with disloyalty and punished him with thirty days in prison. (Incidentally, after the Nazis seized power in Yugoslavia, they appointed Neditch head of their puppet government in Belgrade.)

When German forces entered ruined Belgrade, Mihailovich and a handful of officers fled into Serbia's Sumadija Mountains. First a trickle, then a flood of Yugoslav soldiers followed them into the mountains, where they were joined by men and boys from the mountain villages. By May 1942 it was estimated that Mihailovich commanded 150,000 guerrillas; they were known as Chetniks, after the Serb guerrillas who for centuries had resisted the Turks.

Another large guerrilla group, the Partisans, was led by Josip Broz Tito, an avowed Communist. Tito had two goals—to drive the Nazis from Yugoslavia and to establish his country as a 'workers' paradise'. Tito saw Mihailovich, who was pro-monarchist, pro-Allies and anti-Communist, as a dangerous rival. The two guerrilla leaders also differed in the way they conducted their resistance activities— Mihailovich was cautious, unwilling to attack the Germans if civilians might also be killed; Tito, on the other hand, attacked the Germans wherever he found them, giving no thought to collateral damage among his own people. The Nazis retaliated against the actions of both groups by vindictively and mercilessly targeting Yugoslav civilians, killing over 500,000 in the four years they occupied the country.

## 'Americanski!'

Anthony Orsini had been at the Allied air base in southern Italy barely a week when he received his first assignment as navigator for a US bombing mission over the Ploesti oil refineries in Romania. During the pre-mission briefing, Orsini learned about the anti-aircraft guns and fighter planes the Germans used to defend the refineries, but it was all meaningless information until the squadron reached Ploesti and the pilots found their planes in a firestorm of exploding anti-aircraft shells and strafing German planes. Orsini's plane was struck by a shell that knocked out two of the four engines. The pilot pulled out of formation, turning the B-24 back towards Italy. As the plane lost altitude, Orsini realised they could not possibly reach their base, and the pilot gave the order to bail out.

Falling through the sky frightened Orsini so much that he vomited. As his parachute floated gently down he saw a big woman running in his direction. Distracted by her appearance, Orsini failed to guide his parachute towards a safe landing spot; he smashed into a tree, breaking his collarbone, hit the ground hard and passed out. When he came to, the woman was cradling him in her arms. She helped him up and led him to her village, where they arrived at the same moment as the bombardier from Orsini's crew.

Villagers surged out of their houses to welcome the two Americans and serve them bread and goat's milk. No one spoke English, but their kindness and goodwill reassured Orsini and his crew mate that they were among friends. After a few restful hours enjoying the villagers' hospitality, a group of men gave the two flyers to understand that they should follow them into the woods. About two hours later the village men led the Americans into Mihailovich's camp. The guerrillas looked intimidating, but Orsini's fears were dispelled when they were greeted with cries of 'Americanski!' and powerful bear hugs—hugs which unfortunately aggravated the break in Orsini's collarbone and made him wince in pain.

## Fuelling the Nazi war machine

In 1944 the Allies set up airfields in the south of newly liberated Italy, the closest they could get at the time to the oil refineries of Romania. Romania had fought against Germany in World War I, but after September 1939, having seen the Third Reich conquer Poland in a matter of days, Romania feared that it too would fall victim to the destruction wrought by the Nazis, and so had joined the Axis.

The Germans regarded Romania as a valuable prize—it was especially rich in oil, and the Third Reich needed fuel oil to keep the war machine moving. The biggest refinery was at Ploesti in the north, at the foot of the Transylvanian Alps.

The shattered ruins of Belgrade after the German air offensive of April 1941 form a bleak backdrop to this image of a German soldier pecking out a report on his typewriter.

The refinery buildings and storage tanks sprawled over 50 square kilometres (31 square miles), churning out 907,000 tonnes (1 million tons) of high-grade 90-octane fuel for aircraft, tanks and battleships every month. Ploesti was so productive it delivered a third of the fuel Germany needed.

The first Allied bombing mission over Ploesti was led by an American, Colonel Harry A. Halverson, in June 1942. Halverson and his squadron of twenty-three brand-new B-24 bombers flew from an airfield outside Cairo in Egypt, striking at dawn. They damaged some of the refineries and got away without losing any planes, but that first mission revealed the true extent of the complex and what it would take to destroy it.

After more than a year of planning and months of intense practice, in August 1943 the Allied High Command authorised Operation Tidal Wave, which sent formation after formation of B-24s flying very low over the refineries and storage tanks to ensure they would not miss their targets. Of course, in flying so low the B-24s made excellent targets for the anti-aircraft guns that defended Ploesti. Operation Tidal Wave ended in disaster: of the 177 B-24s sent on this mission, fifty-four were shot down and another fifty-three were severely damaged.

Once Italy was in Allied hands, however, it was no longer necessary to send bombing missions to Ploesti from Cairo. The new route crossed the Adriatic Sea and took the bombers over Yugoslavia to Romania. The flying distance was less, but the resistance the bombers encountered was as stiff as ever. Literally hundreds of flight crews were forced to bail out over Yugoslavia where, if they were lucky, Mihailovich's guerrillas found them before the Nazis did.

## Careful planning

The American Office of Strategic Services had opened a branch in Bari, a seaport town on the heel of the Italian boot, headed by twenty-eight-year-old George Vujnovich, the son of Serbian immigrants who had settled in Pittsburgh. He had been studying at the university in Belgrade when the Nazis bombed the city in Operation Punishment in 1941. Having escaped from Yugoslavia along with his fiancée Mirjana Lazic, Vujnovich joined the OSS to help drive the Nazi invaders from eastern Europe.

US aircraft carried out hundreds of sorties in eastern Europe through 1944, and many planes did not return. OSS field agents reported in to Bari that large numbers of downed airmen were stranded in the mountains of Yugoslavia, some tended by Serbian peasants or Serbian guerrillas, others hiding out and trying to fend for themselves. It was worse for those who suffered shrapnel wounds when their planes were hit, or broken bones when they bailed out—in the mountains there were no hospitals and few doctors. When George Musulin reported that there were 100 Americans in the village of Pranjane, the OSS at Bari agreed that the men must be rescued—the question was how to bring out so many safely.

If it had been a single crew of a dozen men, the Allies could have sent in a small plane, snatched them up and taken off before the Germans realised. But taking out 100 men would require several large aircraft, which would attract a great deal of undesirable attention, and an airstrip, which did not exist in Pranjane or anywhere near it. This mission, code-named Operation Halyard, would require careful planning.

George Vujnovich worked with officers of the Fifteenth Air Force to coordinate the rescue. They agreed that the OSS should send agents to Pranjane to get the men ready and that the Air Force would supply six C-47 cargo planes, each of which could carry perhaps twenty men. But nothing could happen until, somehow, the Americans and the Serbs could build an airstrip. Since the only implements available were those the peasants used on their farms—hoes, shovels, picks and crowbars, axes, wheelbarrows, carts—the work would be hard and progress slow. Furthermore, they would have to keep what they were doing secret from the Germans—not an easy task, because the Germans had garrisons only a few miles from Pranjane. And the C-47s would have to go in at night, when they were less likely to be spotted—which meant providing some kind of lighting to outline the airstrip. Absolute secrecy was essential, because not only the lives of the airmen were at stake. If the Germans learned of the rescue mission, they would attack Pranjane, capture or kill the downed flyers, and massacre by the score the villagers and the guerrillas and anyone else who could possibly have been involved. To ensure that everything went as smoothly as possible, Vujnovich decided to parachute into Yugoslavia and supervise the Pranjane end of Operation Halyard personally, but the State Department sent him a direct order forbidding him to go. Vujnovich's staunch anti-Communist stance and his support for Mihailovich irritated the men at the State Department, who thought that in post-war Yugoslavia they would be able to work more easily with Tito and his Communist Partisans. Since Vujnovich could not go, he sent the one man in whom he had complete trust, George Musulin.

Vujnovich assigned another OSS agent, also an American of Serbian background, Sergeant Mike Rajacich, to assist Musulin. Communication was essential, and when Arthur Jibilian, a communications agent, volunteered for the mission, Vujnovich decided to burden the group with a suitcase-sized radio (which passed as portable in the 1940s). The son of Armenian immigrants, Jibilian did not speak Serbian, but he had combat experience and was an expert radio operator.

## 'Prepare a reception'

Nicholas Petrovich, just seventeen years old, was one of Mihailovich's youngest guerrillas, but he was physically and psychologically tough, a kid who had once stolen an SS officer's sub-machine gun and endured hours of beatings without admitting that he had taken it, let alone revealing where he had hidden it. Petrovich was one of the guerrillas assigned to pick up downed American flight crews and lead them to safety. 'If any one of you comes to me with news that anything has happened to a single one of these airmen,' Mihailovich had said, 'I shall have the man who bears the news executed on the spot.'

Mihailovich might have been overstating the case, but Petrovich was extremely careful about the safety of downed flyers. His standard procedure was to block the road with trees and rocks near any place where an American airman had been spotted. He and his squad would conceal themselves in the forest, waiting for the German patrol sent out to capture the airman. When the troops climbed out of their vehicles to clear the roadblock, Petrovich and his men would open fire, killing them all.

Petrovich was interested in the American bombers that crashed in the mountains, especially their .50 calibre machine guns. If these valuable items could be salvaged, he took them to a blacksmith in Pranjane nearby who custom-designed for each one a sturdy mount so they could be used against enemy patrols. Their large-calibre bullets would tear apart any German foolish enough to approach Pranjane.

Despite the courage and resourcefulness of people such as Petrovich, it was dangerous for the downed airmen to remain in Pranjane—dangerous for them as well as for the Serbs who protected them and cared for them. And although it was risky to send a radio message—the Germans had equipment that could trace an intercepted message back to its source—the airmen at Pranjane managed to send out a brief SOS on a radio cobbled together from salvaged parts: 'There are many sick and wounded. Call back.' And they received an answer: 'Prepare reception for July 31ᵗ or first clear night following.'

On that July night in 1944, Petrovich and everyone else in Pranjane watched the skies for the plane that would drop OSS agents and badly needed supplies. After two nights keeping vigil, they heard the familiar drone of a C-47. Soon they saw the plane overhead, followed immediately by the appearance of three large parachutes—bearing Musulin, Rajacich and Jibilian—and a few smaller parachutes with crates of food, medicine and ammunition, and the portable radio. Jibilian made a soft landing in a cornfield, Rajacich's parachute became tangled in a tree, but Musulin dropped squarely and heavily onto the roof of a chicken shed, shattering it and scattering its hysterical inmates in every direction. He was still trying to extricate himself from the ruined shed when the woman who owned the chicken shed ran towards him, hailing him as a liberator and kissing him repeatedly on both cheeks. As Jibilian and Rajacich joined them, she insisted that they come to her house to rest and have something to eat. Musulin begged off, but gave her 15,000 dinars—about US$10—to cover the expense of the chicken shed. After lavishing with more kisses, she told them where to find Mihailovich.

The arrival of the three agents set off an impromptu celebration with music; the villagers crowded around Musulin, welcoming him back. Musulin eventually spotted Lieutenant Richard Felman, the unofficial leader of the Americans in Pranjane, at the edge of the crowd. Freeing himself from his well-wishers, Musulin introduced himself, and the two men went off to discuss the rescue mission.

Felman was candid—building an airstrip and evacuating the airmen without being noticed would be extremely difficult, maybe impossible. The Germans had garrisons in every city and town within 50 kilometres (31 miles) of Pranjane; there were 4500 troops at the village of Chachak only 20 kilometres (12½ miles) from

Great Rescues of World War II

Pranjane, and 250 in a camp just 8 kilometres (5 miles) away. Musulin had expected there would be Nazis in the vicinity, but what came as a complete surprise were the number of airmen now in Pranjane—he thought he had to evacuate 100, but Felman told him that in fact 250 airmen were harboured in the village.

## Building an airstrip

Outside the village was a commons, a pasture about 640 metres (2100 feet) long and 45 metres (148 feet) wide, where the farmers grazed sheep and other livestock. From a pilot's perspective the area was a nightmare: on one side was a forest, on the other a cliff; it was surrounded by mountains so there was no easy descent path. Furthermore, at a bare minimum a C-47 required a landing strip as long as the pasture—the least miscalculation of speed at the point of landing and the aircraft would slide off the improvised runway and explode in flames.

Using the farmers' sturdy tools, their hoes, rakes, axes, handsaws, picks and shovels, the airmen and 300 villagers and guerrillas set to work clearing the pasture. The farmers provided sixty ox-carts to help carry away rocks and other debris and haul gravel from streambeds to pave the airstrip. To provide protection in the event of Nazi attack during construction, Mihailovich brought in between 6000 and 8000 of his Chetnik guerrillas. Every person involved in the project was alert to the sound of passing aircraft, which sent one and all scurrying into the woods. While one work crew worked at levelling the pasture, removing rocks and shrubs and filling in the smallest hole or soft spot, another was chopping down trees and digging up their stumps to increase the length of the landing strip by 70 metres (230 feet). Only a week after the transformation began, the airstrip looked good, or at the very least a better proposition than when sheep and cows were grazing on it. Persuaded that everything possible had been done to make it safe, Musulin told his radio operator, 'Jibby, tell Bari we're ready. We'll start evacuation tomorrow night.'

## Saved by the cows

The night of 8–9 August, before the first scheduled evacuation, Musulin, Rajacich and Jibilian could not sleep. The sound of machine-gun fire had the three OSS agents leaping out of their beds, grabbing up their weapons and heading into the woods. The shooting

# The tragedy of Draza Mihailovich

By February 1945, Franklin D. Roosevelt and Winston Churchill had admitted to each other that they had made a serious error in backing Josip Tito rather than Draza Mihailovich in Yugoslavia. It had become clear that Tito would not form a post-war government that was friendly to the West, that he had entered Joseph Stalin's orbit instead. On 5 April 1945, Tito signed a document permitting the 'temporary entry of Soviet troops into Yugoslav territory'. Following Germany's surrender to the Allies on 8 May, Tito's Partisans began hunting down General Mihailovich. His friends and allies outside Yugoslavia urged him to escape to Switzerland, but Mihailovich refused to abandon his country. The Partisans captured him in late March of 1946 and Tito charged him with collaborating with the Nazis during the occupation of Yugoslavia.

When the story was picked up by American newspapers, the OSS agents and rescued airmen who had known Mihailovich were outraged to see him characterised as a traitor who had sold out his country. Arthur Jibilian went to the offices of the *Washington Post* to set the record straight. Richard Felman wrote articles praising Mihailovich for the Hearst syndicate of newspapers. Within a matter of weeks, hundreds of the rescued American airmen were lobbying Congress and the US State Department to step in and save Mihailovich from a show trial that would certainly end with his execution. Their visit to Washington received a great deal of press coverage, but Secretary of State Dean Acheson refused to see Felman, and the State Department declined to forward to the court in Belgrade documentary evidence collected by the men of Operation Halyard that would exonerate Mihailovich.

The public outcry against the railroading of a man who had saved the lives of hundreds of American servicemen finally had some impact. Acheson authorised a letter to Tito that urged him to consider the testimony of the OSS agents and the rescued air crews at Mihailovich's trial. Tito rejected the recommendations.

On 10 June 1946, in the auditorium of a military school in Belgrade, General Draza Mihailovich appeared before a court that had already concluded he was guilty, appearing utterly worn out. The trial dragged on for a month, with the prosecutors digressing occasionally to denounce the United States and Great Britain for opposing Tito's alliance with Stalin and the imposition of a Communist government on the people of Yugoslavia.

On 15 July the court found Mihailovich guilty and sentenced him to death. Two days later he was executed by firing squad and his body dumped in an unmarked grave.

In 1948, President Harry Truman posthumously awarded the Legion of Merit to Draza Mihailovich for his contributions to the Allies' victory in Europe. If the award had been publicised at the time, it would have gone a long way to rehabilitate Mihailovich's reputation, but the State Department insisted that such recognition would antagonise Tito and damage US relations with his government. Public recognition was suppressed until 2005, when the award was at last presented to the general's granddaughter, Gordana Mihailovich.

'I reminded the Court of Hitler's message to Mussolini saying that I was the greatest enemy of the Axis, and was only waiting for the moment to attack … I strove for much, I undertook much, but the gales of the world have carried away both me and my work.' Draza Mihailovich, closing speech at his trial, July 1946.

Operation Halyard

had stopped, but they needed to know what had happened. One of the guerrillas assured them there was no problem. 'One of my men saw something moving and challenged it,' he explained. 'When it did not say anything he fired his machine gun.'

'Oh, so there's nobody out there?' Musulin asked.

'Only cow,' the guerrilla replied. 'Now dead cow.'

For the first evacuation Musulin had selected seventy-two wounded men. The uninjured would be evacuated by a seniority system based on how long they had been waiting for rescue. On the morning of 9 August a group of German Stuka dive-bombers flew over the empty pasture, turned and came over it again, flying more slowly and closer to the ground. Musulin cursed himself for not putting a few farmers there to make things look normal; if the Stuka pilots recognised the pasture as an improvised landing strip and bombed it, the C-47s would not be able to land that night, and every German trooper within a 50 kilometre (31mile) radius would be sent to Pranjane. Miraculously, a herd of cows appeared out of nowhere and began to graze on what was left of the grass. During the previous week all livestock had been barred; the cows seemed happy to get back to their grazing ground, which with their presence could not be imagined to resemble an airstrip. The German planes flew on.

For the rest of the day the Americans and the Serbs worked on the field, cutting down a few more trees, bringing up a few more cartloads of gravel and earth to level out a few spots, positioning the oil drums and bales of hay which would be set ablaze to guide the C-47s. After dinner, when it was dark, Musulin led the wounded men who would be flown to Bari that night out to the field; they were followed by a large crowd of villagers and guerrillas. The rescue planes were due about 10 pm, and as the hour approached everyone around the field grew still. When they heard the roar of aircraft engines in the distance, the guerrillas stationed beside the oil drums and hay bales ignited them.

Only four C-47s came into view—Musulin had expected six. (In fact, six had set out, but engine trouble had forced two to turn back.) The first to attempt a landing touched down, but immediately lifted off again. The crowd groaned with disappointment—the landing strip was too short. The second pilot began his descent further back, taxied down the runway, and came to a stop with just metres to spare. The other three pilots followed his example, and soon all four C-47s were on the ground. The spectators ran across the field to welcome them, and suddenly it was a party, with bottles of plum brandy appearing from coat pockets and women pelting the pilots with flowers. Eyewitness Nicholas Petrovich thought that with the about-to-be-rescued airmen cheering, and the Serbs singing and kissing the pilots, it looked like a scene from an American movie.

## The man who saved their lives

With only four planes available only forty-eight of the injured men could be evacuated; Musulin picked the most severe cases. The pilots argued that they could take more than twelve men apiece, but Musulin was afraid that given the abbreviated runway and the extra weight, the planes wouldn't clear the tree line.

Once all four C-47s were in the air, most of the crowd remained along the perimeter of the field, just in case the planes came back before dawn to pick up more evacuees. At 8 am, just as they were thinking of going home for a few hours of sleep, they heard the sound of aircraft again—a whole fleet of aircraft, six C-47s escorted by thirty P-51 Mustangs and P-38 Lightning fighter planes. The crowd erupted into fresh cheers as the C-47s landed and the fighters flew cover overhead. The twenty-four wounded who could not make the night-time flight were loaded first, followed by forty-eight able-bodied airmen.

An hour later, six more C-47s arrived, escorted by twenty-five fighter planes. Before the day was out, 241 American, six British, four French, nine Italian and twelve Russian airmen had been evacuated to Bari. Musulin also sent two badly wounded Serbs who needed specialist treatment available at a US army hospital. That humanitarian act almost got him court-martialled by the Americans. The State Department still thought that Tito was the USA's best friend in Yugoslavia, and that Mihailovich could not be trusted—in blatant contradiction of the testimony of the OSS agents and the many rescued flyers who knew from first-hand experience that they owed their lives to Draza Mihailovich.

Operation Halyard continued for six months, eventually bringing 512 men out of the mountains of Yugoslavia. In those six months, not a single plane was lost, not a single man killed. It remains the largest and most successful rescue of downed airmen in history.

# CHAPTER 11

# THE HERO OF BUDAPEST

### Raoul Wallenberg

With a sickening crash, the Gestapo guards slammed shut the heavy doors of the freight car, locking them from the outside. Crammed together inside each car were between seventy and one hundred Jewish men, women and children. The only 'facilities' were a single bucket of water, and a second, empty bucket to serve as a toilet. The only place where fresh air and sunlight could enter was a tiny barred window.

The train was about to pull out of Budapest's Jozefvaros station, bound for a Nazi death camp, when two automobiles drove up, coming sharply to a halt. Out of the lead car leaped the Swedish diplomat Raoul Wallenberg as his Hungarian aides stepped from the second one. Wallenberg made straight for the German officer in charge. After a short but impassioned conversation, the Nazi ordered the freight car doors be unlocked, and made an announcement—anyone with an authentic protective passport issued by the Swedish government should step down and form a line so the paper could be authenticated. Anyone who presented forged papers would be shot.

Immediately following the Nazi occupation of Hungary in April 1944,
all Jews in the country, like this couple in the Budapest ghetto,
were forced to wear yellow stars to identify their Jewishness.

157
The Hero of Budapest

Wallenberg's assistants set up a folding table on which they piled massive registry books from the Swedish Embassy. In front of the books, as a not-so-subtle reminder, the Nazi officer placed his pistol.

Stephen Lazarovitz, an intern who had been forced out of a Budapest medical school after the fascist Arrow Cross Party came to power in Hungary, did not dare emerge at first—his protective passport was a forgery. But then he saw among Wallenberg's aides Leslie Geiger, a star of Hungary's national hockey team and a personal friend. Lazarovitz decided to take a chance, and took his place at the end of the long line.

Geiger spotted his friend and came over to talk. Lazarovitz whispered that his papers were no good, could Geiger help? Geiger strolled casually back to Wallenberg and held a whispered conversation.

When Lazarovitz reached the table, Wallenberg took the false passport from his hands and announced in a commanding tone, 'I remember this doctor. I gave him his passport personally. Let's not waste our time, because it's late. We need him now at the Emergency Hospital of the Swedish Embassy.'

Wallenberg's air of authority impressed the Nazi officer. 'Let's not waste our time,' he said. 'Next!'

## A special mission

By 1944, the thirty-two-year-old bachelor Raoul Wallenberg, a member of a prominent Swedish family, found himself profoundly dissatisfied with his life. Fresh from his studies in architecture at the University of Michigan in the United States, and looking for change, he had taken a job with a trading company in South Africa, but found the work did not interest him. He next found a position as a banker in Palestine, where he met German Jewish refugees who told him how the Nazis were persecuting Jews. Banking bored him, too, so he returned home to Sweden where he hoped to find work in the profession in which he had trained. When no opportunity presented itself, he went to work for an import-export firm owned by Dr Kalaman Lauer, a Hungarian Jew residing in Sweden. This job required Wallenberg to visit clients in Nazi Germany and Nazi-occupied France, where he learned first-hand of the atrocities of the Third Reich. He also made frequent business trips to Hungary, where he picked up the language, became acquainted with the customs of the country, and made a number of contacts with members of the Jewish community and the Hungarian government.

When the Nazis occupied Hungary in March 1944, the situation of its large Jewish community—estimated at 725,000—became desperate. The Swedish Embassy in Budapest was especially active in issuing protective passports, but something more daring was needed if significant numbers of Jewish lives were to be saved.

Norbert Masur, a German Jew who had escaped to Sweden and was a member of the World Jewish Congress, wrote to Sweden's chief rabbi, Professor Marcus Ehrenpreis, asking for his help in finding a non-Jewish citizen of Sweden who enjoyed the confidence of his government, could receive full diplomatic status, and had the courage and resourcefulness to rescue Hungarian Jews from imminent death. The special envoy he had in mind to appoint would also require almost unlimited funds, and for that reason it would be best if the United States were included in planning this special mission.

Masur's idea appealed to Rabbi Ehrenpreis, but he was not yet convinced that it could be put into operation, nor could he think of any Swede suited to the awesome task. By chance, the rabbi consulted Dr Lauer, who immediately nominated his colleague Raoul Wallenberg. True, Wallenberg was young, he had no direct experience as a diplomat, but he knew Budapest, he was imaginative, well spoken, brave, and he possessed a personality that could be charismatic or commanding depending upon the circumstances. Furthermore, as a bachelor Wallenberg would not have to balance the dangers of his assignment with any obligations to a wife and children.

When he was approached about the mission, Wallenberg expressed his interest but listed several conditions that would have to be met before he would take it on: a free hand to operate as seemed best to him, authorisation to pay bribes as necessary, and unlimited funds to hire support staff and purchase food, medicine and other necessary supplies. One by one, Rabbi Ehrenpreis (who initially thought Wallenberg too inexperienced for such an assignment), representatives of the World Jewish Congress, the International Red Cross and the US Department of

State agreed that Wallenberg was the right man, and acquiesced to his demands. And last of all, Sweden's King Gustav V agreed to inform the government of Hungary that Raoul Wallenberg would act as his personal representative.

On 6 July, Wallenberg left Sweden for Budapest. In his luggage were lists of individuals to whom he could turn for help—Scandinavians living in Hungary, pro-Allied members of the Hungarian government, and members of the anti-Nazi underground. He also had access to a secret bank account in which had been placed an initial deposit of $30,000—about $350,000 in contemporary US dollars.

## A dreadful, familiar pattern

Adolf Eichmann was absolutely jubilant at the prospect of exterminating almost three quarters of a million Hungarian Jews. 'If everything goes as planned,' he told his staff, 'in less than six months we will announce to the Führer that the Jewish vermin of Hungary has been wiped out. It will be the fruition, the crowning of three years' effort, work and thought. It will be another glorious page in the history of the Third Reich.'

After the Nazi occupation of Hungary in March 1944, the dehumanisation of the country's Jews followed the dreadful, familiar pattern. Jewish businesses were closed or taken over; Jews were expelled from the universities, schools and government, from the legal and medical professions, even from the entertainment industry. Their automobiles, bicycles, radios and telephones were confiscated. They were barred from hotels and theatres, and from any other public buildings that were used by non-Jews. And all were obligated to display on their clothing a yellow Star of David.

On 7 April, across Hungary the mass arrests of Jews began. Tens of thousands were confined inside ghettos; they were permitted to bring enough food for fourteen days, but no money, jewellery or valuables of any kind. Tens of thousands more were herded into makeshift camps near railway stations where they awaited deportation. Over the next eight months approximately 285,000 Hungarian Jews would be murdered in the gas chambers of Auschwitz. To facilitate such large numbers, the Nazis built a new railway line connecting Hungary to Auschwitz: its terminus stood only 200 metres (656 feet) from the gas chambers.

On 7 July, seven weeks after the deportations began, Eichmann was delighted to learn that he was on schedule—he had sent more than 435,000 Jews from the provinces to their deaths or to labour camps. Now he turned his attention to Budapest, home to more than 200,000 others.

## A little extra documentary protection

The first protective passports the Swedish Embassy in Budapest had issued were very simple: a page of embassy letterhead with a photo of the individual attached. However, Wallenberg had discovered during his many business trips through Germany and Nazi-occupied Europe that German officials were invariably impressed by elaborate documents. He called for a newly designed passport printed in blue and yellow, the colours of the Swedish flag, bearing the three crowns, the emblem of the Swedish royal family, embellished with official seals, and bearing the signature of the minister of the Swedish Foreign Office.

While the new passport was in production, Wallenberg called upon Admiral Miklos Horthy, once the regent of Hungary, now reduced to a figurehead in the puppet government controlled by the Nazis. Together they worked out the details of how the Swedish protective passports would work. Recipients would have to renounce their Hungarian citizenship and declare themselves citizens of Sweden; as Swedish citizens they would not be required to wear the incriminating yellow star.

In the summer of 1944 Wallenberg's office issued 5000 protective passports, in early autumn another 2500. Because the Swedish Embassy's passport printshop could not meet the demand, a number of printers in Budapest assisted by issuing convincing counterfeit passports. One of them, Joseph Kovacs, a Jewish attorney, issued false baptismal certificates along with his false passports to give the carriers a little extra protective documentation.

Any Hungarian in possession of a valid passport from a neutral country was entitled to live in what was referred to as the 'international ghetto', a number of large buildings and houses in various parts of Budapest rented by Wallenberg and the Swedish Embassy, by the papal nuncio, Monsignor Angelo Rotta, by the directors of the International Red Cross, and by the embassies of other neutral nations. These buildings flew the flags of the neutral countries, and were considered as immune from any incursion or search as the embassies themselves were. To underscore this point, Wallenberg tended to give his safe houses names, such as the Swedish Library and the Swedish Cultural Centre. By January 1945, when the Soviet Red Army drove the Nazis from Budapest, Wallenberg had thirty-two safe houses in the capital, among them an orphanage and two hospitals.

## A hated man

Seven months after the occupation began, on 15 October 1944, the Nazis deposed Admiral Horthy as head of the puppet government and put in office Ferenc Szalasi, head of the Arrow Cross Party, the Hungarian fascist party. Szalasi's first public statement was directed at Wallenberg, Monsignor Rotta and the representatives of neutral countries who had been working feverishly to save as many Jews as possible. 'This is a war of independence against Jewry,' Szalasi proclaimed. 'Whoever impedes the nation's war effort and disrupts the unity is a traitor.'

Szalasi's proclamation was followed by a new statement of policy from Gabor Vajna, the new Minister of the Interior. 'I will not acknowledge the validity of any safe-conducts or foreign passports issued by whomsoever to a Hungarian Jew,' Vajna said. 'At present all Jews living in Hungary are subject to the control and direction of the Hungarian state. And we will tolerate interference from nobody, whether in Hungary or abroad.'

In fulfilment of this new policy, Arrow Cross thugs brutally invaded the safe houses. Eliezer Grinwald was nine years old and living with his two-year-old brother Isaac in the safe house that served as an orphanage when the Arrow Cross raided the place. Some of the children were hauled off to the railway station for deportation, and others the Arrow Cross men threw into the Danube, where they drowned.

Even after Hungarian fascists arrested the entire staff of the Swedish Red Cross and shut it down, Wallenberg continued his efforts. He would appear wherever Jews were being held for deportation and personally demand the release of those whom he declared were under the protection of his government. Sometimes he came away with twenty people, sometimes with as many as 150. When he learned that hundreds of Jews were trapped in Budapest's Dohany Street Synagogue, Wallenberg ignored the Arrow Cross guards at the door, entered the building and walked up to the sanctuary to announce: 'All those who have Swedish protective passports should stand up.' A few hundred rose to their feet, all of whom Wallenberg took away.

The new fascist Hungarian government despised Wallenberg, the Arrow Cross hated him, yet when Wallenberg confronted them they always backed down. Joseph Kovacs, the lawyer-turned-printer of forged passports, had accompanied Wallenberg to the synagogue that night. Kovacs attributed Wallenberg's success in facing down the fascists to the man's personality: 'Raoul Wallenberg was forceful, determined, and never hesitated in saying what he had to say and doing what he had to do.'

## The saviour of 50,000

In a report to the king of Sweden dated 8 December 1944—the day the Soviet Red Army laid siege to Budapest—Wallenberg stated that 7000 Jews were living in Swedish institutions, 23,000 in Swiss institutions, 2000 in Red Cross installations, and several thousands more in buildings flying the Vatican flag. Nonetheless, as the Russians closed in on Budapest and it became clear that the war would soon be over and the Third Reich defeated, gangs of Arrow Cross men violated the diplomatic immunity of the safe houses. Thousands were dragged out of buildings that were under the protection of the Vatican and the government of Switzerland: some were sent at once to Auschwitz for extermination, others were forced into the Jewish ghetto to await deportation at some later date.

To frustrate the Arrow Cross, Wallenberg recruited blond-haired, blue-eyed young Jewish men, dressed them in SS and Arrow Cross uniforms, and sent them to assembly points where Jews were kept until trains were available to take them to the death camps. There, on one pretext or another, these unbelievably daring young men would pull out as many Jews as they could. Another tactic was to send them into the streets of Budapest, where they would confront Arrow Cross men, demand to see their papers, declare these to be forgeries and confiscate them. These identity documents Wallenberg would use in a future rescue mission.

Yet this daring was scarcely a match for the brutality of the Arrow Cross. On one occasion the Arrow Cross raided a safe house, declaring that the inhabitants had fired upon them, and ordered hundreds of Jews onto the street—some of them were murdered on the spot, the others herded empty-handed into the ghetto.

During the week between Christmas and New Year's Day, the Arrow Cross unleashed a fresh wave of atrocities. They raided two Jewish orphanages, forcing the children outside and shooting many of them. They invaded safe houses, stripped the residents naked and made them run to the ghetto. Other Jews were taken to detention centres where they were tortured to death.

Finally, in January 1945, with Budapest about to surrender, the SS prepared to massacre all the Jews still in the ghetto. In a confrontation with General August Schmidthuber, commander of an SS panzer division, Wallenberg made a bold threat: if Schmidthuber went forward with the massacre, Wallenberg swore that he would denounce him to the Russians and see to it that he was executed as a war criminal. Schmidthuber backed down. Through this last-minute act of daring Wallenberg saved the lives of between 50,000 and 70,000 people. It was the final and greatest achievement of the man the Jews of Hungary had come to call 'the Angel of Rescue'.

## What became of Raoul Wallenberg?

'I'm going to Malinovsky's,' Raoul Wallenberg told a colleague on 17 January 1945, 'whether as a guest or prisoner I do not know yet.'

More than sixty years after he made this offhand remark, Wallenberg's joke is not so funny, because on that day he was arrested by the NKVD—the forerunner of the KGB, the secret police of the Soviet Union—and sent to Moscow, where he was incarcerated in the notorious Lubyanka Prison and never seen again. His sudden arrest and disappearance set off decades of conspiracy theories, reports of sightings—including one as late as 1989—and deep suspicion that the Russians still have not revealed everything they know regarding his fate.

This much is certain. On 13 January 1945, after the Hungarian puppet government surrendered Budapest to the Soviets, Wallenberg asked the Russian army for food and other supplies needed for the Jews in his safe houses. Four days later, accompanied by his driver Vilmos Langfelder, Wallenberg set out for the town of Debrecen, about 220 kilometres (137 miles) east of Budapest, to meet Marshal Rodion Malinovsky. Some witnesses have said that Wallenberg had with him suitcases stuffed with cash to sweeten any deal he could make regarding the peace and security of the Jews living in the 'international ghetto'. That same day, agents of the NKVD arrested Wallenberg and Langfelder.

Why would the Soviets arrest Wallenberg, a diplomat and humanitarian? That question, like so many others associated with this mystery, remains unanswered. Some students of the case believe the Soviets regarded Wallenberg as a spy because of his contacts with the US State Department. Others believe the Soviets wanted to use him as a bargaining chip to regain Russian air force pilots who had defected to Sweden during the war.

In Moscow on 21 January, Wallenberg was thrown into the Lubyanka Prison, where he shared a cell with the notorious Nazi Gustav Richter, the Adviser on Jewish Affairs in German-occupied Romania, who had been handed over to the Russians when the Allies liberated that country. On 1 March, Richter was moved to another cell; he never saw Wallenberg again.

For ten years Wallenberg's family, the Swedish government and William Averell Harriman of the US State Department petitioned the Soviet government for information about Raoul Wallenberg and the reasons for his arrest and imprisonment. These inquiries were always answered with a formal assurance that Wallenberg was healthy and safe.

On 6 February 1957, the Soviets published a brief statement which said that on 17 July 1947 Wallenberg had suffered a massive heart attack in his cell and died. He would have been 34 years old. In 1989, more than thirty years after that announcement, Wallenberg's personal belongings were returned to his family in Sweden.

In 2000, Alexander Nikolaevich Yakovlev, a former member of the Politburo, the main governing body of the Communist Party in the Soviet Union, went on record in Stockholm as saying that Wallenberg had not died of a coronary in 1947, but was shot by the NKVD. Yakovlev's revelation sounds plausible, but in the absence of any documentation it is impossible to be certain.

'Here is a man who had the choice of remaining in secure, neutral Sweden when Nazism was ruling Europe. Instead, he ... went to what was then one of the most perilous places in Europe ... to save Jews ... [I]n this age when there is ... so very little on which our young people can pin their hopes and ideals ... the story of Raoul Wallenberg should be told.' Attorney Gideon Hausner, Chairman of Yad Vashem and prosecutor of Adolf Eichmann.

# CHAPTER 12

# GOING FOR BROKE

## The Nisei Regiment
## Rescues the Lost Battalion

For five brutal days the men of the 442nd Regimental Combat Team—the 'Nisei soldiers', all of them Japanese Americans, nearly all from Hawaii—had fought to break through German lines and rescue a battalion of 275 Texans pinned down on a ridge in the Vosges Mountains of eastern France. Six thousand Nazi troops were dug in on the high ground around the embattled Texans. They had tanks, artillery and air support, but still the men of the 442nd persevered with their mission, despite freezing rain, no shelter and no dry clothes, despite little food and even less rest, despite heavy casualties and no sign of reinforcements.

On 29 October 1944, the men of the 442nd's I and K Companies became trapped themselves on a narrow hilltop. The slopes of the hill were too steep and the terrain gave no cover. German machine guns up ahead poured down a deadly barrage on the Nisei soldiers. Within minutes Private Barney Hajiro of I Company saw eight of his buddies killed and another twenty-one wounded. That was it; he'd had enough. Leaping up, he charged the German position, firing non-stop as he ran. Single-handedly

In an Italian town in late 1944, Nisei soldiers of the US 442nd Regiment scramble for cover from an incoming German artillery shell.

Hajiro knocked out two machine-gun nests and killed two enemy snipers—and survived. The 442nd was 100 metres (328 feet) closer to its objective.

## 'We know but one loyalty'

On 19 February 1942, US President Franklin D. Roosevelt signed Executive Order 9066, which authorised the military to round up 11,000 American citizens and residents of Japanese ancestry and force them into internment camps. Within days these Japanese Americans—most of whom lived on the West Coast—were forced to leave their jobs, abandon their homes and businesses, pull their children out of school, leave behind virtually all their personal possessions and relocate to bleak camps in the desert or in isolated corners of Arkansas. People of Japanese descent in the then American territory of Hawaii were spared this indignity for one simple reason—there were too many of them. According to the 1940 US census, the population of the Hawaiian Islands numbered 423,000, of whom 158,000 were of Japanese descent. Of these, 120,000 were Nisei, Hawaiian-born children of Japanese parents. Not only would it not have been practical, it would have been too disruptive to the islands' society, not to mention the economy, to lock up 37 per cent of the population. Nonetheless, the Hawaiian Japanese did not entirely escape suspicion and discrimination.

In the days after Japan's attack on Pearl Harbor on 7 December1941, the US Army assumed command of the Hawaii Territorial Guard (HTG). The HTG was a kind of local militia comprised of college and high school boys; they stood guard at the harbours and ports, and patrolled the islands. Like Hawaii itself, the HTG was multi-ethnic, although the majority of its members were Nisei. White troops from the mainland who arrived in the islands in the weeks after Pearl Harbor were shocked to see so many Japanese. As one Texan put it when he saw a young Nisei in the uniform of the HTG, 'My God, we got here too late. The Japs have got the place already.'

On 19 January 1942, the Army mustered out all the Nisei members of the HTG because commanding officers could not overcome their fear that the Nisei had been infiltrated by Japanese spies and saboteurs. Ted Tsukiyama, twenty-one years old, was a junior at the University of Hawaii. Years later he recalled the day he was forced out of the HTG. 'The bottom dropped out of my life,' he said. 'And because the enemy had the same kind of face as you, suddenly you are distrusted.'

Nevertheless, in barely a month the Nisei rallied. On 25 February, five weeks after being dismissed from the HTG and only six days after Roosevelt ordered the internment of all Japanese Americans on the mainland, hundreds of young Nisei men formed themselves into a new service organisation, the Varsity Victory Volunteers (VVV). In a letter to Lieutenant General Delos C. Emmons, the Army commander in Hawaii, 130 of the founding members, all students from the University of Hawaii, declared:

> *Hawaii is our home; the United States, our country. We know but one loyalty and that is to the Stars and Stripes. We wish to do our part as loyal Americans in every way possible and we hereby offer ourselves for whatever service you may see fit to use us.*

Emmons accepted the VVV's offer, and assigned them to construction work with the 34th Combat Engineers Regiment.

## A multitude of volunteers

The Nisei's real chance to participate in the war came during the first weeks of 1943 when Lieutenant General Emmons announced the formation of a new regimental combat team, the 442nd, to be comprised entirely of men of Japanese ancestry who had been born in America. Emmons said the decision was a tribute to Japanese Americans— although they had suffered from 'distrust because of their racial origin, and [been] discriminated against in certain fields of the defense effort, they nevertheless have borne their burdens without complaint'.

The men who had been members of the HTG and were now part of the VVV were among the most eager to join up. In a speech before the VVV, Ted Tsukiyama urged the Nisei to enlist in the 442nd and so demonstrate to their fellow Americans and to all the world their loyalty to the United States, their commitment to help win the war, and their desire to establish a reputation for themselves that future generations of Japanese Americans could look back on with pride. About 10,000 Nisei came forward; from this multitude of volunteers 3000 were selected for the 442nd.

President Roosevelt, as Commander-in-Chief, authorised the internment of ethnic groups with 'Foreign Enemy Ancestry' (citizens and residents of Japanese, German and Italian ancestry) in internment camps, such as this at Santa Anita in California, for the duration of the war.

Going for Broke

On 28 March 1943, at a ceremony at Iolani Palace in Honolulu—the residence of the last queen of Hawaii—the 3000 men of the newly formed 442nd Regimental Combat Team were inducted into the US Army. A throng of 15,000 family members, friends and well-wishers filled the palace grounds. A few days later another huge crowd turned out to line the streets and cheer as the 442nd marched to the docks to board the ocean liner *Lurline* for the voyage to San Francisco and the beginning of their military training at Camp Shelby in Mississippi. Many of the recruits were not yet in good physical condition, and some staggered under the weight of their heavy duffel bags. Years later Daniel Inouye, who would become a US senator from Hawaii, could still feel the humiliating sting of appearing weak in front of his parents.

Leaders of the Japanese American community in Hawaii were concerned when they heard the 442nd was headed for Mississippi—they feared the young Nisei would meet the type of racial discrimination black Americans suffered in the Deep South. And in fact there were confrontations with white GIs at Shelby and with white civilians outside the camp, but surprisingly the greatest tensions sprang up between the Nisei from Hawaii and the Nisei from the mainland. The Hawaiians had not been sent to internment camps and did not understand the bitterness of the mainlanders towards them. And the mainlanders, who spoke standard English, intimidated the Hawaiians, whose island dialect included vocabulary drawn from Japanese, Chinese, Hawaiian and Portuguese languages, all mixed with English. The mainland Japanese called the Hawaiians 'Buddhaheads', because they seemed more connected to the old world. The Hawaiian Japanese called the mainlanders 'Katonks' because, during the frequent fistfights that broke out between the two factions, *katonk* was the sound a mainlander's skull made when it hit the floor.

The conflicts between the Buddhaheads and the Katonks became so serious that the Army considered disbanding the 442nd. But before that could happen an officer at headquarters had an inspired idea: he sent a group of the Hawaiians to visit two internment camps in Arkansas. When the Hawaiian Japanese saw the mainland Japanese living behind barbed-wire fences, in tiny shacks where no one enjoyed any privacy, with machine guns mounted on guard towers pointing at the internees, they felt for the first time sympathy for the mainland Japanese and respect for those who had enlisted. Back at Camp Shelby they told their fellow Hawaiians

Frank Sinatra signs autographs for members of the Nisei Regiment after a post-war concert in Hollywood, 6 January 1946. The regiment was en route to Hawaii and their return to civilian life.

what they had seen, and almost overnight the clashes ceased. By the time the 442nd shipped out for the European front on 22 April 1944, the men had coalesced into a resolute fighting unit. They took as their motto 'Go for Broke', a phrase they used often in craps games, which meant 'risking everything to win big'.

## 'Follow me?'

In October 1944 American troops had penetrated the Vosges Mountains in eastern France, very close to the German border. Hitler sent thousands of fighting men into the Vosges with orders to drive back the Allies before they took one step on German soil. They were not to retreat, Hitler commanded, they were not to surrender, they were to crush the enemy.

Covered by dense, dark pine forests with paths so confusing even lifelong residents lost their way in the woods, the Vosges region was a fearsome place. The Nazis had made it even more terrifying by planting land mines through the forests, and setting up roadblocks on every significant road and track. Despite this combination of perils Major General John Dahlquist had ordered the 275 men of the 141st Texas Regiment deep into the forest to break through the German lines. The Texans had got a daring 6.5 kilometres (4 miles) beyond enemy lines before a force of 6000 Germans completely surrounded them. Short on food, short on ammunition, with no hope of fighting their way out, the men of the 141st were in a hopeless situation. On 27 October, again on Dahlquist's orders, the men of the 442nd moved into the woods to rescue the Texans. The sky was dark with storm clouds, the forest was thick with fog, and an unaccustomed freezing rain soaked the Nisei soldiers as they slogged through the mud and picked their way across the minefields to reach the hilltop where the 141st was stranded.

German tank artillery relentlessly pounded the route the 442nd was obliged to follow. A machine-gun nest on one of the hilltops decimated their ranks. Company K, led by Second Lieutenant Edward Davis—the only officer in Company K not yet killed or wounded—was ordered to neutralise the nest. Davis, suffering from a severe case of dysentery, staggered to his feet, clutching his stomach. Looking at Sergeant Etsuo 'Etchan' Kohashi, he asked the question: 'Follow me?' Kohashi's answer was a shrill battle-cry; the men of Company K took up the yell, rising to their feet and running forward. Machine-gun fire rained down; overhead, a rocket exploded in the upper branches of a towering pine, sending shrapnel and long sharp splinters flying. Lieutenant Davis fell to the ground, his leg shattered. Jim Tazoi had the radio battery for the transmitter strapped to his back, yet he was running easily among the trees until a bullet passed through his shoulder, knocking him to the ground. He was just beginning to comprehend that he had been hit when shrapnel from an exploding grenade buried itself in his abdomen. Twenty-one-year-old Sergeant Fujio Miyamoto had a reputation as a gentle young man, dutiful son and faithful fiancé. As he ran from tree to tree, firing at the enemy, he became a different person—all he could think of was killing the Nazis who were killing his friends.

## The banzai charge

At the edge of the forest, where the woods gave way to the outskirts of the village of Biffontaine, stood the cottage of the Voirin family. It was tiny, but it was warm and dry, so the medics of the 442nd carried their wounded there. In a short time every scrap of floor space in Josephine Voirin's two rooms was occupied by wounded and dying Nisei. She had almost nothing with which to comfort these strangers—very little food, not enough mattresses, not even water—a stray German shell had destroyed her water supply. When there was no more room in the cottage, the medics took the wounded to a large two-storey farmhouse nearby, the home of Alexander Tarentzeff and his family. Tarentzeff, a Cossack and veteran of World War I, had settled in this remote corner of France after the Bolsheviks massacred his family. In a short time his house too was filled to overflowing. Those who didn't make it Tarentzeff wrapped in canvas, laying their bodies in neat rows in the field near his front door.

Up on the slope I and K Companies were pinned down on a narrow ridge by small arms and mortar fire, taking heavy casualties. They had tried to flank the German stronghold, but the sides of the ravine were too steep. It was about two-thirty in the afternoon of 29 October when, unexpectedly, the commander of 3rd Battalion, Lieutenant Colonel Alfred Pursall, stepped out from behind the tree where he had taken cover. He was a burly individual, and with a .45 calibre pistol in each hand he looked like the hero from a Western cowboy movie. He even delivered a classic Western line: 'Okay, boys—let's go!'

The men of Companies I and K surged forward, hurling hand-grenades, firing their rifles and sub-machine guns, and screaming ferociously. '*Make!*' bellowed Sergeant Joe Shimamura. '*Make! Make!*' It was the Hawaiian word for 'death'. In little more than an hour the Nisei soldiers had reached the German stronghold, taking heavy casualties. When they spilled over the top of the defences, still firing, still screaming, they found only a handful of terrified young Germans, eager to surrender, too frightened to defend themselves. Their advance became known as the 'banzai charge', and Lieutenant Colonel Pursall came through it without a scratch. They had advanced a few hundred metres, but they still hadn't reached the 141st.

## A backhanded compliment

On the morning of 30 October, the day after the banzai charge, the Germans made a simultaneous attack on the beleaguered 141st from three sides. Sergeant Bill Hull was certain this was the final assault, that the Nazis were throwing everything they had at them to wipe them out completely. 'That was the first time I thought I was going to die,' Hull recalled later. He was manning a machine gun, and now he poured a steady stream of deadly fire into the advancing enemy, giving no thought to conserving ammunition. When he heard a new commotion behind him, Hull was certain the Nazis had broken through their rear defences. He turned around for one last fight, but instead of a German stormtrooper a Nisei soldier jumped into his dug-out. 'It was the Japanese Americans who broke through the enemy and saved us,' Hull recalled. 'I was giving thanks to God, and that Japanese American soldier looked real special to me.'

The first Nisei soldiers to reach the Lost Battalion were the men of the first and second platoons of I Company. After the banzai charge, only six men were left in the First Platoon, and only two in the Second.

The Texans cheered, slapped each other and their rescuers on the back, and even cried a little, but the 442nd could not stay to celebrate—their orders were to advance and drive the Germans from their position. The Nisei soldiers moved on to spend another night in the forest—and another, and another … In fact, they were not relieved for ten days, until 9 November. The whole time German artillery pounded their position relentlessly while German aircraft ran bombing missions over the woods as they huddled in waterlogged foxholes. When at last the order came to pull back, most were so exhausted they could barely walk, many were suffering from combat fatigue, and a few, such as Rudy Tokiwa, bore wounds that had become infected.

On the afternoon of 12 November 1944, after three days of rest, hot showers and hot meals, the men of the 442nd were called out for assembly—General Dahlquist wanted to congratulate them for rescuing the 141st and for breaking through the German defences. But as he reviewed the troops the general looked distinctly displeased. Turning to the 442nd's executive officer, Colonel Virgil Miller, Dahlquist said, 'I ordered that all the men be assembled.'

'Yes sir,' Miller replied. 'All the men are what you see.'

In the beginning of October, when the 442nd marched into the Vosges region, the regiment's strength stood at 2943 men. In the intervening weeks 161 men had been killed in action (including thirteen medics), forty-three were listed as missing, and 2000 were wounded—800 of them seriously. The 442nd had taken most of those casualties rescuing the two hundred and eleven survivors of the Lost Battalion.

# CHAPTER 13

# THE MEN WHO DIDN'T NEED RESCUING

## George S. Patton and the Siege of Bastogne

General George S. Patton, commander of the US Third Army, had just lit a cigar, and after-dinner drinks were being poured for the general and his guests, when the telephone rang. Colonel Paul D. Harkins, Patton's deputy chief of staff, took the call. It was General Lev Allen calling on behalf of General Omar Bradley and instructing Patton to transfer his 10th Armoured Division to VIII Corps in Belgium's Ardennes Forest.

As Harkins replaced the phone in its cradle he knew Patton was not going to like this—the general was assigned to lead the 10th Armoured in an attack on Dillingen scheduled for 19 December 1944—three days hence. Steeling himself, Harkins walked over to the general, bending down to whisper the new order in his ear.

'What!' Patton exclaimed. He was so angry he bit off a chunk of his cigar. Then he leaped from his chair to the phone, and called General Bradley.

A still from captured Nazi war footage showing German soldiers advancing into Belgium in the harsh, wet winter of 1944.

The Men Who Didn't Need Rescuing

'Look Brad,' he said, 'don't spoil my show! Third Army has sweated and bled to bring this damn thing to a head. Without the 10th Armoured we won't be able to exploit the breakthrough at Saarlautern.'

Bradley was sympathetic, but for security reasons he couldn't explain the situation to Patton. 'I've got to hang up, Georgie,' he said. 'I can't discuss this matter on the phone.'

The date was 16 December, and the discussion with Bradley was the first inkling that Patton had received of *Wacht am Rhein*, Hitler's massive last-ditch effort to crush the Allies in Europe.

By the time he hung up, Patton had regained control of his temper. 'I guess they're having trouble up there,' he said to his aide-de-camp, Colonel Charles Codman. 'I thought they would.' The comment wasn't a display of arrogance. The general had never been contemptuous of the professionalism of the German war machine. Now that the Third Reich was crumbling, Patton imagined himself in Germany's position and knew what he would do—mount a major offensive that would take the enemy completely by surprise. As he mulled over these things in his headquarters in the French town of Nancy, 200,000 German troops were attacking the Allies' line in Belgium, Luxembourg and north-eastern France.

## 'Watch on the Rhine'

By autumn 1944 the conquered peoples of Europe were beginning to believe that they could be delivered from the Nazis, that the Third Reich could be defeated. Only weeks earlier, on 20 July, assassins had nearly succeeded in killing the Führer by planting a bomb in his office. From the east, the Soviet Red Army was advancing into Romania, Bulgaria, Yugoslavia and East Prussia, while the Americans, the British, the Canadians and the French were driving towards Germany. France and Belgium had been liberated by the Allies, and US troops had even crossed into German territory, holding ground outside Aachen, the ancient capital of Charlemagne. The Allies were in possession of a great swathe of western Europe, from the Dutch city of Nijmegen in the north, all along the Franco-German border to the Swiss city of Basel in the south. But in spite of these signs that defeat was near, Hitler was not remotely ready to surrender.

On 16 September 1944 at Wolf's Lair, Hitler's fortress-residence in Poland's Goerlitz Forest, the Führer met in secret with his most trusted generals—Wilhelm Keitel and Alfred Jodl and Chief of Staff Heinz Guderian. Reichsmarschall Hermann Goering could not attend, and sent General Werner Kreipe in his place. General Jodl gave a report of the military situation: although Germany had more than 9 million men under arms, in the last three months they had suffered more than a million casualties, mostly in the west fighting the Allies. The general was beginning to describe the Wehrmacht's difficulties in the Ardennes, the region that spreads across southern Belgium and Luxembourg, when Hitler interrupted him: 'Stop!' Silence fell. After a long pause Hitler announced, 'I have made a momentous decision. I am taking the offensive. Here,' he said, pointing at the map spread across the table, 'out of the Ardennes! Across the Meuse and on to Antwerp!' He ordered Jodl to draw up plans for an offensive that would be the Third Reich's answer to the D-Day invasion of France. Hitler believed—correctly—that the Allies were spread too thin along the Franco-German border, and that their weakest spot was the Ardennes.

Four weeks later Jodl presented Hitler with a daring plan that would deploy twelve panzer and eighteen infantry divisions—200,000 men—against the Allies. To maintain secrecy, details would be revealed in person, on a need-to-know basis, only to those officers who would be involved in the offensive. Jodl could not risk transmitting even a hint of his plan via radio—he knew the Allies had cracked Ultra, the German secret code.

For the success of this campaign, Jodl required three things: surprise, speed and bad weather. To mislead the Allies, he had General Keitel issue an order withdrawing the Reich's armies from the Western Front to defend Germany's eastern borders. Furthermore, Jodl and Hitler agreed to call the operation *Wacht am Rhein*, 'Watch on the Rhine', the title of a popular patriotic song that called upon the German soldier, 'respectable, pious and strong' to defend 'the country's sacred border'. The name was not only nationalistic, it was deceptive—the German assault force was not heading for the Rhine, but the Meuse.

To pull off this attack, Jodl calculated all 200,000 men, their tanks and other equipment, must cross the Meuse in two days and be in Antwerp within a week. The logistics of the move were a gamble, but Jodl believed his officers and men could

The Men Who Didn't Need Rescuing

accomplish it. One more thing remained—to neutralise the Allies' superiority in the air. For that Germany required heavy snow or rain, and their best chance of attacking under the benefit of bad weather was scheduling the offensive for mid-December.

Hitler chose two generals to lead the attack through the Ardennes—Field Marshal Walter Model and Field Marshal Gerd von Runstedt. But when he met with them on 22 October they expressed misgivings, arguing that they would need more troops and that Jodl's plan mirrored the Allies' flaw by stretching German forces too thin. This was not what Hitler wanted to hear. He praised the boldness of the plan, and invoked the memory of Frederick the Great's victory at Rossback and Leuten. 'Why don't you people study history?' he stormed. 'The Ardennes will be my Rossback and Leuten. And as a result another unpredictable historical event will take place: the Alliance against the Third Reich will suddenly split apart!'

Rather than enrage the Führer further by disagreeing with him, Model and von Runstedt accepted their orders and spent the next six weeks assembling the men and supplies they would need for this massive undertaking. To supplement the veteran soldiers, the generals conscripted factory workers in their forties and fifties who had been working in essential industries, and thousands of Hitler Youth, some as young as fifteen. They called up hundreds of Panzer and Tiger tanks, carefully camouflaging them so Allied pilots would not spot them from the air.

Angered by Model and von Runstedt's lukewarm reception of the plan, Hitler gave command of the most critical assault to an old ally, SS General Sepp Dietrich, a veteran of World War I and a loyal Nazi since the 1920s.

## 'A wave of terror'

At Hitler's new headquarters near Ziegenberg the commanders of *Wacht am Rhein* were told to disarm themselves before going in to meet the Führer. Since the assassination attempt in July, Hitler had become increasingly suspicious. Inside the meeting room he harangued the commanders for nearly an hour, first on the genius of Frederick the Great, then on the great things National Socialism had done and would yet do for Germany. Finally, he got to the point: the assault would begin at five-thirty on the morning of 16 December. The Seventh Army would strike southern Belgium and Luxembourg to scatter the Allies and shield the main thrusts of the attack, led by Dietrich and the Sixth Panzer Army in a drive to Antwerp, and by General Hasso von Manteuffel's Fifth Panzer Army, which would race through the Ardennes to capture Brussels.

In planning this offensive Jodl had emphasised the importance of surprise and speed. Hitler added another factor for the success of the attack. 'I want all my soldiers to fight hard and without pity,' he ordered. 'The battle must be fought with brutality and all resistance must be broken in a wave of terror.'

## Counterattack

On 19 December, in the stark, sparsely furnished boardroom of the barracks at Verdun in France, General Dwight D. Eisenhower met with his chief generals, including Bradley and Patton. Although the German assault was driving back the Allies in almost every sector, Eisenhower was calm and clear-headed as he gave his orders. He wanted Patton to take charge of the counterattack with at least six divisions. 'When can you start?' Eisenhower asked.

'As soon as you're through with me,' Patton replied.

Everyone seated around the table perked up.

'I left my household in Nancy in perfect order before I came here,' Patton said, 'and I can go to Luxembourg right away, straight from here.'

'When will you be able to attack?' Eisenhower asked.

'The morning of December 22nd, with three divisions,' Patton replied.

Patton's aide-de-camp, Colonel Codman, recorded that at this announcement, 'the current of excitement leaped like a flame'. General Patton was promising the impossible: he would disengage three divisions that were already fighting the Germans, march them 160 kilometres (99½ miles) through snow and ice in only three days, and without any rest send them into battle against one of the most, if not *the* most, desperate German onslaughts of the war.

Eisenhower read this as vintage Patton, pure hubris and bluster. 'Don't be fatuous, George,' he said.

Patton did not lose his cool. 'This has nothing to do with being fatuous, sir,' he replied. 'I've made my arrangements and my staff is working like beavers this very moment to shape them up.'

Patton's confidence was reassuring, even persuasive. The Allies needed a strong counterattack, and Patton had one in the works. By the end of the meeting, Patton had even won over Eisenhower, who walked him to the door. Aside from the German attack, the latest news was that the US Congress had appointed Eisenhower a five-star general. As they said goodbye, Eisenhower alluded to his promotion. 'Funny thing, George,' he said, 'every time I get another star I get attacked.'

Patton smiled. 'And every time you get attacked, Ike, I bail you out.'

## The keystone

*Wacht am Rhein* began with a heavy artillery bombardment that took the Allies completely by surprise—as General Jodl had hoped—and all along the line Allied troops were in retreat. As the Allied forces attempted to regroup, their high command recognised that for the Germans to pull off their operation they needed Bastogne, a Belgian town with 4000 inhabitants. The seven major roads through the Ardennes Forest all converged on Bastogne—it was key to keeping German lines of supply open as they drove towards Antwerp and Brussels. But by the time the Allied commanders realised Bastogne's significance, the Germans were only 18 kilometres (11 miles) from the town. General Troy Middleton ordered the 101st Airborne Division, a veteran outfit of 805 officers and 11,035 enlisted men, to get there before the Germans and hold the town. With the 101st's commander, General Maxwell Taylor, in the United States, and Taylor's deputy, Brigadier General Gerald Higgins, in England, the division's artillery commander, Brigadier General Anthony McAuliffe, became responsible for the defence of Bastogne.

On the night of 18 December the 101st, along with about 6000 men of the 10th Armoured Division and the 463rd Artillery Battalion, took possession of Bastogne. This surprised the Germans, who had assumed they could seize the town and hold it with one division; now that the Americans had dug in, they would have to fight for it. 'The importance of Bastogne was considerable,' von Manteuffel said after the war. 'In enemy hands it must influence all our movements to the west, damage our supply system and tie up considerable German forces. It was therefore essential that we capture it at once.' Suddenly this minor town became, as Hermann Goering described it, 'the keystone of the entire offensive'. Von Manteuffel called a halt to the advance and arranged his forces to completely encircle Bastogne. The 17,000 American defenders found themselves surrounded by three German divisions with a total of 45,000 men.

## Trench foot

Getting troops to Bastogne had been so urgent that the men of Easy Company, 506th Parachute Infantry Division, were sent into action before they could collect their winter gear. Three days after they were in place on the perimeter of the town, on 21 December, a heavy snow began to fall, piling up more than 30 centimetres (12 inches) deep as the temperature fell well below freezing and a bitter wind blew through the forest. The men were not wearing their winter boots; they had no woollen socks, no long underwear, no warmly lined heavy winter trenchcoats—and of course starting a fire was out of the question.

Melted snow in the bottom of the foxholes soaked their boots, setting off an epidemic of trench foot, a condition which causes open sores to develop, leaving the feet vulnerable to fungal infections and even gangrene. Corporal Gordon Carson, who'd heard someone say that frequent massage would reduce the risk of getting trench foot, had taken off his soggy boots and socks to massage his cold, bare feet when a German shell struck a pine tree above his foxhole. A nasty spray of giant splinters rained down on him—a large shard of wood pierced one of Carson's feet and another lodged in his thigh. He was evacuated to the makeshift hospital set up in Bastogne.

General McAuliffe had given orders that all wounded men in the hospital were to receive a bottle of alcohol because supplies of painkillers were very low. A medic treated Carson's wounds, then handed him a bottle of crème de menthe. That night, after Carson had drank about half of it, the Luftwaffe ran a bombing mission over the town. Several of the shells fell so close to the hospital they shook the building and threw Carson to the floor. The violent jolt of the bombing and the fall from his bed combined with the sweetness of the crème de menthe to make Carson very unwell; he vomited into his helmet. Years later he told historian Stephen Ambrose, 'It was all green!'

## McAuliffe's reply

The Americans in Bastogne were not so much under attack as under siege. The Germans launched sporadic mortar attacks or sprayed machine-gun fire against American positions, the Luftwaffe bombed the town and snipers picked off men who were careless about keeping their heads down, but there was no massive frontal assault. From General von Manteuffel's perspective there was no reason to squander the lives of his men—he had the Americans outnumbered more than two to one, they were short on food and medical supplies, and were shivering almost to death in their foxholes. Soon they would surrender. Meanwhile a steady stream of trucks kept the German soldiers well supplied with food, equipment and ammunition.

The Americans had 105-mm and 155-mm howitzers. They had blazed away at the Germans during the first days of the fight, but as Christmas Day grew closer they were almost out of shells. An artillery crew manning a gun on the road to the village of Foy was down to three shells—and they were hoarding them in case German tanks attacked their position.

On 22 December, von Manteuffel sent four men under a white flag of truce with a message for General McAuliffe, calling upon him to offer 'honourable surrender to save the encircled USA troops from total annihilation'.

McAuliffe sent back a written reply: 'NUTS!'

The Germans were mystified by McAuliffe's answer until an American POW explained that 'NUTS' was an idiom for 'Go to hell'.

The next day, 23 December, the defenders of Bastogne got a break. The snow stopped, the skies cleared, and American C-47 cargo aircraft flew over the town to air-drop supplies. The food would supply the men for only a day or two, and they needed more ammunition than the C-47s had brought; nonetheless, the delivery lifted everyone's morale.

## They didn't need rescuing

As he had promised Eisenhower, at six in the morning of 22 December, General Patton and the 4th Armoured Division set off for Bastogne. That afternoon it began to snow, and the snow fell heavily all through the night. At daybreak the storm came to an end and the skies, for the first time in a week, were perfectly clear. Making the most of the opportunity, Allied fighter-bombers and medium bombers filled the skies, dropping relief supplies over Bastogne and bombing and strafing the enemy.

Patton attributed the break in the weather to the Third Army's chaplain, Colonel James H. O'Neill, a Catholic priest. On 18 December the general had telephoned O'Neill requesting a prayer for an end to the rain, snow and fog that was so badly slowing the advance of the army and making air support all but impossible. Father O'Neill could not find such a prayer in any prayerbook, so he'd written his own:

*Almighty and most merciful Father, we humbly beseech Thee, of Thy great goodness, to restrain these immoderate rains with which we have had to contend. Grant us fair weather for Battle. Graciously hearken to us as soldiers who call upon Thee that, armed with Thy power, we may advance from victory to victory, and crush the oppression and wickedness of our enemies, and establish Thy justice among men and nations. Amen.*

Jubilant, Patton called for his deputy chief of staff. 'Goddamnit, Harkins, look at that weather! That O'Neill sure did some potent praying. Get him up here, I want to pin a medal on him.'

When O'Neill arrived the next day, Patton exclaimed, 'Chaplain, you sure stand in good with the Lord and soldiers.' Then he pinned a Bronze Star to the startled priest's chest.

For the next three days Patton's men moved as fast as they could to Bastogne. Just after midnight on 26 December, the 4th Armoured Division arrived behind German lines. With Patton's permission, Colonel Wendell Blanchard led a tank charge that smashed through the enemy lines and rolled into the besieged town. After sunrise more men and more tanks entered Bastogne, followed by supply trucks and ambulances to carry the wounded to hospitals. Rather than risk battle with the American reinforcements, the Germans abandoned their position.

Historians describe Patton's drive to Bastogne as a rescue, a term that still irritates surviving members of the 101st, who insist that they were doing just fine holding off the Germans, they didn't need rescuing.

The Men Who Didn't Need Rescuing

## The Malmedy massacre

On 17 December a regiment of the 1st SS Panzer Division under the command of Lieutenant Colonel Jochen Peiper. The men of the 1st Panzer had a reputation for brutality: in Russia they had left a trail of devastation, burning homes, barns, and entire villages and towns, and on two occasions they had massacred the inhabitants of Russian villages. Their German comrades called them 'the Blowtorch Battalion'.

On spotting the American convoy the Panzers opened fire, destroying the lead vehicles; the tanks kept firing until the Americans surrendered. The Germans herded their prisoners into a field south-east of the Belgian village of Malmedy. Then an SS tank commander ordered a private to shoot the prisoners. The man opened fire, and was joined by dozens of others who used machine guns to mow down the defenceless prisoners.

When not a man was left standing, the Germans walked among the bodies, calling out in English if anyone needed help. Those who responded were executed with a pistol shot through the skull. The Germans murdered 113 prisoners of war that day.

Three of the Americans escaped the slaughter, running through the woods until they reached the town of Malmedy, where they found a US colonel to whom they reported the massacre.

After the war, Lieutenant Colonel Peiper and seventy-four men of the 1st SS Panzer Division were arrested and tried before the US Military Tribunal for War Crimes in Dachau. The tribunal found all the defendants guilty, and sentenced forty-three—including Peiper—to death. The rest were sentenced to long terms in prison.

None of the death sentences were ever carried out. Complaints regarding the alleged unfairness of the trial, along with political pressure not to antagonise and alienate the German people after the Soviets blockaded Berlin, worked in favour of the former SS men. All the death sentences were commuted, all the prison terms reduced. The last prisoner, Jochen Peiper, was released in 1956.

Eventually Peiper settled in France. There, on Bastille Day, 14 July 1976, his house caught fire. Peiper died in the blaze. The fire was almost certainly the act of an arsonist—when the firefighters arrived at the burning house, they found that their hoses had been cut.

Christmas Day 1944: The bodies of fallen comrades lie in the rubble as three American soldiers search the ruins of bombed-out Bastogne for survivors.

The Men Who Didn't Need Rescuing

# CHAPTER 14

# THE IMPOSTOR
## Giorgio Perlasca and the Jews of Budapest

They were children of striking appearance—dark complexions, curly brown hair, beautiful faces. They were twins, brother and sister, about twelve or thirteen years old, and they were alone, with no mother or father to comfort them as the cattle car was crammed with yet more candidates for the death camp.

Out of nowhere Jorge Perlasca, the assistant to Spain's ambassador in Budapest, reached out and grabbed the children from the crowd of doomed Jews. As he pushed them inside the embassy Buick, he shouted, 'These two people are under the protection of the Spanish government!' An SS major immediately stomped over and demanded that Perlasca hand back the children.

Placing himself between the officer and the car, Perlasca answered, 'You have no right to take them! This car is Spanish territory. This is an international zone!'

At their feet are heaped the filthy, tattered clothes that were all they had to wear—a group of Jewish women from Budapest rescued from a concentration camp and supplied with fresh, clean garments.

Giorgio Perlasca unwittingly faced down Adolf Eichmann one day in Budapest. At his trial in Jerusalem in 1962 for war crimes against the Jews, Eichmann was found guilty and later executed.

The argument turned into a shoving match until the major lunged for the door handle and began to pull. Perlasca threw his weight against the door to keep it shut. The embassy chauffeur hurried to help, adding his weight to secure the door.

Then another man joined the quarrel, Raoul Wallenberg, the Swedish diplomat and humanitarian. 'You don't know what you're doing,' he told the SS major. 'You are committing an act of aggression against the territory of a neutral country. You'd better think very carefully about the consequences of your actions.' But instead of backing down, the major drew his pistol, pointed it at Perlasca's face, and said, 'Give me back those two, you're interfering with my work.'

Before the situation could degenerate further, an SS colonel intervened. The major made his complaint. Perlasca stated his case. With a wave of his hand the colonel dismissed the major, then turned to Perlasca. 'You keep them,' he said in a calm, almost friendly tone of voice. 'Their time will come. It will come for you, too.'

As the colonel walked away Wallenberg drew close to Perlasca and whispered, 'You realise who that was, don't you?'

'No,' Perlasca replied.

'That was Eichmann.'

## A fascist hero

While still in his teens, Giorgio Perlasca had become an ardent fascist. He believed wholeheartedly in Benito Mussolini's dream of an Italian empire that would dominate the Mediterranean and North and East Africa, an empire that would revive the vanished glory of ancient Rome and be on a par with the modern empires of Great Britain and France. When Mussolini began his dream of empire by declaring war on Abyssinia (now Ethiopia) in 1935, Perlasca volunteered. In eight months the Italian fascists defeated the Abyssinian army; Abyssinia and its neighbours, Eritrea and Somalia, became the first provinces of the new Italian Empire.

From Ethiopia, Perlasca travelled to Spain to fight with Francisco Franco and his fascist followers, who called themselves Nationalists, in the civil war against Communist forces, who called themselves Republicans. He fought so valiantly that when the fascists won Franco presented him with a safe conduct entitling him to the help and protection of any Spanish Embassy or consulate anywhere in the world.

Ironically, Giorgio Perlasca had become a fascist hero at the same time that he had become disillusioned with fascist ideology, particularly the virulently anti-Semitic version espoused by the Nazis.

Mussolini's dreams of Italian grandeur, even when Italy became one of the Axis powers, did not last long. In 1943 King Victor Emmanuel III dismissed him as leader and installed Marshal Pietro Badoglio as head of the government, which shortly afterwards signed an armistice with the Allies, taking Italy out of the war. Adolf Hitler considered Italy's actions pure treachery. So in March 1944, when Perlasca found himself alone in Budapest just as the Germans entered the city and seized the government of Hungary, he was in a precarious position. The other members of the Italian legation had fled. If the Nazis realised who Perlasca was they would arrest him and ship him to a concentration camp. As he moved unobtrusively through the centre of Budapest, he saw a little boy, about ten years old, running down the street. A moment later a Nazi soldier raised his rifle and fired; the child fell dead on the pavement. As Perlasca and several passers-by cautiously approached the little body, Perlasca asked one of them: 'Why did this happen?' The man replied, 'He was a Jew.'

## A citizen of Spain

Perlasca still had with him the safe conduct from Franco. 'No matter where you are in the world,' it read, 'you can turn to Spain.' He slipped the document inside his pocket, collected his possessions, and called a cab to take him to the Spanish Embassy. The chargé d'affaires, Angel Sanz Briz, welcomed Perlasca and put him up, with a handful of other refugees, in a fine villa. Perlasca was safe and, if not living in luxury, living as close to it as was possible in Budapest in 1944.

On the basis of the Franco document, Sanz Briz provided Perlasca with a Spanish passport and a copy of a letter he had sent to the Hungarian Ministry of Internal Affairs stating that Francisco Franco had complied with a request made by Giorgio Perlasca two years earlier and granted him Spanish citizenship. His Spanish name was Jorge Perlasca. Sanz Briz asked Perlasca to work with him at the embassy, completing the necessary paperwork for safe conducts and citizenship documents to be distributed to the Jews of Budapest, who were becoming increasingly desperate to find some way to escape deportation to the Nazis' slave labour and death camps. For this assignment Perlasca received a third document declaring that he was on the staff of the Spanish Embassy.

From the time of the Nazi occupation of Hungary in March, up until June, over 400,000 Hungarian Jews, most of them from the countryside, rural towns and small cities, were exterminated. More than 200,000 Jews remained in Budapest, and every day hundreds were packed into freight cars and sent to the gas chambers, or forced at gunpoint to the banks of the Danube where they were murdered, or were confined in the ghetto where 500 people died every day of disease or starvation. Sanz Briz was working feverishly with Raoul Wallenberg from the Swedish Embassy, Monsignor Angelo Rotta, the pope's representative in Hungary, leaders of the International Red Cross, and diplomats from other neutral countries to save as many lives as possible. Now Perlasca was helping too.

A few days after receiving his Spanish documentation, Perlasca took the embassy car to the railway station where the Hungarian police, supervised by the SS, were loading Jews into cattle cars. In the crowd stood an elderly man who wore his yellow Star of David badge beside the medals he had been awarded for heroism during World War I. Acting on impulse, Perlasca took the old veteran by the arm and helped him into the car. An SS officer objected, but backed away when Perlasca presented his impressive array of documents.

That World War I veteran was the first Jewish person Perlasca saved.

## A man of authority

Eva Lang, twenty years old and newly married, had a few square feet of living space to herself on the sixth floor of a Spanish safe house overlooking St Stephen's Park, a section of Budapest where the embassies of neutral nations operated safe houses for Jews and other individuals hunted by the Nazis. Her husband, Pál, was not with her—shortly after their wedding he and Eva's brother had been rounded up by the Nazis for forced labour in Germany. But Eva had succeeded in obtaining letters of protection for herself, her mother and other family members from the Spanish Embassy; in both German and Hungarian the letters stated: 'Relatives resident in Spain have requested Spanish citizenship for these persons ... The Spanish legation

Great Rescues of World War II

A lone Red Army soldier peers at the desolation of Budapest after its capture from the Germans by Soviet forces in early 1945.

requests that the competent authorities take this matter into consideration in the application of any measures and that the above-named persons be exempted from forced labour.' These letters were a godsend, but men of the Arrow Cross Party, a fanatically anti-Semitic Hungarian fascist organisation, did not always respect them.

One one occasion in December 1944 Eva managed to get a small, round can of sardines, a delicacy that she could share with her family. A few days earlier she had burned herself quite badly picking up a hot cooking pan; she was trying to carry the can in her heavily bandaged hands when she lost her grip and it rolled down the stairs. She caught up with the little can on the fourth floor when it landed on a step just behind a tall, handsome, elegantly dressed man who was blocking the path of a band of Arrow Cross men. They tried to push him out of the way, but the gentleman pushed back. In a loud, angry voice he told the intruders they had no business in the building, that it was under the protection of the Spanish government. Had they not seen the flag of Spain flying over the door? They had violated Spanish territory, and he ordered them to get out at once.

Eva was astonished by this man's courage—the Arrow Cross thugs would beat or shoot anyone who got in their way. But this time they backed down, perhaps because the gentleman was a person of authority who showed no fear. Then Eva recognised him—he worked at the Spanish Embassy, he had provided her letters of protection. His name was Jorge Perlasca.

## 'A flag is not enough'

To make the safe conducts and other protective documents he issued to Hungarian Jews plausible to the Nazis and the Arrow Cross, Sanz Briz often identified the receiver as being 'of Sephardic origin', meaning that he or she was descended from Jews who resided in Spain during the Middle Ages. Another ruse was to declare that the person had relatives in Spain who were Spanish citizens, or had business interests in Spain, and was waiting for the formalities to be completed so he or she could emigrate. 'While awaiting departure,' Sanz Briz wrote on these documents, 'the X family shall be under the protection of the Spanish government.' All of the papers Sanz Briz created were backdated to the period before the Nazis installed Ferenc Szalasi, head of the Arrow Cross Party, as Hungary's head of state.

Despite holding protective papers, it was too dangerous for these 'Spanish' Jews to remain in their own homes; at any moment the SS, the police or the Arrow Cross might break in, deport them or kill them. Consequently, Sanz Briz opened eight safe houses in Budapest where they could live under the protection of Spain.

Sanz Briz, like his fellow diplomats, understood that flying their nation's flag over the door of the safe houses was not enough, even though the puppet government in Budapest must have known that violating the immunity of these houses operated by Spain, or Sweden or the Vatican, or any other neutral nation, would create an international incident. In a group meeting in mid-November 1944, Sanz Briz and his fellow diplomats agreed to visit their safe houses often, to 'let themselves be seen', so the SS and the Arrow Cross would know the embassies took a personal interest in the wellbeing of the residents.

On 29 November, however, the situation in the Spanish Embassy took a dramatic turn. The Soviet Red Army was closing in on Budapest and the city could fall any day. Francisco Franco, who had risen to power by defeating the Communists in the Spanish civil war, did not want to risk his diplomats falling into the hands of the Soviets. He ordered Sanz Briz and all other Spaniards in the embassy to return home via Switzerland. Perlasca's safe conduct from Franco made him eligible to escape, too. After a sleepless night during which he debated his options, Perlasca decided to remain in Budapest. At six the next morning he said goodbye to Sanz Briz and went to visit the safe houses.

As he feared, Sanz Briz's departure had emboldened the Arrow Cross— a group of them was arresting the Jews in the house on St Stephen's Park. Marching into the midst of the uproar, Perlasca shouted, 'Hold everything! You're making a mistake. Sanz Briz has not fled, he has simply gone to Bern to communicate more easily with Madrid.' The Arrow Cross men hesitated, and in that moment Perlasca took an enormous chance. 'Sanz Briz left a specific note naming me as his replacement during his absence,' he said. 'You are speaking with the official representative of Spain!'

Unwilling to suspend the clearance simply on Perlasca's word, an Arrow Cross officer went to a phone and called the Minister of Foreign Affairs; he suggested they postpone the arrest for a few days until they could confirm his statement.

## A gift before Christmas

A few hours later, a secretary ushered Perlasca into the office of József Gera, leader of the Arrow Cross Party. Perlasca waited until the secretary left and had closed the door before he began to speak. He adopted a weary attitude as he reviewed with Gera the series of annoyances he was enduring solely because Sanz Briz had left the city on sensitive diplomatic business. So much misinformation was

### Perlasca after the war

On 29 May 1945, Giorgio Perlasca stood at Budapest's East Railway Station, waiting to board the train that would take him to a seaport where he would catch a ship to Italy. Friends had come to see him off, among them a group of Jews from the safe house in St Stephen's Park. They presented Perlasca with a declaration that read in part:

*There are no words to praise the tenderness with which you fed us and with which you cared for the old and the sick. You gave us courage when we were on the verge of desperation and your name will never be missing from our prayers. May Almighty God reward you.*

Back in Italy, Perlasca turned to the meat export business, married and had a family, but he never told anyone about his activities in Budapest during the war. In the 1980s, a group of Jewish women whose lives he had saved began to look for him. They found him in 1987, living in a modest apartment on the outskirts of Padua in northern Italy. And once they found him, they told his story to anyone in the media who would listen. Almost overnight Giorgio Perlasca became a celebrity. The officials at Yad Vashem, the Holocaust Museum in Israel, named him one of the Righteous Among the Nations. Italy awarded him the Gold Medal for Civil Bravery, Spain presented him with the Order of Isabella the Catholic, and Hungary gave him the Star of Merit. He was invited to countless awards ceremonies, seminars and international conferences. And he gave countless interviews to news reporters who always asked the same question: Why did he do it?

Perlasca's answer was simple: 'Because I couldn't stand the sight of people being branded like animals. Because I couldn't stand seeing children being killed.'

circulating throughout Budapest, and now the Arrow Cross men were violating the immunity of Spanish safe houses under the mistaken notion that diplomatic relations between Spain and Hungary were at an end. Perlasca asked for Gera's help, and as a token of his appreciation, in advance, he had brought a gift. He drew an envelope from his coat pocket and placed it on Gera's desk. Inside were 25,000 pengo, the equivalent of about US$750 at the time.

As Gera accepted the envelope, he expressed regret for the actions of some overzealous individuals. He assured Perlasca that such errors in judgment would not be repeated. Then he walked Perlasca to the door, congratulating him on his new assignment at the embassy.

The next day Perlasca presented his false credentials to the Minister of Foreign Affairs. That afternoon radio stations across the country reported that Spain's ambassador had been called away on official business, but in his absence all diplomatic business should be directed to the embassy secretary, Jorge Perlasca.

It wasn't just the bribe that brought Gera around; no one doubted that the Soviets would capture Budapest, and once that happened the Arrow Cross men—not the Jews—would become the hunted. Gera hoped he and his men would find refuge in Spain, which had a fascist government, and that maintaining friendly relations with Perlasca now might save his neck later.

And Perlasca took advantage of this new relationship with Hungarian officialdom by escorting more Jews from their hiding places to the safe houses.

On Christmas Eve 1944 the Arrow Cross, on the verge of panic as the Red Army surrounded Budapest, broke into the Swedish Embassy and arrested the entire staff, Raoul Wallenberg included. In the days after Christmas they violated the immunity of numerous safe houses, forcing the residents into the ghetto; en route, they shot dozens of Jews, and inside the ghetto murdered hundreds more. But the Spanish safe houses were left intact. On 16 January 1945, the Soviets captured the portion of the city where the Spanish safe houses were located. Inside were perhaps as many as 5000 Jews (an accurate number has never been established), alive and safe through the efforts of Jorge Perlasca.

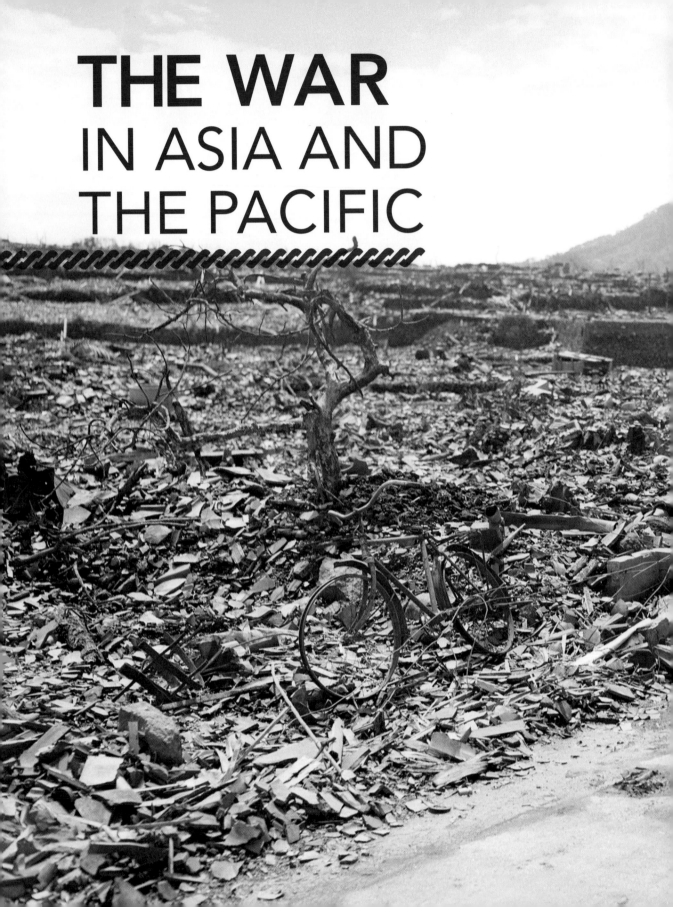

# THE WAR
## IN ASIA AND
## THE PACIFIC

# CHAPTER 15

# THE JAPANESE SCHINDLER
## Chiune Sugihara

In 1940 there were only two options for a traveller from Lithuania who wanted to reach Japan: a seventeen-day journey overland by the Trans-Siberian railway, through the Soviet Union to the Pacific port of Vladivostok, to connect with a ship bound for Kobe in Japan, or a three-day rail journey through Nazi-occupied Europe to a seaport on the Mediterranean, there to catch a ship to Asia and on to Kobe.

For Stanislaw Kaspcik and his wife Stella Kaminskaya neither choice was appealing, for they had good reason to fear both the Soviets and the Germans. Stella had grown up as the stepdaughter of a vehemently anti-Bolshevik Russian aristocrat; Stanislaw had been a high-ranking member of the Polish secret service until the Nazis conquered Poland. If, during their transit of the Soviet Union, the Russians learned of Stella's White Russian connections and Stanislaw's secret service career, they would be taken off their train and shot. If they went south through German-occupied countries and the Nazis learned that Stanislaw had been a member of the

Typical of scenes enacted at railway stations across occupied Europe, SS troops gather together a group of nervous Jews to be sent off to concentration camps. It was to prevent such a fate that Chiune Sugihara aided Jews in Lithuania.

Polish military, the best he could hope for would be deportation to a concentration camp; Stella would probably be deported as well. It was a Catch-22 situation, but ultimately the couple decided to risk the shorter journey.

The night before they were to leave Lithuania, Stella and Stanislaw celebrated with a farewell dinner with family, friends and the man who had provided them with their visas for Japan, Vice Consul Chiune Sugihara. The prospect of being at the mercy of the Nazis for three days frightened Stella, but Sugihara had a plan. After dinner he presented her with an envelope containing a pair of gloves, a gift for Japan's Foreign Minister. The envelope bore the stamps and seals of an official diplomatic document. 'Show this envelope at all border crossings,' Sugihara instructed her. 'You will be like diplomatic couriers.'

At each of the heavily guarded borders of Lithuania, Poland, Germany, Austria and Italy, Nazi or Italian fascist police threw open the Kaspciks' compartment door with a violent crash and demanded to see their papers. To look the part on their journey, Stanislaw had purchased a beautifully tailored suit, and Stella was stylishly dressed. The attractive young couple betrayed no sense of their uneasiness as they presented their visas and their diplomatic package. It always produced the same reaction—the police instantly became courteous and respectful as they murmured to each other, 'Diplomatic courier'.

Shielded by Sugihara's envelope, the Kaspciks arrived safely in Naples and boarded a steamship to carry them to safety in Japan.

## A new consulate in Kaunas

By Japanese standards, Chiune Sugihara was an unconventional man. From his mother, descended from a long line of samurai, he learned reverence for Japan's traditions and loyalty to his family and his country, yet independence, even rebelliousness, was the dominant facet of Sugihara's personality, and it was already asserting itself by the time he was in his teens. His father wanted him to become a doctor, but Sugihara insisted upon studying English literature at Waseda University, a college with a reputation in Japan for its progressive, Western-style education. For this act of filial disobedience, Sugihara's father disowned him.

Japanese troops entering Manchuria during the Sino-Japanese War.
The Japanese set up a puppet government and renamed the region Manchukuo.

The Japanese Schindler

In 1919, still at Waseda University and just nineteen years old, Sugihara was awarded a scholarship by the Foreign Service Ministry to study Russian and German in Harbin, the capital of Manchuria. Manchuria was at the time coming under Japanese control; by 1931 it would be a Japanese colony and renamed Manchukuo. Harbin possessed a sizable White Russian population, nearly all refugees from the Soviet regime, many of them descended from Russian aristocrats. While studying there, Sugihara met a Russian woman, Klaudia Semionova Apollonov, married her, and converted to the Russian Orthodox Church. The year he married, Sugihara was twenty-four. As a boy he had been a good athlete, as a young man he was of moderate height at 165 centimetres, broad-shouldered and trim, handsome, with piercing eyes and thick black hair.

Although his private life was unusual, in all other ways Sugihara was an excellent candidate for the Japanese diplomatic service: he was multilingual, diligent, imaginative and attentive to details. And his first assignment could not have been more convenient—he was named deputy consul for Manchuria, where he proved himself by negotiating the purchase of the Manchuria Railroad from the Soviet Union on terms favourable to Japan.

At the same time that Sugihara's career was beginning to advance, Japan was expanding its empire in China. While this expansion was a cause for celebration back in Japan, to Sugihara, who witnessed the brutality employed by the Japanese troops to subdue the Chinese population, it was sickening and shameful. The soldiers slaughtered millions of Chinese civilians, often in ways that could only be described as sadistic. In 1934 Sugihara resigned as deputy consul of Manchuria in protest, requested a transfer to a post in Europe, and returned to Japan to await his next assignment. There he met and fell in love with Yukiko Kikuchi; in 1935 he divorced Klaudia and married Yukiko.

After a twelve-month stint in Helsinki, Sugihara received a new posting in 1939: he was to open a Japanese consulate in Kaunas, the capital of Lithuania. He was also expected to observe the movements of Nazi and Soviet troops to determine whether the Nazis were preparing to invade Russia, or if the Soviets were preparing to absorb Lithuania into their empire. A Nazi invasion of Russia would be advantageous for Japan—if the Soviet Red Army was obliged to concentrate its forces along its western border, Japan would be able to expand its empire in Asia with minimal Russian interference.

In the autumn of 1939, Sugihara and his wife and children arrived in Kaunas, where they rented a house large enough to serve as the consulate and their home.

## Safe in Japan

In general, the Japanese people did not distinguish Jews from Gentiles any more than they distinguished Protestants from Catholics. Jews were simply Westerners and foreign, no different to any other British, American or Russian person who on any given day the ordinary citizens of Japan might encounter in the business districts of their large cities.

In the 1930s the Japanese government developed closer ties with Nazi Germany, primarily for commercial reasons—Japan's military wanted to purchase the technologically innovative weapons Germany was producing. The Japanese believed in the superiority of their race to all other races as fervently as did any German Aryan, but they never persecuted the Jews. Joseph Rosenstock, a Polish Jew, was welcomed in Japan where he founded and served as the first conductor of the Nippon Philharmonic Orchestra. The executives of the Nippon Columbia Records Company rejected pressure from Germany to stop selling music recorded by Jewish artists. Western classical music was popular in Japan, and the music executives were not about to ban top-selling recordings by Jascha Heifetz, Fritz Kreisler or Yehudi Menuhin just to please the Nazis.

When World War II began, Japan's tolerance of the Jews stood in sharp contrast to the treatment of other non-Japanese people. Thousands upon thousands of Chinese, Korean, Filipino, not to mention British, American, Dutch, French and Australian soldiers and civilians suffered torture and death at the hands of Japanese troops, but Jewish refugees, perhaps because they did not represent any Allied government, were left in peace.

In 1940, when Japan allied itself with the Third Reich, the Jews living in the country not unnaturally became anxious about their future. To allay their fears, Foreign Minister Matsuoka Yosuke invited a group of Jewish business leaders to meet with him on New Year's Eve. Yosuke introduced himself, saying,

Japanese Foreign Minister Yosuke meets Hitler in Berlin. Yosuke was a major advocate of a Japanese alliance with the Nazis, but refused to carry out any of the Nazis' anti-Semitic policies in Japan.

The Japanese Schindler

'I am the man responsible for the alliance with Hitler.' Then he added, 'But nowhere have I promised that we would carry out his anti-Semitic policies in Japan. This is not simply my personal opinion, it is the opinion of Japan, and I have no compunction about announcing it to the world.' Yosuke's statement proved to be the truth: the Jews living in Japan were left free and undisturbed throughout the war. Furthermore, the government and the military consistently refused to comply with Germany's repeated demands that they deport or exterminate the large Jewish refugee community in Shanghai, a Chinese city under Japanese control.

## A nation of 'provocateurs'

Japan's policy regarding Jewish refugees took second place to Sugihara's own experiences which stirred up in him, as he expressed it in 1985, the year before his death, 'the kind of sentiments anyone would have when he actually sees the refugees face to face, begging with tears in their eyes. He just cannot help but sympathise with them.'

By the time Sugihara and his family arrived in Kaunas, the Jewish community of Lithuania was trying to find housing, food and means of support for 15,000 refugees from Poland. The stories the Polish Jews told of Nazi atrocities were horrifying. At Czestochowa the Nazis had dragged more than 100 Jews from their homes and shot them in the street. In the town of Mielec, on Rosh Hashanah, the Jewish New Year, they had rounded up about thirty-five Jewish men, forced them to strip naked, herded them into a butcher's shop and set it on fire. As a 'special tribute' to Joseph Goebbels during his visit to Lodz in October 1939, the SS had rampaged through a Jewish neighbourhood, killing dozens of men and women outright, and hurling children out of windows.

Roving bands of Nazi soldiers tore out the beards of elderly rabbis, or set the beards on fire. They forced men to clean out latrines with their prayer shawls. In the town of Cisna they forced a Jewish congregation to pile their Torah scrolls and prayer books in the marketplace, set them afire, then dance around the flames singing, '*Wir freuen uns, wie das Dreck brennt*' ('How glad we are the filth is burning').

The question in everyone's mind was how long Lithuania would remain a safe haven. The German army had stopped at the western border; the Soviet army might march across the eastern border at any time. Lithuania was surrounded, and it was becoming clear to citizens, refugees and the diplomatic corps that it would not survive much longer as an independent nation.

In the spring of 1940, six months after Sugihara arrived in Kaunas, representatives of the Soviet government began publishing absurd claims that Lithuanian citizens were creeping across their borders to harass and even take captive soldiers of the Red Army. Soviet Foreign Minister Vyacheslav Molotov declared to the world that if Lithuania were invaded by the Soviet Union, it would be the little country's own fault: 'Lithuania's fate was threatened by no one else but its own provocateurs'.

On 15 June 1940, Soviet tanks accompanied by between 300,000 and 400,000 troops poured across the eastern border, occupying every city and town, seizing control of the airports, the  power grid and the communications network. To escape Russian retribution, Lithuania's president, Antanas Smetona, who had advocated armed resistance, fled through Germany to exile in Switzerland.

One month later, on 15 July, the Soviet occupation forces held a rigged referendum and reported that 99 per cent of the Lithuanian electorate had voted to become part of the Soviet Union. Immediately after the referendum the Soviet secret police, the NKVD, assisted by Red Army troops, began rounding up anti-Soviet Lithuanians. Members of the Lithuanian Cabinet and leaders of the various political parties were among the first to be arrested and deported to Russia for execution. But at least twenty-three other groups were also targeted, including members of the National Guard, police officers, journalists, prosperous business people, farmers and landowners, leaders of labour unions, ship owners, investors in the stock market, priests and rabbis and prominent individuals within the Catholic and Jewish communities. Between 15 July 1940 and 21 June 1941— the day the Nazis seized Lithuania—approximately 75,000 Lithuanians were deported, executed or simply disappeared; of that number, at least 7700 were children under the age of eighteen.

# Defying protocol

Because the independent nation of Lithuania no longer existed, there was no longer any need for foreign embassies or consulates in Kaunas—all diplomatic matters would now be handled through Moscow. Consequently, in late July 1940, the Soviet authorities in Lithuania ordered the diplomatic corps to close their offices and return to their homelands. For the convenience of the diplomats, a twenty-day extension would be granted upon request. Sugihara requested the extension, but for reasons the Soviets could not predict.

Early in the morning of 26 July the consul and his wife had woken to find a line of Jews standing outside the consulate, waiting for the office to open. The crowd wanted visas to Japan, where they hoped to catch a ship to Shanghai, or the United States, or any place where they would be safe from the Nazis and the Soviets. That first day Sugihara issued seventeen visas. The next day he issued forty-one. The third day, Sunday, the consulate was closed, but on Monday he issued 121 visas. These were family visas—a single document was all that was necessary for a husband, a wife and all their children to travel under the protection of Japan. As a formality, Sugihara wired his Foreign Minister requesting permission to issue a large number of visas to Jewish refugees, saying, 'Daily, hundreds of Jews are thronging our building asking for visas to go to the US via Japan.' But he did not wait on a response—on 30 July he issued 257 visas.

As word spread through Kaunas that the Japanese consul was sympathetic to their plight, the throng of Jews in the street outside grew to the point that Sugihara, looking out his window, could not see the end of the line. Many people had out-of-date passports, safe conducts issued by the defunct League of Nations, papers that were obvious forgeries, or no papers at all, but Sugihara did not allow such inconsistencies to trouble him—in defiance of protocol and diplomatic standards, he simply handed out as many visas as he could each day.

Yukiko Sugihara assisted him. In 1940 there was no time-saving technology to expedite the process—each visa had to written out by hand. It has been reported that Sugihara spent up to twenty hours a day writing visas, and that his wife spent many hours each day helping him. While he was trying to save lives, Sugihara received a definitive answer from the Foreign Office in Tokyo:

*Concerning transit visas requested previously STOP Advise absolutely not to be issued any traveller not holding firm end visa with guaranteed departure ex Japan STOP No exceptions STOP No further inquiries expected STOP (signed) K Tanaka Foreign Ministry Tokyo*

By the time this cable, which he ignored, had arrived, Sugihara had made up his mind to continue handing out visas until he was compelled to leave the country. In one of his more memorable acts, he wrote out 300 visas to save the entire faculty and all the students of the Mir, or Mirrer, Yeshiva. Thanks to Sugihara they travelled safely to Kobe, where they re-established the school.

By the end of August the Soviets had lost patience with the vice consul—they ordered Sugihara to close the consulate and leave the country. On 4 September 1940, Sugihara and his family boarded a train—not for Vladivostok and then Japan, but for Berlin. For the rest of World War II, he would fulfil his consular duties in Nazi-occupied Europe.

By the time the train moved out of Kaunas station, Sugihara and his wife had written 2139 family visas, saving the lives of between 6000 and 10,000 Jews (an accurate count has never been established). There are two legends told about the day Sugihara left Kaunas: one claims that he was still writing visas and passing them out his compartment window as the train left the station; the second claims that he passed the visa stamp to a Jewish man standing on the railway platform so more visas could be created. The truth of either story has never been established, but like other such legends they tell us something of the character of the man and how he was revered by the people whose lives he saved.

## Friends in Kobe

Sixteen-year-old Chaya Liba Szepsenwol and her eighteen-year-old sister Fejge were among the lucky 2139 who had secured a visa from Chiune Sugihara. About the same time Sugihara was closing down the consulate in Kaunas, the sisters were boarding a train heading east to Vladivostok. Their journey was funded by relatives in America who ran a candy store and gift shop, hard-working Jewish immigrants

## The Sugiharas after the war

In spring 1945, Chiune Sugihara was serving as Japan's consul in Bucharest in Romania when the Soviet Red Amy drove out the Nazis and occupied the city. The Soviets arrested Sugihara, his wife and their four sons, along with seventeen consulate staff. The reason for the arrests is uncertain: perhaps it was because the Russians believed that Japan, as a member of the Axis, was not entitled to diplomatic immunity, or perhaps it was because they knew or suspected that Sugihara had monitored Soviet troop movements before the Russian invasion of Lithuania in 1940.

The Russians confined the Sugiharas in a prison camp on the Black Sea, later moving them to a more remote camp further inland. They were not beaten or abused, but their diet was paltry—only 500 grams (1 pound) of meat and a kilogram (2 pounds) of fish per month, a kilogram of bread per day, and some tomato paste. They were held for eighteen months.

The Russians released the Sugiharas at the beginning of 1947. On 10 April of that year they arrived via the Trans-Siberian railway at Vladivostok, where they boarded a ship for Japan—ironically, following the same route as the thousands of Jews who had escaped from Lithuania thanks to Sugihara's visas.

Only weeks after arriving home, the Japanese Foreign Ministry summoned Sugihara to its offices in Tokyo, where he was ordered to submit his resignation. Records show that the Foreign Ministry at this time was requiring the resignation of many of its diplomats—in 1947 Japan was under occupation by US forces, and an occupied nation has no need for a large body of diplomats. Nonetheless, Sugihara's family always believed the Foreign Minister forced him out of the diplomatic corps because he had disobeyed orders. The fact that his visas had saved the lives of thousands of Jewish refugees did not enter into the equation.

Chiune Sugihara and his wife Yukiko in the Japanese consulate office in Bucharest.

who had dipped into the family savings and even taken out a loan against a life insurance policy to ensure that Chaya and Fejge could escape Lithuania before the Nazis closed in.

From Vladivostok the girls sailed to the Japanese port of Kobe, but there they encountered a problem—they did not have what is known in diplomatic circles as an 'end visa', as specified in the cable from the Foreign Ministry which Sugihara had ignored. The Sugihara visa gave them entrée to Japan, but the Japanese wanted to know where the sisters intended to go next, because they would not be permitted to remain. Chaya and Fejge replied that their destination was the United States, but they had no documentation to prove that the United States would accept them, nor could they appeal to the US consulate in Kobe, because on the day they arrived it was closed in observance of an American holiday.

While the immigration officials debated what to do next, Chaya and Fejge got in touch with leaders of the Jewish community in the city, who sent two men to promise that the Jews of Kobe would take full responsibility for them. With that assurance, the Japanese released the two émigrées from Lithuania.

The Szepsenwol sisters were deeply moved by the generosity of Kobe's Jews, who welcomed them into their homes and provided for them, as well as by the kindness of their Japanese neighbours, who welcomed them with small gifts such as baskets of fruit.

After two months, the paperwork finally cleared and the sisters received visas to continue to America. Many years later, in an interview with author Hillel Levine, Chaya Szepsenwol, who now went by the name Lucille Camhi, said, 'I think of Mr Sugihara as my saviour.'

# CHAPTER 16

# RESCUING CAESAR

## General Douglas MacArthur's Escape from Corregidor to Australia

The cable from the president seemed to drain all energy and spirit from General Douglas MacArthur. It had arrived at his subterranean headquarters in the Malinta Tunnel on Corregidor, late in the morning of 23 February 1942. US President Franklin D. Roosevelt was ordering MacArthur to leave the island fortress for Mindanao, the big island in the south of the Philippine Archipelago, then continue on to Melbourne in Australia, where, the cable read, 'you will assume command of all United States troops'.

At any other time the president's cable would have been welcomed—it came, after all, with a promotion to commander of all US troops in the Pacific. But given the situation in the Philippines, MacArthur read the order as a personal humiliation. The army of the Empire of Japan was rolling over the islands. On the nearby Bataan Peninsula of Luzon, 76,000 troops—64,000 Filipinos and 12,000 Americans—were pinned down, with no hope of escape, reinforcement or rescue. On tiny, rocky, tadpole-shaped Corregidor, MacArthur commanded

The Japanese air raid on Pearl Harbor on 7 December 1941 brought the United States into World War II on many fronts, perhaps none more critical than the War in the Pacific, which was fought in such places as the Philippines, Guam and Papua New Guinea.

12,000 troops, almost all of them American, and their situation was just as desperate. He had sworn he would never leave his men, that he would fight and die with them on 'the Rock'.

To obey the president, his Commander-in-Chief, meant breaking his word and abandoning his troops, but to disobey meant court martial and disgrace. MacArthur called for his chief of staff, Major General Richard K. Sutherland; together they went to find MacArthur's wife, Jean. Sequestering themselves in MacArthur's bungalow on the hill above the tunnel, they discussed the cable at length. When the general emerged from the bungalow he ordered his staff to meet with him inside the tunnel; there MacArthur rehashed his concerns and anxieties. At the end of this meeting the general announced his decision: he would resign his commission, find a boat to take him across to Bataan, and enlist as a common soldier.

MacArthur's staff objected. He was misreading the cable, they argued. Roosevelt was sending the general to Australia to collect reinforcements and supplies to relieve the siege of Bataan and Corregidor. In a few weeks he would be back, and he would return a hero. Over the objections of his staff MacArthur wrote a draft of his proposed letter of resignation, but on Sutherland's advice he put it aside until the next morning.

After a night's sleep MacArthur was able to be persuaded that Roosevelt did intend to send him back to the Philippines with fresh troops, but he remained worried about the timing of his departure. He cabled Roosevelt: 'I know the situation here in the Philippines, and unless the right moment is chosen for so delicate an operation a sudden collapse might result.' Roosevelt knew that the general's departure could damage the already shaky morale of the US troops in the Philippines as well as the morale of the public back home, so he agreed to let MacArthur make this decision.

Nine days went by and MacArthur showed no sign of leaving Corregidor; Roosevelt sent another cable: 'The situation in Australia indicates desirability of your early arrival there'. Still MacArthur hesitated—the idea of abandoning his men haunted him. Five days later Roosevelt sent yet another cable, urging him to go while there was still time. This time MacArthur responded; he cabled Roosevelt that he planned to leave on 15 March and arrive in Australia on 18 March. According to historian William Manchester, MacArthur was in one of his 'Caesarean moods' when he announced his decision to his staff. 'We go with the fall of the moon,' he declaimed, 'we go during the ides of March.'

## The day after Pearl Harbor

Corregidor rises 190 metres (623 feet) from the sea at the entrance to Manila Bay. It lies 40 kilometres (25 miles) from the city of Manila, about 3 kilometres (2 miles) off the Bataan Peninsula. In the sixteenth century the Spanish transformed the island into a fortress to guard the harbour. At the onset of World War II, Corregidor was a fortress once again: fifty-six gun emplacements circled the island, including eight 12-inch (305-mm) mortars that had a range of 13.5 kilometres (8 miles) and two other 12-inch mortars that could strike a target 24 kilometres (15 miles) away. Also, there were twenty 3-inch (76-mm) anti-aircraft guns and forty-eight .50 calibre machine guns, and for night-time raids there were five 60-inch (152-cm) searchlights.

Between 1922 and 1932, beneath Malinta Hill, the US Army Corps of Engineers had blasted a series of tunnels 3.6 metres (12 feet) high as a bomb-proof storage facility. They were never intended for human habitation, as Corregidor was well stocked with housing: barracks and a Filipino village at Bottomside, the lowest part and mid-section of the tadpole-shaped island, a military hospital and barracks on the western plateau (the 'head' of the tadpole) known as Middleside, and more barracks and the officers' quarters on the highest, eastern 'tail' section, Topside.

The remnant of an ancient volcano, Corregidor is a beautiful island with dense tangles of emerald jungle where brilliantly coloured tropical birds flash against the vivid green of the vegetation. There is a sandy beach at Bottomside and clear blue waters for swimming, and picturesque roads that lead through the jungle up to the cliffs where visitors enjoy breathtaking views of the Pacific, Manila Bay, the Bataan Peninsula and, in the distance across the bay, the white colonial churches and palaces of old Manila.

MacArthur had lived in the Philippines since 1936; with the rank of field marshal, he had been responsible for training the Filipino armed forces to resist possible invasion by empire-building Japan. But the first blow against America's

General MacArthur and his staff contemplate the damage from a Japanese bomb strike at the entrance to the Malinta Tunnel complex on Corregidor.

territorial interests had fallen not on the Philippines, but on Hawaii: on 7 December 1941, Japan launched a surprise attack on the US naval base at Pearl Harbor, crippling the US fleet in the Pacific and bringing America abruptly into World War II. The next day, however, shortly after midday, a fleet of Japanese heavy bombers, dive-bombers and fighter planes attacked Clark Field, 65 kilometres (40 miles) north-west of Manila, where the planes of the US Far East Air Force—ninty-one P-40 Warhawk fighters and thirty-five B-17 Flying Fortress bombers—were lined up, wingtip to wingtip, for refuelling. The Japanese pilots began their raid by bombing the airfield, but discovered that by flying low and strafing the planes with tracer bullets they could set off a domino effect of exploding fuel tanks. In about an hour they had virtually demolished US air power in the Philippines, reduced the hangers and maintenance facilities to burning ruins, and killed eighty men.

Two days later Japan struck again, this time targeting the Cavite Navy Yard 13 kilometres (8 miles) south-west of Manila. Vice Admiral John Bulkeley was a lieutenant at the time and commander of Motor Torpedo Boat Squadron 3: 'They kept beautiful formations, all right,' he said. 'The first big V had fifty-four planes in it, and they came in with their fighters on up above to protect them from ours—only ours didn't show!' By employing swift evasive manoeuvres, Bulkeley's squadron of PT boats survived the attack, but the submarine USS *Sealion* took a direct hit and sank. Two other submarines and a destroyer were damaged; two minesweepers were sunk and a third damaged.

With great precision the Japanese bombed a cache of more than 230 torpedoes and many thousands of litres of 100-octane fuel; they levelled the signal station, the power plant, Canaco Hospital and the officers' quarters, and attacked the city itself. In less than two hours, the navy yard had been flattened, the city of Cavite was in flames, and casualties ran to at least a thousand dead and many more wounded.

After the disastrous attacks on Clark Field and Cavite Navy Yard, the US Asiatic Fleet, stationed in Manila, withdrew to Java: with no hope of air cover, it was virtually defenceless against another Pearl Harbor-type attack.

On 22 December 1941, a Japanese force of 40,000 men landed at Lingayen Gulf on the west coast of Luzon Island. On Christmas Eve MacArthur's wife, their three-year-old son Arthur, along with Ah Cheu, the little boy's Chinese amah, or nanny, evacuated to Corregidor. The President of the Philippines, Manuel Quezon, also moved to Corregidor, along with his government. The refugees had no viable option: the Japanese were bombing Manila, and the Japanese army was advancing so rapidly across Luzon that on Christmas Day, General MacArthur, acting on the advice of Quezon, would declare Manila an 'open city', meaning that Filipino and American forces would not defend the capital, that the Japanese could march in peacefully and take possession. (The purpose of such a declaration is to spare the lives of civilians as well as save artistic and historic monuments from destruction.) On 2 January 1942, the Japanese occupied the city.

## Life in the tunnel

On the Rock, the US garrison had prepared accommodation for President Quezon and the MacArthurs inside the Malinta Tunnel. The main chamber ran for 430 metres (1411 feet) and was 10.6 metres (35 feet) wide; twenty-five lateral tunnels, each 120 metres (394 feet) long and 3.6 metres (12 feet) high, ran off this main passageway. Army engineers had hung neon lights from the ceiling, which gave the gloomy tunnels an eerie glow. They had also installed portable toilets, but these facilities were inadequate. In addition to their ever-present suffocating dampness, the tunnels reeked of raw human waste, dank earth and unwashed bodies. The atmosphere was unhealthy and depressing.

By the time the MacArthurs arrived it was nearly midnight on Christmas Eve. A Catholic priest had improvised an altar in the main chamber, and President Quezon, along with all the Filipino and American Catholics, packed into the tunnel for Midnight Mass. The MacArthurs also attended the mass; afterwards, the garrison's commanding officer, Major General George Moore, showed the general and his family to their quarters. MacArthur was appalled—a cave was no place for women and children. 'Where are your quarters?' he asked Moore. 'Topside,' Moore replied. 'We'll move up there tomorrow morning,' the general said.

The MacArthurs moved into a bungalow where they enjoyed an unobstructed view of Manila Bay. Unhappily, their new home was a perfect target for Japanese bomber planes, which launched the first attack against the Rock on 29 December, dropping 54 tonnes (60 tons) of bombs, hitting the barracks at Bottomside and

Topside, the fuel depot and the hospital. Three days later a second wave of aircraft bombed Corregidor for three hours. During these raids Jean MacArthur and little Arthur hurried down to the Malinta Tunnel, but the general refused to take cover— he stood outside the bungalow, in plain view, as if he could stare down any Japanese gunner who dared to take aim at him. Such acts of bravado distressed his wife so much that during later raids he joined his family in the tunnels.

While the tunnel complex itself was bombproof, its large entranceway was vulnerable. Any kamikaze pilot who dive-bombed the entrance would have caused horrific casualties. There was also the possibility that a skilful pilot might fly low enough to drop a bomb that could bounce into the entrance. Against such contingencies the Army engineers strung heavy cable between telephone poles along the approach to the tunnel—these would bring down any plane before it reached the entrance—and in front of the entrance they erected a heavy wall to deflect any bombs. The tunnel complex was now more secure, but it was also more difficult to live in, for the wall at the entrance severely obstructed the inflow of fresh air.

And fresh air was a precious commodity for the hundreds of people living and working inside the tunnel. The hospital had been moved inside, and the general's staff had their offices there. Carlos Romulo, a journalist who later became the Philippines' ambassador to the United States, and then president of the General Assembly of the United Nations, was on Corregidor at the time and recalled the horrors of this underground life:

> The smell of the place hit me like a blow in the face. There was the stench of sweat and dirty clothes, the coppery smell of blood and disinfectant coming from the lateral where the hospital was situated, and over all the heavy stink of creosote, hanging like a blanket in the air that moved sluggishly when it moved at all.

## 'We are near done'

Supplies of food were already dangerously low, and from the end of December the Japanese navy and air force kept American and Filipino ships from resupplying the garrison. Even water was in short supply—the Rock had few sources of drinkable water, and even in peacetime water had to be brought in by barge. The 12,000 troops and civilians on Corregidor were limited to two cups of water per day, some rice and a little fish. Any transport mules that were killed in bombing raids were butchered and served up to the garrison. On such a limited diet the men were losing their strength, falling ill, looking gaunt; MacArthur ate the same rations as his troops and had the same haggard appearance.

In mid-February MacArthur learned that Singapore had surrendered; 130,000 British, Indian and Australian troops were now prisoners of war. MacArthur understood that the fall of Singapore ensured the fall of Bataan and Corregidor, for now Japan could devote its air force, navy and infantry almost exclusively to the conquest of the Philippines.

The Rock was becoming too perilous a place for some of the civilians who had taken refuge there. On 22 February 1942 the submarine USS *Swordfish* managed to reach the island and carry Manuel Quezon to Panay Island, an interim place of sanctuary until he could evacuate to the United States, where he established the Philippine government-in-exile. Quezon and MacArthur had been friends and colleagues for more than ten years, and their parting was an emotional one. The usually aloof general embraced his friend, saying, 'Manuel, you will see it through. You are the father of your country and God will preserve you.' Quezon, barely able to hold back tears, slipped a ring from his hand and put it on MacArthur's finger. 'When they find your body,' the president said, 'I want them to know you died for my country.'

A week after Quezon left Corregidor, the *Swordfish* returned to pick up US high commissioner Francis Sayre, his wife and son, and eleven other American civilians. Their destination was Australia.

About this time MacArthur got a report through to Washington of the situation on Corregidor. In a dispassionate tone he itemised the garrison's troubles: they had suffered 50 per cent casualties; they had been on half rations for a month; they were in desperate need of rest. 'We have pulled through a number of menacing situations,' MacArthur wrote, 'but there is no denying of the fact that we are near done … Since I have no air or sea protection, you must be prepared at any time to figure on the complete destruction of this command.'

# 'Young, cocky, and brash'

In many ways Douglas MacArthur and John Bulkeley, commander of Motor Torpedo Boat Squadron 3, were alike: both loved adventure, both thrived on danger, both were born to command. Bulkeley brought a dash of swagger and old-fashioned gallantry to every ship he commanded; routinely, his biographers use the terms 'swashbuckling' and 'buccaneer' to describe him. Bulkeley didn't dispute this characterisation: he described himself during World War II as 'young, cocky, and brash'. When MacArthur finally admitted to himself that he must obey President Roosevelt's orders and leave Corregidor, John Bulkeley was the man he asked to see.

The general invited Lieutenant Bulkeley to lunch at his bungalow on Topside; when he arrived, MacArthur led him not to the dining room, but outside, to an open field pockmarked with bomb craters where they could speak candidly without fear of being overheard. MacArthur explained that the president had ordered him to leave Corregidor to take command of US forces in Australia. He wanted Bulkeley to carry him and his family south to Mindanao, where he would rendezvous with US Army Air Force B-17s that would fly them to Australia. The tricky part would be breaking through the Japanese air and sea blockade of Corregidor, then travelling hundreds of kilometres across open sea in what were essentially Japanese waters.

Bulkeley was a bit surprised by this plan. 'But General MacArthur, sir,' he said, 'wouldn't it be safer for you to get to Mindanao by submarine or by air?'

MacArthur replied that the Japanese would expect him to take either of those routes if he tried to escape the island. 'They won't be expecting me to make the break-out by PT boat,' he said. Then he asked, 'Well, Johnny, do you think you can pull it off?'

'General,' Bulkeley replied, 'it will be a piece of cake.'

Forty-five years later, when he wrote an account of his mission, Bulkeley admitted that the challenges of getting MacArthur to Mindanao were greater than he had been willing to acknowledge at the time. He would be taking his PT boats through 'nearly 600 miles [965 km] of largely uncharted waters with unseen jagged coral reefs waiting to rip apart our thin-skinned wooden boats'. Furthermore, the Japanese expected MacArthur to make a run for safety. In radio broadcasts designed to undermine American morale, Tokyo Rose declared that the Japanese would capture MacArthur alive, then give him a public hanging in front of Emperor Hirohito's palace in Tokyo.

# The farewell

President Roosevelt's orders had been for General MacArthur to leave Corregidor alone, but that order was amended to include his wife and son. MacArthur, however, planned a much larger exodus. His passenger list included young Arthur's amah, thirteen army officers—including his chief of staff Sutherland—two naval officers and a staff sergeant. The general was not being high-handed; if he was to command US troops in the Pacific he would need his staff, men who he knew and trusted.

Before he left, however, MacArthur wanted to meet with General Jonathan Wainwright, who was commanding the forces on Bataan. The day Wainwright came ashore on Corregidor, Sutherland met him, and at the Malinta Tunnel disclosed what the general probably already suspected—that MacArthur was evacuating from the Rock. Then they walked up to MacArthur's bungalow on Topside.

The two generals looked terrible: MacArthur had lost 14 kilograms (31 pounds) from living on half rations, and his khaki bush jacket had grown shabby from heavy use and repeated washings. Wainwright's uniform looked several sizes too big for the man—he and his men on Bataan had been reduced to three-eighths rations. Sitting in lounge chairs on the bungalow's porch, the two men alternated between forced good cheer and realistic assessments of the future.

MacArthur promised, 'If I can get to Australia you know I'll be back as soon as I can with as much as I can. In the meantime you've got to hold.'

Wainwright replied that holding Bataan was 'our aim in life'.

'You'll get through,' Wainwright said.

'And back!' MacArthur replied.

'Goodbye, Jonathan,' MacArthur said, shaking Wainwright's hand. 'When I get back, if you're still on Bataan, I'll make you a lieutenant general.'

'I'll be on Bataan if I'm still alive,' Wainwright replied.

# Racing into the night

Escaping via PT boat was risky. They were compact wooden vessels, 23.5 metres (77 feet) long, 6 metres (19½ feet) wide, with small fuel tanks; to make the run to Mindanao all four boats in the squad that would carry MacArthur and his party would have to strap twenty extra drums of fuel to their decks. But what PT boats lacked in size they compensated for in speed. As Bulkeley put it, a PT boat was designed 'to roar in, let fly a Sunday punch, and then get the hell out, zigging to dodge the shells'. Unfortunately, with the extra weight of passengers, their luggage, and those extra fuel drums, Bulkeley's PT boats would be lucky if they made half their normal speed of 45 to 50 knots.

For several days MacArthur and Bulkeley met to work out the details of the escape. At dusk the four PT boats would pick up groups of evacuees from four different points around Corregidor, then rendezvous at the mouth of Manila Bay. From here Bulkeley would lead the boats, single file, through the minefields off Corregidor. Then the boats would head for the Cuyo Islands, 400 kilometres (248½ miles) south in the Sulu Sea, where they would lie up in some secluded inlet or stream until nightfall, then set out for the next leg of the journey.

If the squad encountered a Japanese vessel, Bulkeley's PT boat—the one which would be carrying the MacArthur family, was to peel away from the pack, leaving the remaining three boats to fight off the enemy.

The general and the lieutenant worked out rendezvous points if the boats were separated, as well as places where they could hide from the Japanese, and even locations where, if necessary, they could be rescued by submarine.

The greatest anxiety for MacArthur and Bulkeley were Japanese aircraft. If they spotted the little convoy, it was questionable if the PT boats could fight them off with .50 machine guns.

Since speed and manoeuvrability were essential, Bulkeley set a limit of how much luggage the evacuees could bring along—one suitcase each, weighing no more than 16 kilograms (35 pounds). Meanwhile, Jean MacArthur was collecting food for the voyage. Not much was available, but she managed to find canned salmon. Since water was in such short supply, she took along cans of orangeade. She divided the rations equally and packed them into four duffel bags, one for each PT boat.

Then circumstances obliged Bulkeley and MacArthur to move up their departure date: Japan's spies had reported that the general was preparing to leave Corregidor. The Americans noticed Japanese ships patrolling the waters around the Rock, and MacArthur's staff had received word that Japanese destroyers were en route to Manila Bay. MacArthur and Bulkeley agreed they must leave immediately.

As the sun set on 11 March, the MacArthur family and their nanny Ah Cheu made their way to the South Dock at what had been Bottomside. The Filipino village and the entire dock area had been destroyed in bombing raids. The earth was scarred by bomb craters, the buildings were fire-blackened hulks, there were even scorch marks on the rocks near the remnants of the pier. The general was the last to board Bulkeley's *PT-41*. He looked deathly pale, and he had developed a nervous twitch at the corner of his mouth. Before he climbed aboard he lifted his cap—a signal to artillery crews to begin diversionary fire to cover their escape. As the big guns opened fire, the general stepped aboard. 'You may cast off, Buck, when you are ready,' he said.

As *PT-41* pulled away from the wrecked dock, the three other PT boats emerged from the darkness. Led by a minelayer, they crept single file through the Japanese minefield. Once they were in the clear, the four skippers opened their throttles to full speed and raced into the night.

## The getaway

There was no moon the night of 11 March, and the sea was rough, with waves 4.5 to 6 metres (15 to 19½ feet) high crashing against the PT boats, soaking anyone on deck. Bulkeley edged his boats closer to Cabra Island, where he expected the waters would be calmer. The PT boats were about 3 kilometres (2 miles) offshore when the light from several bonfires suddenly shattered the darkness: Japanese coastwatchers had spotted the little convoy and were alerting the forces on Luzon and Mindoro. By dawn Japanese bombers and destroyers would be searching the area for the PT boats; their only hope of escape was to find a secure island hiding place before the sun came up. Bulkeley led his boats out to the open sea.

Before they sailed everyone had been concerned about Jean MacArthur, who always got seasick, but in the choppy waters that night, all three MacArthurs were ill, suffering violent bouts of nausea. The general wrote later that the first night aboard Bulkeley's *PT-41* was like 'a trip in a concrete mixer'.

Given the rough seas and the moonless night, the four PT boats lost each other in the dark. Their plan called for the boats to rendezvous in the Cuyo Islands and be tied up and camouflaged before dawn—none of them got there on time. It was full morning when Bulkeley eased *PT-41* into a secluded cove. The plan also called for the party to rest for the day and depart at sunset, but MacArthur and fellow evacuee Admiral Francis Rockwell were worried that any further mishap would delay their reaching Cagayan on Mindanao Island, where the Flying Fortresses would be waiting. If they were significantly late, the pilots could well assume that the evacuees were dead or captured, and fly back to base in Australia without them. Reluctantly, MacArthur decided to risk travelling in daylight. At two-thirty in the afternoon he told Bulkeley, 'Well, let's go.'

They had been at sea only fifteen minutes when Bulkeley's lookout spotted a Japanese cruiser; fortunately, the high seas concealed the little PT boats and they escaped undetected. After dark they reached Negros Island, where the Japanese had placed artillery batteries along the shore. Fortunately, when the artillery crews heard the engines of the PT boats they mistook them for American bombers; as searchlights scanned the skies, the little convoy sped away into the dark.

Still concerned about losing time, Bulkeley and MacArthur insisted that they press on. At six-thirty in the morning they spotted Cagayan on Mindanao's north coast, where they were to meet the B-17s. Bulkeley led the way into the harbour. On shore, Colonel William Morse was waiting with a guard of infantrymen. He remembered that seeing MacArthur standing erect in the bow of the PT boat reminded him of Emmanuel Leutze's famous painting, *Washington Crossing the Delaware*.

In a little over thirty-five hours Bulkeley and his men had brought the MacArthurs and their party through 896 kilometres (557 miles) of Japanese-held waters. The general stepped ashore, helped his wife off the boat, and turned to the commander of *PT-41*. 'Bulkeley,' he said, 'I'm giving every officer and man here the Silver Star for gallantry. You've taken me out of the jaws of death, and I won't forget it.'

## The last leg of the journey

The day the MacArthurs landed on the north of Mindanao, 25,000 Allied troops were defending the island from Japanese invaders who had captured Davao. The evacuees were exhausted; nevertheless, they expected that Colonel Morse would escort them to the B-17s and on to Australia. But Brigadier General William F. Sharp, commander of US forces on Mindanao, had planned a reception. The preparations were made by the Filipino staff, who unfortunately let it be known that General MacArthur was on Mindanao. By the afternoon word had reached the Japanese, who promptly sent a detachment of troops to capture the general, and dispatched two bombers on a reconnaissance mission over the plantation.

In fact, there were no B-17s waiting. After four days on the plantation, with Japanese planes flying daily missions overhead, the best that could be found was a battered specimen that had barely survived the bombing of Clark Field. The general stood waiting on the improvised airstrip at Cagayan as the B-17, its engine spluttering, made a wobbly landing. Damning the plane as 'dangerously decrepit', MacArthur refused to set one foot on board, and sent an irate radio message to George Brett, who was responsible for getting the party to Melbourne, and to George Marshall at the White House, demanding 'the three best planes in the United States or Hawaii [crewed by] completely adequate, experienced' pilots. The general's message to Washington did the trick; two new B-17s were sent from Townsville to transport the entire party.

Already carrying ten crew each, the planes could barely fit everyone. And having just recovered from seasickness, they now experienced air sickness. They were near the end of their flight when the pilots received a message that Darwin, their destination, was under attack by Japanese bombers; the B-17s changed course for remote Batchelor Field, 80 kilometres (50 miles) south. The passengers barely had time to disembark for breakfast when a message came in warning that Japanese bombers were heading even for this location. The passengers scrambled hastily aboard two Australian DC-3s, and their pilots charted a course for Alice Springs in the Australian outback.

By now Jean MacArthur was out of patience. She refused to get on another plane; and insisted they make the next leg of their journey, the 1645 kilometres (1022 miles) from Alice Springs to Adelaide, by train, then catch another train to Melbourne, their final destination. As a courtesy, John Curtin, Prime Minister of Australia, sent a 'special train' to Alice Springs.

It took three days to reach Adelaide. Realising that a crowd of reporters and spectators would be waiting for him there, MacArthur had prepared a brief speech. 'The President of the United States ordered me to break through the Japanese lines … for the purpose, as I understand it, of organising the American offensive against Japan, a primary object of which is the relief of the Philippines. I came through, and I shall return.'

Great Rescues of World War II

General MacArthur, accompanied by Major General Patrick J. Hurley, already stationed in the country, waves a greeting as he arrives in Australia to take command of US forces in the Pacific after his rescue from Corregidor.

Rescuing Caesar

# CHAPTER 17

# AGAINST ALL ODDS
## Chinese Peasants Rescue the Doolittle Raiders

It was 18 April 1942. The sixteen planes involved in the Doolittle Raid had launched from the aircraft carrier USS *Hornet*, hit a number of industrial and military targets in Tokyo, Yokohama, Yokosuka, Nagoya, Kobe and Osaka, and flown on towards intended landing sites in mainland China. But for pilot Travis Hoover of Aircraft #2, the only option at this point was to risk a crash landing. He was out of fuel and cruising at too low an altitude to bail out. He spotted a long, flat rice paddy, ideal for a landing. As his navigator, Lieutenant Carl Wildner, positioned a seat cushion to protect his face, Hoover cut the ignition and the B-25 Mitchell eased down into the soft muck of the paddy with barely a bump.

Japanese air raids on the Chinese mainland during the war resulted in countless scenes of carnage similar to this. Chinese soldiers inspect the damage.

Hoover, Wildner, co-pilot Lieutenant William Fitzhugh, bombardier Lieutenant Richard Miller, and engineer/gunner Sergeant Douglas Radney piled out of the plane. It was night, they had no idea where in China they had landed, although they were convinced they had come down in a Japanese-occupied sector. Rather than leave the plane to be made use of as spoils of war, they decided to destroy it, building a small fire in the engine and feeding it until the fuselage caught and the fuel tanks exploded into flame. Hoover and his crewmen could now see dozens of people silhouetted against the night sky, peering at the burning B-25 over the dykes that surrounded the paddy. Believing the fire was being observed by Japanese, the five Americans slipped quietly away into the darkness, walking in single file, each man holding onto the man in front so as not to get separated. They moved rapidly due west, hoping to get to Free China before the Japanese at the landing site caught up with them, or they encountered more Japanese along the way.

For three days the five men walked west, with no idea where they were. They had only one canteen, one container of rations and a few candy bars to sustain them. By day they avoided farms and villages for fear they might run into a Japanese patrol, or be betrayed; at night they slept in abandoned huts. But once the food and water were gone, the Americans had no choice but to ask for help from the Chinese. The first two people they met were a farmer and his young son. Using signs and drawing a rough map, the boy was able to assure the airmen there were no Japanese troops in the area.

The Americans kept moving, hoping to reach Chu-hsien, a city in Free China that had an airfield; from there they could hop a plane back to an Allied base. By chance they met a band of Chinese guerrillas who led them to Ninghai, a town about 520 kilometres (323 miles) north of Shanghai, where the guerrillas and the downed crewmen hoped they would find someone who spoke English. Once again, their luck held—Hoover and his friends met Tung Sheng Liu, twenty-four years old, a recent graduate of the university in Beijing where he had learned English. Years later Liu remembered his first meeting with the Americans: 'They'd spent three days on the run, up in the mountain in the rain, so they were dirty, and hungry, and their uniform pants had shrunk three inches.'

The guerrillas had a house in Ninghai that they used as their headquarters; here they laid out an immense quantity of food, filling three tables. As the famished airmen ate, Liu translated back and forth in English and Chinese. The guerrillas asked where the Americans wanted to go; drawing a map from his shirt pocket, Hoover pointed to Chu-hsien. The guerrillas said that Chu-hsien was only 160 kilometres (99½ miles) away; that they would provide guides and bearers to take the Americans there, and arrange places to stay along the route.

Once again the Americans travelled by night, with Liu and their guides leading them along footpaths through rough country. At dawn they camped in ancient, abandoned Buddhist temples where the guerrillas had secreted food and bedding. When they reached a range of mountains the bearers carried the Americans in sedan chairs. It became a contest among them—who would carry the slender navigator Carl Wildner, and who would have to carry the hefty bombardier, Richard Miller, who weighed some 90 kilograms (198½ pounds).

One week later, when the party arrived in Chu-hsien, they learned they couldn't get a plane out—the Japanese were bombing the airfield almost every day. For a week they rested in Chu-hsien, reviewing their options; the guides and bearers went back to Ninghai, but Liu remained with the Americans. The six young men had become good friends, and the Americans knew how much they were indebted to him.

Finally, it was arranged that the crewmen could take a bus to Hengyang, from where a US Army C-47 would fly them to Australia. Hoover and his friends persuaded Liu to come with them to Australia, but as Liu began to climb aboard the C-47, the pilot barred his way—Army regulations banned foreign nationals from military aircraft. Hoover and his crew argued and pleaded and cursed, but the pilot would not make an exception, even for someone who had saved the lives of five Americans. In the end, Hoover, Fitzhugh, Wildner, Miller and Radney had no choice but to leave Liu behind.

## 'A day that will live in infamy'

At seven-forty-eight on Sunday morning, 7 December 1941, wave after wave of Japanese bombers and fighter planes, 360 in all, attacked the US naval base at Pearl Harbor in Hawaii. The attack caught the Americans completely by surprise, not least because Japan and the United States were not at war. In ninety minutes the Japanese sank five battleships and two destroyers, damaged three other battleships and three cruisers, destroyed 188 aircraft and damaged another 155, killed 2345 servicemen and fifty-seven civilians, and wounded 1247 servicemen and thirty-five civilians.

The sneak attack both enraged and humiliated the people of the United States. And more bad news was coming: within hours of the assault on Pearl Harbor, Japanese forces attacked Malaysia, Hong Kong, the Philippines, Guam, Wake Island and Midway Island. It was clear that Japan intended to be master of the Pacific. The day after the attack the President of the United States, Franklin D. Roosevelt, addressed a joint session of Congress in the House of Representatives. After describing the events of 7 December—'a day which will live in infamy'—Roosevelt made a promise to Japan and to the world: 'No matter how long it may take us to overcome this premeditated invasion, the American people in their righteous might will win through to absolute victory.' Then he called upon Congress to pass a declaration stating that in light of the attack on Pearl Harbor, a state of war existed between the United States of America and the Empire of Japan.

Thirty-three minutes after Roosevelt left the chamber, Congress passed a declaration of war; the vote was unanimous in the Senate, and nearly unanimous in the House—only Jeannette Rankin, a committed pacifist representative from Montana, voted against it.

## The right bomber for the job

During the four months following the attack on Pearl Harbor, US newspapers were filled with reports of more defeats and more disasters as Japanese forces seized Singapore, Hong Kong, the Philippines, the Dutch East Indies and the Solomon Islands, invaded Burma, Borneo, New Guinea and Bali, the Andaman Islands in the Bay of Bengal off the coast of India, and bombed Darwin in northern Australia. In February 1942 the United States was struck again when a Japanese submarine shelled an oil refinery near Santa Barbara, California. On 9 April, America suffered another humiliating defeat when the 76,000 American and Filipino troops on the Bataan Peninsula on Luzon in the Philippines surrendered. Since the attack on Pearl Harbor, the Japanese had killed, wounded or captured approximately 320,000 Allied troops in the Pacific.

To avenge the Japanese attacks on US territory, combat the endless string of bad news from the Pacific, and lift the morale of the military and the American people, President Roosevelt urged his commanders to launch an air assault on Tokyo.

In the first weeks of 1942, General Henry Arnold, Chief of Staff of the Army Air Force, called Lieutenant Colonel James Doolittle with a question: 'Jim, what bomber do we have that will get off [an aircraft carrier] in five hundred feet [152 metres] with a two-thousand-pound [907 kilogram] bomb load and fly two thousand miles [3218 kilometres]?'

Doolittle promised Arnold an answer in a day or two.

James Doolittle was one of the leading experts on aeronautics in the United States. He had been a flight instructor during World War I; he had studied aeronautical engineering at the Massachusetts Institute of Technology and at the Air Service Mechanical School. He had helped develop the horizontal and directional gyroscopes that enabled pilots to fly 'blind' in fog, darkness or bad weather; and he was considered one of the finest pilots in the US military.

The day after his conversation with Arnold, Doolittle reported that the B-25 Mitchell could do the job, once it was fitted with extra fuel tanks to enable a 3200 kilometre (1988 mile) run. His report complete, Doolittle asked, 'Now, what's behind all this?'

Arnold replied that he was planning a bombing raid on Japan. Without hesitation Doolittle volunteered to take command of the mission, supervise the modification of the planes and train the flight crews.

In the weeks that followed Doolittle assembled a fleet of sixteen B-25s, each with a highly trained five-man flight crew, himself among them—they became known as Doolittle's Raiders. Meanwhile, Arnold's intelligence staff selected targets for the bombers: oil refineries, aircraft manufacturing plants, and iron, steel and other major factories in Tokyo and other industrial cities. The aircraft carrier selected for the mission was the new USS *Hornet*, launched in Newport News, Virginia, only a week after the attack on Pearl Harbor. After a successful test run with two of the bombers, the *Hornet* set sail for California via the Panama Canal. The *Hornet*, accompanied by another carrier, the USS *Enterprise*, and escorted by fourteen destroyers, cruisers and other support ships, was headed for a launch site 720 kilometres (447 miles) from Japan—at that distance the Raiders could bomb Tokyo and still have plenty of fuel to reach safe airfields in Free China—from which they could make their way to Allied bases. Unexpectedly, 1040 kilometres (646 miles) out from Tokyo, the convoy encountered Japanese fishing boats that had been posted to watch for possible air and naval assaults. The light cruiser USS *Nashville* fired on the fishing boat *Nitto Maru*, sinking it, but not before the fishermen had radioed a warning to Tokyo, where Rear Admiral Ugaki Matome ordered five carriers, six cruisers, ten destroyers, nine submarines, ninety fighter planes and 116 bombers to intercept the US ships.

Doolittle had lost the element of surprise. If the Raiders took off from their present location they would not have enough fuel to bomb their targets in Japan and reach the safety of Free China. Nonetheless, Doolittle and Vice Admiral William F. Halsey, commander of the escort fleet, agreed that the raid should proceed. At eight in the morning of 18 April, Doolittle assembled his men. 'If there's any of you who don't want to go, just tell me,' he said. 'Because the chances of your making it back are pretty slim.' None of the other seventy-nine Raiders opted out.

Then Doolittle reviewed their orders: bomb military and industrial targets in and around Tokyo, then turn west towards China and the rendezvous in Chungking (now Chongqing).

## The best pilot in the Air Force

The weather on the morning of 28 April 1942 was terrible. Heavy crosswinds, drenching downpours, and 9 metre (29½ feet) waves crashing against the *Hornet*. 'I've never been in worse weather in my life,' recalled Robert Bourgeois, the bombardier on Aircraft #13, nicknamed 'The Avenger'. 'The rain! Oh, the rain! I've been in a bunch of hurricanes right here in Louisiana. And they were tame compared to this thing.'

It took two or three sailors to help one airman with all his equipment get across the lurching deck to his plane. Some of the Raiders went down on hands and knees and crawled to their planes. Adding to the chaos on deck was the presence of a film crew and the Oscar-winning director John Ford—the Navy had hired him to document the Raiders' takeoff. If the raid proved successful, President Roosevelt and the Joint Chiefs of Staff planned to distribute Ford's film to movie theatres across the country to give an added boost to American morale.

At 8.25 am, Lieutenant Colonel Doolittle, pilot of Aircraft #1, was ready to take off. The wind was howling, the giant 18,143 tonne (20,000 ton) carrier was pitching relentlessly in the unforgiving seas, yet years later Doolittle could still remember how he felt at that moment: 'Confident'. His navigator, Lieutenant Henry Potter, felt the same way. 'We were particularly confident since we had the best pilot in the Air Force flying with us,' he said. Doolittle's co-pilot, Lieutenant Richard Cole, was not so optimistic. Years later, he remembered thinking, 'It would be a pretty bad feeling for everyone behind us if we took off and dropped into the water.'

With the seventy-five Raiders in the other planes and hundreds of the *Hornet*'s crewmen watching intently, Doolittle taxied down the deck, cut to full speed, and flew off into the driving rain. Then he swung around, flying low over the carrier as everyone on board cheered. One by one the other fifteen planes followed him. One terrible accident marred the takeoff: Machinist's Mate Robert Wall slipped on the slick, wet deck, falling into the rotating left propeller of Aircraft #16, 'Bat Out of Hell'. The propeller gouged his back and sliced his arm nearly clean through. Years later the Bat's co-pilot, Robert Hite, recalled seeing the wounded sailor lying on the bloodstained deck: 'We took off not knowing if he was alive or dead.' Wall lost his arm, but he survived.

## Flying from Shangri-La

Three hundred kilometres (186½ miles) from Tokyo the bad weather that had made the takeoff so precarious suddenly cleared, and the Raiders flew through a perfect, cloudless sky. They would be able to see their targets clearly, but in turn would be perfect targets for Japanese guns on the ground as well as the fighter planes that were certain to be sent against them. Sure enough, as the Raiders entered Tokyo airspace they were greeted by a blaze of cannon fire and anti-aircraft guns. Incredibly, not one B-25 was shot down. In his 5 June 1942 report to the War Department, Doolittle characterised the Japanese anti-aircraft fire as 'active but inaccurate'.

The Raiders' bombs struck a steel mill, an oil storage facility, several power plants and a new light cruiser, the *Ryuho*, not yet launched. Several bombs landed inaccurately in civilian areas, damaging homes, schools and an army hospital, killing fifty people and injuring 400. In terms of the damage inflicted on the Japanese industrial and military machine, the Doolittle Raid was a minor irritation. But in two things it did succeed—it shocked the Japanese populace, who had believed absolutely that their homeland was inviolable, and it restored the confidence of the American public, who were thrilled that US bombers had attacked the capital of Japan and escaped without a single plane being shot down.

In a press conference after the raid, President Roosevelt told reporters that Doolittle and his men had set out 'from Shangri-La', the mythical Himalayan paradise in James Hilton's best-selling novel, *Lost Horizon*. In this way Roosevelt kept secret the identity of the *Hornet* so it would not be a target for future Japanese attacks, while giving the raid a sense of romance and mystery. The press and the public were delighted.

## 'Physical and mental torture'

Flying low along the coast of China after the raid, Lieutenant Ted Lawson saw island after island come into view, but none of them offered a suitable place to land. Eventually he spotted a stretch of beach that looked promising. He turned 'The Ruptured Duck' over the sea to circle back towards the beach when both engines died as the fuel ran out, and Aircraft #7 began to plummet. At 180 kilometres per hour (112 miles per hour) the B-25 struck the water at a sharp angle—the nose crumpled, the windshield shattered, then it flipped over. Lawson, co-pilot Dean Davenport, navigator Lieutenant Charles McClure and bombardier Lieutenant Robert Clever were thrown through the broken windshield. Engineer/Gunner Sergeant David Thatcher was knocked unconscious, but the icy seawater pouring into the plane rapidly brought him to; he scrambled out through the emergency door and hoisted himself onto the belly of the plane. From this vantage point he could see his four crewmates trying to swim through heavy surf to the shore, so Thatcher slipped into the water and set out after them.

Thatcher had a deep cut on the top of his head and his back was badly bruised from being thrown around, but the other four were in terrible shape. Lawson had a long, nasty gash that ran down his left thigh from hip to knee; he had serious lacerations on his arm, shin and head; his lower lip was cut almost to the chin, and nine of his front teeth had been knocked out.

Davenport had suffered severe cuts on his right leg, from knee to ankle. McClure's shoulders were both dislocated. Clever had deep gashes all over his head and was bleeding profusely. They huddled on the sand of the deserted beach in a pouring rainstorm, cold, bleeding and afraid that any moment a Japanese patrol would find them. Instead, they were found by eight Chinese peasants, all wearing baggy black shirts and woven bamboo hats. None of them spoke English, nor could they understand any of the Chinese phrases Thatcher had memorised, but by gestures they indicated they wanted to help. They carried Lawson and Davenport, but when they tried to pick up McClure he screamed in pain, so he had to manage on his own two feet. Thatcher walked as well, and Clever, still bleeding, crawled along behind on hands and knees.

Their rescuers took them to a hut in a nearby small village; the family who lived there had no medicine, no bandages, but they placed the wounded airmen on their cots, and wrapped them in quilts. Clever passed out from loss of blood. As the others began to warm up they inspected their wounds and realised that if they did not get to a hospital quickly, infection would set in.

Then they heard footsteps approaching. A moment later a large Chinese man wearing Western clothes—trousers, hunting shirt and heavy shoes—stood in the doorway. Lawson guessed he must be a figure of authority because all the Chinese in the hut treated him with deference. In his account of the Doolittle Raid, *Thirty Seconds Over Tokyo*, Lawson described the visitor:

> *His black eyes, set in that muscular deadpan, darted around the room. Then he stepped forward briskly and went from one of us to the other, looking at our wounds closely and suspiciously examining all buttons, insignia and other identifying markings left on our torn clothes … I just looked at his stony face, wondering if he was planning to sell us.*

Finally the man spoke: 'Me Charlie.' The Americans could hardly believe their good luck—in this isolated village they had come across someone who spoke English. They barraged Charlie with questions. Where were they? Where was the nearest doctor? Would he help them escape the Japanese? Those questions were all too complicated for Charlie, whose English was far from fluent, but he was able to convey some important information: there were Japanese in the neighbourhood, there was no doctor nearby, but he would bring a boat to take them to safety.

Charlie and the other men left. The women brought Lawson and his crew bowls of hot water, some of which they drank, using the rest to wash the blood from their wounds. The women offered them food, but the airmen felt too ill to eat. They lay on their cots, moaning as the shock wore off and the pain set in. With his belt, his necktie and a strip torn from his shirt, Lawson, with Thatcher's help, made a crude triple bandage that closed the ugly gash in his thigh. An elderly Chinese man examined his split lower lip, then made a plaster of rice paper and some kind of powder which stopped the bleeding.

Early the next morning Charlie returned with eight men and four stretchers made of rope and bamboo. Painfully, Lawson, McClure, Clever and Davenport climbed into the stretchers and the pathetic procession, led by Charlie, set off towards the mountains. Thatcher, whose injuries were less debilitating, walked. Charlie led them to a guerrilla camp where he arranged with the guerrillas to send a guard of six armed men with the party to protect the downed flyers. Then the bearers lifted the stretchers, and the group set out again.

Late in the afternoon they arrived at a narrow canal where a flatboat was waiting. The bearers placed the Americans in the bottom of the boat and stepped out, the six guerrillas stepped in and the boatman cast off. About two hours later he edged his flatboat into a landing place where eight new bearers were waiting; and sailing to meet them was a Chinese junk. The bearers lifted the wounded men to the bank and were heading for the junk's mooring spot when one of the bearers called out a warning. The bearers dumped the airmen in a ditch and, along with the guerrillas, jumped in after them, lying flat in the mud and gesturing to the Americans to make no sound. Lawson raised his head enough to peer over the edge of the ditch, and saw a Japanese gunboat alongside the junk. Everyone in the

## What became of the Doolittle Raiders?

Of the eighty men who participated in the Doolittle Raid:

Lieutenant Colonel James Doolittle (fifth from left) and his crew were guided to safety by Chinese guerrillas after they bailed out over Quzhou and landed in a rice paddy.

- one died when he bailed out over China;
- two drowned in a crash landing off the Chinese coast;
- five, the crew of Plane 8, opted to land in Soviet territory rather than China. The Soviets confiscated the plane and imprisoned the crew in an internment camp. After thirteen months as prisoners, all five men escaped, making their way to safety in Iran;
- eight were captured by the Japanese: three were executed by firing squad, the other five were sent to a POW camp where one died of beriberi and malnutrition; the remaining four survived forty months of harsh captivity, much of it spent in solitary confinement;
- sixty-four of the Doolittle Raiders owe their lives to Chinese civilians, most of them poor farmers, fishermen and labourers, who risked their own lives to hide the crewmen, tend their injuries, and get them back to Allied lines;
- four Raiders later became prisoners of the Germans;
- thirteen other Raiders died later in World War II, most of them in action.

Ted Lawson recovered from the amputation of his leg. In 1943 he published *Thirty Seconds Over Tokyo*, an account of what he and his crew experienced during and after the Doolittle Raid. The book became a bestseller, and in 1944 MGM made a movie version starring Van Johnson as Lawson and Spencer Tracy as Lieutenant Colonel James Doolittle. Lawson died in 1992, a few weeks short of his seventy-fifth birthday.

Tung Sheng Liu emigrated to the US in 1946. In 1947 he learned that the Doolittle Raiders were having a reunion in Minneapolis, and surprised the crew of Aircraft #2 by appearing at the reunion. Liu has attended many Doolittle reunions, and has been named an Honorary Tokyo Raider.

After the Tokyo Raid, James Doolittle was given command of the Twelfth Air Force in North Africa, then of the Fifteenth Air Force in the Mediterranean theatre, and finally of the Eighth Air Force. After the war he served as a director of the Shell Oil Company and Chairman of the Board of Space Technology Laboratories. In 1985, by a special act of the United States Congress, he was promoted to full general. General Doolittle died in 1993, at ninety-seven years of age.

ditch could hear the crew being questioned. 'It was torture to lie there in the ditch, waiting,' Lawson recalled. 'Physical and mental torture.'

Miraculously, the gunboat motored on. Moving quickly, the bearers carried the stretchers to the water's edge, then waded out to the junk and raised the stretchers high. The crew of the junk hauled the wounded men over the side, then got them into the hold, where they remained out of sight until they reached their destination, Yai Hu, a town with a China Relief station. The Chinese doctor in charge at the station spoke English and apologetically explained that he had no antiseptics, no painkillers, not even aspirin. But the nurses washed the men, cleaned their wounds, gave them hot tea, fed them and replaced their filthy, bloodstained uniforms with fresh, clean clothes. Best of all, they sent for Chen Shenyan, another doctor, who had access to better facilities.

Dr Shenyan arrived with a dozen bearers and four sedan chairs—Thatcher was still walking wounded—and they set off for Linhai where Chen Shenyan's father, also a doctor, operated a hospital with three British missionaries who had medical training. After more than twelve hours on the road, being bounced and jostled in the uncomfortable sedan chairs, Lawson and McClure were nearly delirious with pain, and Clever was again in shock. Medical supplies at Dr Shenyan's hospital were not extensive, but did include antiseptic, clean bandages and a little chloroform. And in the hospital they were safe from the Japanese, they were well cared for, they could rest, and heal and regain their strength.

A few days after Lawson and his crew reached the hospital, something entirely unexpected happened: another bomber crew from the Doolittle Raid walked into Linhai. These were the men of Aircraft #15—Lieutenant Donald Smith, Lieutenant Griffith Williams, Lieutenant Howard Sessler, Sergeant Edward Saylor and Lieutenant Thomas White MD.

Unfortunately, Dr White's bag of surgical instruments and his supply of medicines had been lost in Aircraft #15's crash landing. McClure, Clever and Davenport were by now recovering quite well, but Lawson's leg was badly infected. For several days, White worked with everything available to clear up the infection, but it was too late. In the end he did the only thing that would save Lawson's life—he amputated the leg.

# Retaliation

The Japanese were infuriated by the escape of the Doolittle Raiders: of the eighty airmen, all of whom had bailed out or crash-landed their aircraft in China, only eight had been captured. The rest had got away because they had been assisted by the local population. With the authorisation of Emperor Hirohito, 100,000 Japanese troops in fifty-three battalions fanned out across Chekiang and Kiangsi provinces, where the Raiders had landed. They destroyed every village and town that had rendered any assistance to the Americans. People who had received trinkets from the Raiders were slaughtered with all their family. A village schoolteacher whose family had fed a flight crew was viciously targeted. 'They killed my three sons,' he said, 'they killed my wife, Angling; they set fire to my school; they burned my books; they drowned my grandchildren in the well.' The Japanese had thrown him down the well, too, but he had survived the fall; when the soldiers took to drinking after the attack and became dead drunk, he climbed out, killed a soldier to avenge each member of his family, and ran away.

For several weeks the Japanese committed horrible atrocities in the two provinces—beheading women and infants, burning men alive. In June and July they turned to bacterial warfare, spraying cholera, typhoid, bubonic plague and dysentery over Chekiang and Kiangsi. No one knows how many Chinese died from the atrocities and the deliberately induced epidemics. The lowest estimate is 250,000 men, women and children.

# CHAPTER 18

# 'WE WERE LEFT'
## The Rescue of John F. Kennedy
## and the Crew of *PT-109*

The sun was going down on 2 August 1943 when Lieutenant John Fitzgerald Kennedy, twenty-six years old, hauled himself partway up the beach of Plum Pudding Island. Too exhausted to stand, or sit or even crawl to the shelter of a tree, Kennedy lay motionless, his legs in the surf, his face resting on the sand, panting heavily, trying to regain a little strength. For four hours he had swum, towing Motor Machinist's Mate Patrick McMahon, a strap from McMahon's kapok life vest clenched between his teeth. Without Kennedy, McMahon would have been helpless—he had been in the engine-room of *PT-109* when the boat was struck amidships and cut in half by the Japanese destroyer *Amagiri*. In the collision the fuel tanks had exploded and McMahon suffered severe burns, to his hands particularly. He could not swim; if Kennedy had not made that Herculean effort to save him, McMahon would have floated alone in the sea until death by shark attack, by Japanese patrol or from exposure.

PT crewmen Lieutenant James Reed, Lieutenant John F. Kennedy, Ensign George Ross and Lieutenant Paul Fay take a moment off during their tour of duty on Tulagi in the Solomon Islands. Kennedy and Ross were aboard *PT-109* when the *Amagiri* struck.

As Kennedy lay gasping on the sand, McMahon dragged himself out of the water. For four hours his burns had been immersed in saltwater; his whole body was alive with pain, yet he tried to get Kennedy on his feet and lead him to cover—they were in the Solomon Islands, where the Japanese were very active. They could not risk lying exposed on the beach, an easy target for any sniper.

With McMahon's help Kennedy got to his feet, and immediately doubled over, vomiting up all the seawater he had swallowed. When the retching stopped, Kennedy did not have the strength to stand again, nor did McMahon have the strength left to help him. The two men crawled on hands and knees to the shelter of some bushes, and once again collapsed. Several minutes passed. Kennedy sat up, in time to see the other nine surviving members of his crew come ashore—they had swum to safety together, clinging to a long wooden plank, a piece of the wreckage of *PT-109*.

## No place too deadly

It could be argued that Kennedy had no business being in the US Navy. Initially he had tried to enlist in the Army, but the medical board rejected him because he had a weak back. He also suffered from spastic colitis, a chronic condition that had begun during childhood. In fact, he had been a sickly little boy who was always underweight.

Having been rejected by the Army, Kennedy tried the Navy. This time he had better luck, thanks to the intervention of his father, Joseph P. Kennedy, a multimillionaire and former US ambassador to Britain's Court of St James. The elder Kennedy had political ambitions for his sons, and understood that candidates who had served in the military, especially in wartime, impressed the voters. Unwilling to see 'Jack' sitting out the war in the family mansion in Massachusetts, Ambassador Kennedy asked his friend Captain Alain Kirk, director of the Office of Naval Intelligence, to pull some strings. Thanks to Captain Kirk, in October 1941 Kennedy was appointed an ensign in the Naval Reserves.

For nearly a year Kennedy performed office work until he was selected for Motor Torpedo Boat training on Lake Michigan at the Naval Reserve Officers Training School at Northwestern University in Chicago. He wanted to see action, and he wanted to skipper his own PT boat, but so did lots of other young men. To give him an edge, Kennedy senior pulled a few more strings.

At the time Lieutenant John D. Bulkeley was touring the country, addressing crowds at bond rallies and recruiting young men to captain PT boats. Bulkeley was both a celebrity and a war hero—he had commanded the PT squadron that evacuated General Douglas MacArthur and his family from Corregidor, bringing them safely to Mindanao through hundreds of kilometres of Japanese-patrolled waters (see chapter 16). For this exploit, President Franklin D. Roosevelt invited Bulkeley to the White House, where he presented him with the Medal of Honour.

Over a thousand men had volunteered to command PT boats, but the Navy needed only fifty. Jack Kennedy's odds of being among the select few were slim. Then Bulkeley received an invitation from Ambassador Kennedy to join him for lunch at the Plaza Hotel in New York City. Many years later Bulkeley recalled that luncheon conversation: 'Joe wanted to know if I had the clout to get Jack into PT boats, and I said that I did, and would interview his son the next time I was at Northwestern. If I thought Jack could measure up, I would recommend his acceptance, I told Joe.'

Joseph Kennedy thanked Bulkeley, then asked for one more thing—that Jack be assigned to some place in the Pacific that 'wasn't too deadly'.

Bulkeley, along with Lieutenant Commander John Harllee, who was also responsible for selecting officers for PT boats, met with Jack Kennedy at Northwestern; they liked what they saw. In spite of his boyish appearance, Kennedy was intelligent, enthusiastic about serving and eager to get into combat. Furthermore, he had been sailing since he was a boy. The fact that his father had used his influence on Jack's behalf did not trouble Harllee. 'There's a lot of people who use political influence to keep *out* of combat,' he said, 'but Jack Kennedy used it to get *into* combat.'

In April 1943, Kennedy sailed aboard the carrier USS *Rochambeau* to Tulagi in the Solomon Islands, where he took command of *PT-109* in Motor Torpedo Boat Squadron 2.

## 'Superb rescuers'

The day Kennedy stepped aboard *PT-109*, the boat was barely a year old. It had been built by the Elco Naval Division of the Electric Boat Company in Bayonne, New Jersey, and outfitted at the New York Naval Shipyard in Brooklyn. It first saw action one night in December 1942 with seven other PT boats, attacking eight Japanese destroyers, firing round after round of torpedoes until the Japanese withdrew. *PT-109* and its crew saw more action in January and February of 1943 in New Georgia and the Solomon Islands, an area the Japanese coveted as a launching base for prospective invasions of Australia and New Zealand. But in spite of its youth, *PT-109* was in sad shape—infested with rats and cockroaches, grimy, needing lots of repair work. Kennedy and his crew went to work and made their boat look respectable.

Conventional wisdom has long held that PT boats were unequal to fighting the Japanese, little better than death-traps. But Richard Keresey, who skippered one in the Solomons, had a different perspective. PT boats, he said, '[were] superb rescuers, they saved hundreds from death or capture: downed flyers, sunk sailors, trapped Marines, coast watchers, stranded nuns, and General MacArthur.'

Through 1942 and 1943 the Navy ordered hundreds of PT boats from Elco, which built the most popular model. Elco boats had a wooden hull and were 24.5 metres (80 feet) long with a 6.3 metre (20 foot) beam. With three 12-cylinder engines operating at 4500 horsepower, a PT boat could cruise at a maximum speed of 41 knots. Each boat accommodated up to fourteen men, including quarters for three officers. Typically, they were armed with a 40-mm gun, machine guns and four torpedo-launching tracks, but some also carried depth charges, 37-mm aircraft guns or rocket launchers.

Technically they were Motor Torpedo boats. PT was the abbreviation for 'Patrol Torpedo boat', a name derived from their function—most PT boats patrolled the sea lanes of the Pacific watching for Japanese destroyers, or searching for downed pilots.

PT boats did necessary work, but at a high cost. Of the 495 the US Navy put into service during World War II, sixty-nine were destroyed—twelve through some accident or act of nature; thirty-three through friendly fire, or purposely destroyed by their crews to prevent them from falling into enemy hands; and twenty-four destroyed in action against the enemy; 331 crewmen were killed in action.

## The bubble burst

Kennedy's crew included executive officer Ensigns Leonard J. Thom and George H.R. Ross, Seaman Raymond Albert, Gunner's Mate Charles A. Harris, Motor Machinist's Mates William Johnston, Patrick H. McMahon, Harold William Marney

Lieutenant Kennedy at the controls of *PT-109*; cool sea
breezes were no match for the blazing sunshine of the tropics
and the glare from the bare metal of the engine bay.

and Gerard E. Zinser, Torpedoman's Mates Andrew Jackson Kirksey and Ray L. Starkey, Radioman John E. Maguire and Quartermaster Edman Edgar Mauer.

The crew was stationed at the base on Lumbari Island in the Solomons, a dull place that did not even offer the occasional movie. Life aboard a PT boat at anchor was miserable: below decks the quarters stank of fuel oil, but the crew rarely slept in their quarters—it was too hot and stuffy. Instead they slept on deck.

*PT-109* had no refrigerator, so the men could not keep fresh meat, fish, milk or butter on board; they survived on canned rations, usually beans and fried Spam, washed down with coffee. In a letter to his sister Kathleen, Jack Kennedy conceded that he was not living in a tropical paradise:

> *That bubble I had about lying on a cool Pacific Island with a warm Pacific maiden hunting bananas for me is definitely a bubble that has burst. You can't even swim—there's some sort of fungus in the water that grows out of your ears—which will be all I need.*

Many nights the crew of *PT-109* ran missions in 'the Slot', the Navy's nickname for the New Georgia Sound, which runs virtually through the centre of the Solomon Islands. To supply and reinforce their troops in the Solomons, the Japanese sent a steady stream of destroyers through the Slot; the Allies called these convoys 'the Tokyo Express'. It was the mission of the PT boats to intercept them and turn them back.

After they returned to base the men caught a few hours' sleep on deck, then dragged themselves through the necessary tasks of refuelling, and cleaning and readjusting the guns, torpedoes, radio and engine. The intense heat drained them of physical energy and mental alertness; their poor diet made them susceptible to dysentery; and tropical diseases such as malaria and dengue fever were a constant threat.

## 'We were left'

On 1 August 1943, Allied intelligence reported that the Japanese planned to make a supply run with 900 troops as reinforcements from Bougainville Island through the Blackett Strait to Kolombangara, a nearly perfectly round, heavily forested island where they had a base and an airfield. The troops and supplies would be carried aboard three destroyers, with a fourth, the *Amagiri*, serving as escort. That evening Lieutenant Commander Thomas Warfield sent out fifteen PT boats, including Kennedy's *PT-109*, against the convoy.

It was a moonless night, and in the dark the convoy slipped past the PT boats. By 1.30 am of 2 August, the Japanese had arrived at Kolombangara, unloaded the troops and cargo, and turned back to Bougainville. Kennedy's and two other PT boats were still patrolling Blackett Strait, trying to detect the enemy in the blackness.

About 2.30 am Motor Machinist's Mate Marney, stationed in the forward gun turret, cried out, 'Ship at two o'clock!' Kennedy looked up to see the 1814-tonne (2000-ton) *Amagiri* only 250 metres (820 feet) away and bearing down fast. In a matter of seconds the *Amagiri* struck *PT-109* amidships, slicing the smaller vessel in half.

Marney and Torpedoman's Mate Andrew Jackson Kirksey were killed instantly, crushed to death. Kennedy and the surviving members of his crew were thrown into the water. The stern half sank immediately, but the bow remained afloat.

Harris called to Kennedy, 'McMahon is badly hurt!' Following the voice in the darkness, Kennedy swam until he found them just 100 metres (328 feet) from the bow. Harris's leg was injured, but he could swim; McMahon's burns, however, were so serious that he could barely move. Kennedy towed him back towards the still-floating bow, which a stiff breeze was carrying away from the shipwrecked crew—it took them forty-five minutes to catch up with the remains. Ensign Leonard Thom, a big, blond-haired left tackle from Ohio State, came in towing Motor Machinist's Mate William Johnston, who was deathly ill from inhaling gasoline fumes.

They had a flare gun, but they were afraid to use it lest the *Amagiri* return. So they clung to the ruined bow, waiting for the other PT boats to come pick them up, but no one came. Years afterward Radioman John Maguire was still bitter. 'Those sons of bitches ran away from us,' he said. 'We were left.'

## The coastwatcher

At 9.30 am on 2 August, Lieutenant Arthur R. Evans, an Australian coastwatcher, received a radio message from an Allied base that *PT-109* had gone down in Blackett Strait during the night. Evans passed the word to his Solomon Islander scouts with instruction to watch for any signs of survivors.

Evans was part of an extensive network of about 400 men positioned throughout the islands of the South Pacific and New Guinea, observing the movements of the Japanese. It was dangerous work. If the Japanese had found him, they would have tortured and killed him. In 1942 the Japanese captured coastwatcher Jacob Vouza on Guadalcanal—they had slashed and stabbed him, but he would not reveal anything. They left him to die, but he survived, and managed to get to an American base.

Meanwhile, on Plum Pudding Island, Kennedy and his men had their first scare—a Japanese barge cruised so close to shore they were certain someone would spot them. The barge was the only ship they saw all day—no Allied vessel came looking for them.

At nightfall Kennedy took a battle lantern and his .38 pistol and swam out to the middle of Ferguson's Passage, hoping to find and signal a PT boat. None came and by morning Kennedy discovered that the current had carried him about 3 kilometres (2 miles) from Plum Pudding to an islet named Leorava. He staggered up the beach, collapsed and fell asleep. He woke several hours later, still exhausted from treading water all night, and now he had the same swim back to Plum Pudding. He made it.

His crew was hungry and thirsty—they had found no spring, no stream, no source of water at all on the island. And they were concerned about the injured men, especially McMahon. Kennedy decided they should move to Olasana Island, nearly 3 kilometres (2 miles) distant, where he hoped they would find water and coconuts. In their weakened condition the men took several hours to get there. From Olasana they could see another island, Naru, less than a kilometre away. Still hoping to flag down a passing PT boat, Kennedy, this time accompanied by Ensign George Ross, swam over to Naru.

The first things they found were the wreck of a small Japanese vessel and a dug-out canoe; inside the wreck was a crate of hard candy, inside the canoe a can of water, the first food and drink they had seen in two days. As they were gulping down the water, they saw a second canoe some distance off. The islanders in the canoe saw them too, and thinking they were Japanese, paddled away. The men in the canoe were two of Evans' scouts, Biuku Gasa, twenty years old, and Eroni Kumana, eighteen years old.

As the scouts passed Olasana, Biuku said they should stop—he wanted a drink of coconut water. They had just beached the canoe when one of Kennedy's crewmen crawled out of the bushes. Biuku cried out, 'A Japanese here!' As the two men pushed their canoe back into the sea, Ensign Thom hurried out of the brush calling loudly, 'Navy! Navy! Americans! Americans!' He rolled up his shirtsleeve to show his pale skin. But still Biuku and Eroni kept their distance. Then Thom had an inspiration—he called out the name 'Johnny Kari'; Kari was a well-known Solomon Islander scout. That got Biuku and Eroni's attention, and they came ashore.

Appropriating the canoe he had found, Kennedy paddled back to Olasana with the candy and the water, leaving Ross to rest. As he waded ashore, dragging the canoe, the crew ran down to the beach shouting, 'We're saved! Two locals have found us!'

Biuku and Eroni did not speak English, none of the men from *PT-109* spoke their language. Believing the nearest help was Rendova, 60 kilometres (37 miles) away, Kennedy took a piece of coconut shell and with his knife carved on it the message:

> *NAURO ISL*
> *NATIVE KNOWS POSIT*
> *HE CAN PILOT 11 ALIVE NEED*
> *SMALL BOAT*
> *KENNEDY*

While Kennedy was laboriously carving, Thom, who had somehow located a pencil and a sheet of paper, was writing out something similar. They gave their messages to Biuku and Eroni to take to Rendova. Wisely, before they made such a long and hazardous journey, the scouts went to Kolombangara where they found Benjamin Kevu, an English-speaking scout. Now the rescue mission was gathering speed. Kevu sent a runner to Evans, who ordered his scouts to take a large war canoe to Olasana.

The war canoe had not come to take them away—it was not large enough to rescue eleven men. But it did bring in abundance the things the starving men needed— yams, potatoes, rice, fresh fish, even C-rations of roast beef hash. Evans' men built a hut to shelter McMahon from the sun, climbed trees from which they threw down a blizzard of coconuts, and lit cooking fires to give the crew a hot meal.

Afterwards, the scouts had Kennedy lie down in the bottom of the war canoe; they covered him with palm leaves, then paddled to Evans' hideaway on Kolombangara. Evans had already arranged for a group of PT boats to pick up Kennedy that night

## *PT-109* is found

In July 2002 the US Navy confirmed that underwater explorer Robert Ballard had found the remains of *PT-109*. Ballard discovered the remains two months earlier, about 365 metres (1197 feet) below the surface, in Blackett Strait. At the time of his discovery, he was nearly 100 per cent certain that he had found Kennedy's boat because no other PT boat had gone down in that area.

The remains of *PT-109* are scant—one torpedo and torpedo tube, both covered with a thick layer of rust and coral, and a cranking mechanism used to aim a torpedo tube before firing. Since PT boats were built of wood, most of *PT-109* undoubtedly disintegrated long ago, only the metal parts of the boat would remain—the engine and fuel tanks are probably buried in the sand of the ocean floor.

Representatives of the US Navy confirmed that the place where Ballard found the wreckage agrees with the location identified by Kennedy. The torpedo is a Mark 8 and the torpedo tube is a Mark 18, both of which were used almost exclusively by PT boats during World War II. And the cranking mechanism is also consistent with the type of equipment found on a PT boat.

Ballard did not call for the recovery of the remains of *PT-109*. Speaking to a reporter for *National Geographic News* he said, 'I'm actually content to leave it buried. I think it's a grave, and it's apropos—showing us enough to know but burying the rest.'

At a jungle river anchorage in the Solomon Islands, an unidentified PT boat hides beneath camouflage netting, a peaceful scene at odds with the reason that US forces were in the Pacific.

from nearby Patparan Island; from there the group would move on to Olasana to pick up the crew.

It took place exactly as Evans planned. At ten that night Kennedy climbed aboard a PT boat where his squadron commander, Lieutenant Alvin Cluster, along with Biuku and Eroni, was waiting to greet him. Then the boats went to Olasana.

Kennedy came ashore in a rubber raft calling for Thom: 'Lenny! Hey Lenny!' Out of the darkness came the voice of one of his men shouting, 'The boats are here!' By dawn, the crew was safe, the injured men carried off for medical treatment.

## Afterwards

At their base on Lumbari the men prepared a banquet for Biuku and Eroni, a token of appreciation for the two men. At one point Kennedy stood and drank a toast to the scouts. He promised that if he survived the war, they would see each other again.

Kennedy intended to keep his promise—in 1961 he invited Biuku and Eroni to travel to Washington, DC to be his guests at his inauguration as President. But when the two men arrived at Honiara airport on Guadalcanal, a clerk informed them that they could not go because they did not speak English. In fact, two Solomon Islander politicians had confiscated the tickets so they could attend the inauguration.

In 2002, when Robert Ballard discovered the remains of *PT-109*, Max Kennedy, son of Robert F. Kennedy and JFK's nephew, travelled to the Solomons to visit Biuku and Eroni and thank them on behalf of his entire family for saving the lives of Kennedy and his men. Both were nearly eighty years old, living in traditional palm-leaf huts without electricity or running water, and only a dug-out canoe for transportation. As a gift from the Kennedy family and the National Geographic Society (which sponsored the search for *PT-109*), Biuku and Eroni were given a new house and a powerboat.

Biuku Gasa died in 2005; he was eighty-two years old. At the time of writing, Eroni Kumana was still alive.

On the night their PT boat was rammed, John F. Kennedy saved the lives of eleven of his crewmen. But it was Biuku Gasa and Eroni Kumana who saved all the survivors of *PT-109* from starvation or capture by the Japanese.

# CHAPTER 19

# THE VOYAGE OF THE USS *CREVALLE*

## The Submarine That Rescued Forty American Civilians and Retrieved Japan's Top-secret 'Z Plan'

The small double-outrigger vessel that Filipino fishermen call a *banca* drifted 200 metres (656 feet) off the bow of the USS *Crevalle*, waiting its turn to transfer Sam and Rose Real and their five children to the submarine. As another banca that had just set down its passengers passed close by on its return to shore, its skipper called out, 'The sub is full! There's no more room. You better turn back now.'

This was crushing news. After three years of living in the jungle, hiding from the Japanese, the appearance of an American submarine ready to carry the Real family to safety in Australia seemed like a miracle. To be told at the last moment that they could not go aboard, that they would have to return to the jungle, was more than Rose Real could bear. She burst into tears. Her husband and children sat immobilised, their faces studies in incomprehension and disbelief.

USS *Crevalle* arriving in Pearl Harbor after its seventh and final patrol voyage. It was fitting that the vessel responsible for bringing the captured Z Plan to Australia should survive the war.

The boatman began to turn his banca towards shore when a second voice rang out over the water. 'Ahoy, small boat!', a sailor on the *Crevalle* called. 'Return to disembark your passengers!'

The family's spirits soared. A few moments later the banca bumped against the hull of the submarine. A dozen sailors helped the Reals climb on deck and down the ladder into the vessel. Rose was still weeping as she stepped off the ladder. 'My God,' she said, 'I thought we were going to be left behind.'

At 6.37 pm on 11 May 1944, with the evacuees from Negros Island aboard, Captain Francis D. Walker, Jr. gave orders for the *Crevalle* to get underway. The rescue had gone off flawlessly: it had taken just under forty minutes to get the group aboard—eleven men, eight women and twenty-one children ranging in age from two-and-a-half to seventeen. The forty refugees included sugar planters, Presbyterian missionaries, even four men who had survived the Bataan Death March and escaped from a Japanese POW camp. In truth, the *Crevalle* did not have room for so many passengers. Captain Walker had been expecting no more than twenty-five, but how could he leave behind American families on a Japanese-occupied island?

## A horrific existence

Negros Island lies in the Sulu Sea between the islands of Panay and Cebu. At 225 kilometres (738 miles) in length, and 80 kilometres (262 miles) across at its widest point, it is the fourth largest island of the Philippines. In the early 1940s the coastal plains of Negros were filled with vast fields of sugarcane, and the mountain range that ran down the middle of the island, covered by endless hardwood forests and immense jungles, was the source of valuable tropical timbers. There were hundreds of Americans on the island—sugar planters, engineers, lumbermen, miners, missionaries, and the faculty and administrators of Silliman University in the town of Dumaguete at the southern end of the island. In late May and early June of 1942, Japanese forces under Colonel Kumataro Ota occupied Negros. As the enemy troops came ashore, about one-third of the island's population—Filipinos, some of them wealthy sugar industry people with strong US ties, and Americans—fled into the mountains. The Filipinos formed guerrilla bands to harass the Japanese; the Americans, all of whom had escaped with their families, sought refuge near remote jungle villages.

To the Japanese authorities, the American business executives, teachers and missionaries were not harmless civilians, but enemy aliens. From Singapore to the Dutch East Indies, wherever they conquered, Japanese forces herded civilians of the Allied nations into POW or labour or concentration camps. Conditions in these camps were horrific—minimal sanitation and medical facilities, meagre rations, crippling work details, and always the prisoners were at the mercy of the guards who for any pretext, real or imagined, could beat them, torture them, even kill them.

The Americans on Negros who escaped the Japanese invasion were saved by ordinary Filipinos. They guided the refugees into the mountains, carrying their luggage and their children. They supplied food and water for the journey, opened their homes to them at night, and when they reached some remote place where the guerrillas believed they would be safe, local villagers helped the refugees build huts and collect food, and taught them how to survive in the jungle.

But the Americans were never entirely safe: Japanese patrols hunted for them, and any Filipino who tried to protect them risked torture or death. In the town of Bacolod at the northern end of the island a German national, Edward Weber, volunteered to help the Japanese identify guerrilla sympathisers and track down Americans hiding in the jungle. On one such mission Weber and a Japanese patrol encountered a farmer called Mercades Urbano, and ordered him to take them to the places where Americans were hiding; Urbano said he knew nothing about any Americans hiding in the mountains. Weber and the Japanese did not believe him; they wrapped wire around each of his thumbs and hung him from the limb of a tree. The poor man kept silent until the pain became unbearable—he pleaded to be cut down, swearing that he would take them to an American family's hiding place. The wires were cut, and Urbano, nursing his mangled thumbs, led the patrol to a camp where a wealthy Filipino sugar family named Ossorio had been living. But when they got there the place was deserted, the Ossorios had moved on. Thinking Urbano had made fools of them, Weber and the troops beat him savagely. They would have sent him to a prison camp, but later that day, entirely by chance, Urbano stumbled upon the hiding place of an American Catholic priest, Father LaSage. The Japanese arrested the priest and let Urbano go.

The Japanese demanded absolute obedience and full cooperation of all the people they conquered. Any form of resistance was an excuse for the harshest of penalties. In February 1944, for example, guerrilla leader Salvador Abcede arranged with the US Navy to evacuate two dozen American refugees who had been hiding in the mountains above Balatong Point on the south-west coast of Negros. The rescue went off without a hitch, but an informant reported to the occupying authorities that Filipino villagers had protected and worked with Abcede's guerrillas to help the Americans escape. Five days later terrible retribution was exacted: Japanese troops fell upon the villages near Balatong, burning homes and crops, slaughtering livestock, and murdering eighty-nine men, women and children.

## 'Too hot for us to hold'

On 31 March 1944, Admiral Mineichi Koga, Commander-in-Chief of the Japanese Combined Fleet, and his chief of staff, Admiral Shigeru Fukudome, were en route in separate Kawanishi flying boats from Palau in the Pacific to Japanese headquarters at Davao on Mindanao: their mission—to deliver top-secret documents code-named 'Z Plan', which outlined the Japanese military's strategy for a counteroffensive that would drive the Americans from the Pacific. The planes were in Philippine air space when they were overtaken by a fierce tropical storm. Koga's plane went down in the sea and all on board were lost. Every manoeuvre Fukudome's pilot attempted to escape the storm or at least skirt it failed, and the admiral ordered him to fly to Manila; they would wait out the storm there. By now the plane was so low on fuel that reaching Manila was out of the question, but the pilot saw Cebu Island nearby—he informed the admiral that he would land there. Fukudome leaped out of his seat and rushed to the cockpit, insisting that the pilot was wrong, the island was not Cebu. As they argued, the pilot began his descent; Fukudome, enraged by such insubordination, seized the controls and pulled them sharply to bring the plane out of landing mode. The struggle not unnaturally caused the Kawanishi to spin out of control; the aircraft struck the waters of the Bohol Strait between the islands of Cebu and Bohol, the fuel tanks exploded, and very quickly it began to sink. A dozen staff officers died in the crash, but Admiral Fukudome and thirteen others survived. For three hours they paddled slowly and painfully towards Cebu

Island, where they were met on the beach by members of the Volunteer Guard, a local band of guerrillas.

The Volunteer Guards escorted their prisoners deep into the mountains of Cebu, to the headquarters of Lieutenant James Cushing, an American who had been organising and leading guerrilla raids against the Japanese for two years. The Volunteer Guards did not realise they had captured a Japanese admiral; and when they reached Cushing's camp, one of the captives, who spoke English, identified Fukudome to Cushing as 'General Twani Furomei'. Delighted to have such a high-ranking man as his prisoner, Cushing immediately began arranging for the group's transfer to Brisbane, the Australian headquarters of US General Douglas MacArthur.

Two of the Japanese survivors were missing from the captured group. The current had carried them away from the beach and washed them up on a reef about 400 metres (1312 feet) offshore. A local fisherman saw the stranded men and, thinking they were Americans, paddled his small boat out to rescue them. When he realised they were Japanese, he panicked, leaped out of his banca and swam hastily back to shore. The survivors took over the abandoned banca and headed for Barrio Sangat, a small town on Cebu; here they informed the commander of the local garrison that Admiral Fukudome, along with a box containing important military documents, was missing.

With authorities desperate to recover the admiral and the secret documents, Japanese troops immediately fanned out across southern Cebu, overrunning villages and farms, torturing civilians for information about the survivors of the plane crash and the whereabouts of a mysterious box. Hundreds of innocents were killed, among them small children and even infants. Reports of the atrocities unnerved Cushing's men—it was their families and friends who were suffering and dying. On 9 April 1944, Cushing sent a message to headquarters in Brisbane:

*JAP PRISONERS TOO HOT FOR US TO HOLD. DUE TO NUMBER OF CIVILIANS BEING KILLED. I MADE TERMS THAT CIVILIANS ARE NOT TO BE MOLESTED IN FUTURE. IN EXCHANGE FOR THE PRISONERS.*

Cushing, the Volunteer Guard and the intelligence officers in Brisbane regretted the necessity of releasing 'General Furomei', but other news from Cebu was very interesting. The night the survivors of the crash of the flying boat swam to shore, a shopkeeper named Pedro Gantuangko, in the village of Sitio Bas, had been unable to sleep for the pain of an attack of gout. He had limped down to the beach, and as the sun came up spotted something floating in the water. Gantuangko asked his neighbour, Opoy Wamar, to paddle out in his banca and retrieve the object.

It was a wooden box, slick with fuel oil, and inside was a soggy bundle of Japanese documents bound in a splendid red leather portfolio. It looked valuable, something the two men could sell and split the profits. And there was more: beneath the portfolio Gantuangko and Wamar found two silk bags—one was packed full of condoms, the other contained little nuggets of pure gold. Gantuangko took everything home, where he carefully dried out the documents. Then he placed the portfolio, the condoms and the gold inside a large bag, tucked it inside the oily box, and carefully buried the box in a hole near his mother's house.

The two men were still wondering what to do with their treasure when Japanese troops descended and forced all the villagers at gunpoint to the local church. Speaking through an interpreter, the officer in charge demanded to know if anyone had seen a box wash up on the beach. All the villagers shook their heads—no. The troops ransacked every house and found nothing, but they were certain the missing box had washed up here: several Japanese experts in tides and currents had pinpointed Sitio Bas as the most likely place for it to come ashore.

After the Japanese left, Gantuangko dug up his find and took it into the jungle, handing it over to a guerrilla soldier he knew. He gave the guerrilla everything, even the gold—keeping it in the village was far too risky.

The next day the Japanese returned and interrogated the villagers yet again. This time they brought along a truck loaded with rice and cloth—a promise of what the villagers would be given if they cooperated. But aside from Gantuangko and Wamar, no one had the least idea what the Japanese were looking for. When the soldiers left, Wamar fled into the jungle for safety; Gantuangko collected his family together and sailed his banca to the island of Bohol. Before they reached their hiding place, they saw Japanese troops setting fire to the village.

Gantuangko's guerrilla contact carried the box to Cushing, although it has never been established exactly when the American received the documents. It would be ironic if the Z Plan was in the guerrilla camp while Admiral Fukudome was still a prisoner there. What is known is that by 13 April, four days after Cushing had cabled headquarters that he had released his prisoners, he had the Z Plan. From their elaborate appearance he knew the documents were important, but he did not know what they said because no one in the camp could read Japanese.

## Planning something innocuous

It did not matter that no one could read the documents, for the scorched-earth policy that Japanese patrols were still inflicting on the civilian population of Cebu despite Fukudome's release was enough to convince everyone that they must be vital to Japan's war effort. The question, then, was how to get the documents safely to Brisbane? If a US Navy convoy were now to appear off the coast of Cebu, and if a solitary banca paddled out to it, the Japanese were bound to suspect that the Americans were in possession of the Z Plan; every Japanese ship and bomber in the Pacific theatre would pursue the convoy and do its utmost to blow the ships out of the water.

Headquarters in Brisbane wired instructions to Cushing on Cebu and the guerrilla leader Salvador Abcede on Negros to think up a low-key mission that would appear innocuous and not raise Japanese suspicions. A few months earlier the submarine USS *Narwhal* had rescued a couple of dozen American civilians from Negros, carrying them to safety in Australia. Although the Japanese had mounted a harsh punitive expedition in the area where the refugees had been hiding, the submarine had not been pursued. Abcede and Cushing suggested a similar mission—a lone submarine picking up a few American civilians, not from Cebu, where the Japanese were on high alert, but from Negros again. Cushing would arrange to get the portfolio to Abcede; Abcede would escort the refugees to the rendezvous point. No one would know that one of them would be carrying the Z Plan in his luggage.

It was a simple plan, and Brisbane approved it almost immediately. Abcede was instructed to bring the American civilians to Balatong Point. If it was safe to proceed, he should hang two white sheets from the trees—like laundry hung out to dry. The submarine USS *Crevalle* would surface at sundown on 11 May; Abcede would have his evacuees ready to move. At no time did it occur to the officers at headquarters to inform Captain Walker that he would be transporting the Z Plan to General MacArthur's headquarters.

## The meal they had dreamed of

The *Crevalle*'s crew were not accustomed to having women on board, let alone children. The submarine was just as strange to the refugees: after three years in the warm, fragrant atmosphere of the jungle, the vessel felt uncomfortably claustrophobic, and it stank of old cooking odours, cigarette smoke, the fumes of diesel oil and the unmistakable reek of unwashed bodies.

But the *Crevalle* also held luxuries the Americans had not seen in years. One of the women edged up to the door of the tiny galley where three cooks were at work. Pointing to a large stainless steel coffee urn, she asked if the coffee was real. 'You bet,' one of the cooks replied. 'Help yourself.' Another asked for a slice of 'real bread'. In the jungle there had been nothing but cassava bread. The children were taken to the officers' wardroom, where the crew had made a big pile of candy and chocolate bars.

For dinner the *Crevalle*'s cooks served up platters of meat, potatoes, vegetables, freshly baked bread, butter, canned peaches, pitchers of milk and iced water. The adults forgot their table manners and heaped their plates with food. The children were less enthusiastic—they had grown accustomed to Filipino cuisine, and most of these foods were unfamiliar. Even the milk was odd—it didn't taste at all like the water buffalo milk they had drunk every day in the jungle. The dinner was especially hard on the four rescued POWs: here was the type of meal they had dreamed of, but after years of barely subsisting on rice and a few bits of vegetable their stomachs could not deal with such abundance.

## Battered but still afloat

At dawn on 14 May, the *Crevalle* was surface-cruising across the Molucca Sea through the Sunda Islands of Indonesia. Down below Captain Walker, the evacuees and the off-watch crew were asleep. Almost at the same moment as Lieutenant

Luke Bowdler climbed from the hatch onto the bridge to begin his four-hour stint as officer of the deck, a Japanese bomber burst from cover among thick cumulus clouds; it was only a few hundred metres away, and it was heading straight for the *Crevalle*. Bowdler triggered the alarm as he shouted the orders, 'Clear the bridge! Dive! Dive!' Just before he slammed the hatch shut he saw the bomb fall—thank God, it would miss them.

The screech of the klaxon, the sudden dive and the impact on the vessel from the bomb's explosion greatly alarmed the civilian passengers, but over the next few hours, as the *Crevalle* cruised deep under water and no further bombs were dropped, they regained their composure, and Captain Walker brought the submarine close enough to the surface to up periscope. Shortly before ten that morning, a Japanese convoy of two *marus* (warships), two destroyers, two destroyer escorts and a converted minesweeper was sighted off a tiny atoll called Tifore. The *Crevalle* had five torpedoes in its tubes, and Captain Walker decided to use them; when the convoy turned suddenly and made straight for the *Crevalle*, Walker called the crew to battle stations.

The convoy's unexpected about-turn wasn't an accident—a Japanese bomber, unseen by Captain Walker, had spotted the periscope and dropped a smoke bomb indicating the *Crevalle*'s location. And now the plane had released a bomb known as a 'sub killer'. Shouting 'Get me down!', Walker gave the order to dive. The sub killer missed, but when the *Crevalle* was only 60 metres (197 feet) down the Japanese destroyers dropped a round of depth charges into the sea.

Seven powerful explosions rocked the submarine, throwing passengers and crew to the floor, causing light bulbs to explode, and sending any object that was not bolted down sailing through the air. In the officers' wardroom the books flew off their shelves, striking a group of children playing on the floor. The seals on two hatches were compromised, and water cascaded down from the conning tower, soaking the radar and sonar equipment. Throughout the ship water gushed through cracks and fissures caused by the force of the depth charges.

In the silence that followed the explosions, passengers and crew could hear the sounds of the Japanese vessels above them. Walker had taken his sub down to 120 metres (394 feet), and was inching away from the convoy, hoping to avoid being located by sonar, but the Japanese found their position, and eight more depth charges pounded the *Crevalle*'s hull. Even veteran seamen believed they were about to die.

In a further effort to escape detection, Walker had the noisy ventilation system shut down. The temperature inside the submarine soared to a hideous 49°C (120°F); worse yet, the oxygen supply was being depleted at an alarming rate. The children fell into a deep sleep from the lack of oxygen and the adults felt light-headed, which made it difficult for the crew to keep their minds focused on their duties. The *Crevalle* crept silently through deep water for five hours until the Japanese eventually gave up the search. Before giving the order to break surface, Captain Walker attempted to raise the periscope, but it had been smashed by the depth charges. Some time after they had heard the last sound from the convoy, Walker decided to take the risk. As the *Crevalle* broke the surface, the captain climbed out to the bridge—the horizon was clear, no Japanese ships or bombers anywhere in sight. His sub was battered, but it was still afloat, and most of the damaged equipment the crew could repair themselves. They had been very lucky.

## 'Our precious cargo'

At 6.29 am on the morning of 19 May 1944, the *Crevalle*'s lookouts spotted two Australian ships, a patrol boat and a motor ketch, cruising towards them from the entrance to Darwin Harbour; they had been waiting for the submarine's arrival. Through a megaphone the captain of the patrol boat shouted that he had come to take off the passengers. Walker ordered 'All Stop', and word spread quickly among the excited evacuees that they were about to be transported to shore. The children were excited, the women put on their best dresses, the escaped POWs tried to look like soldiers rather than scarecrows. Walker had the luggage brought up, including the box of Japanese documents, and one by one the evacuees came on deck. It was a brilliantly sunny morning—the first time they had seen the sun in eight days.

Captain Walker made a brief speech to the assembled evacuees. He apologised for the scare they had suffered, but his submarine was a vessel of war, and since he had had five torpedoes on board he had felt obliged to try to sink some of the enemy's ships. (If anyone at headquarters had told him that he was transporting

## Life in the jungle

For the American refugees on Negros Island life in the jungle was rough but bearable, and at least food was abundant. The Filipino farmers grew corn and camote, a kind of sweet potato; there were coconuts fresh from the tree, and milk directly from the water buffaloes. At local markets the Americans bought or bartered for sugar and chickens, some of which they kept for their eggs while others found their way into the cooking pot.

The Filipino women taught the refugee women skills that were virtually unknown in the United States—how to make thread from plant fibres, how to derive lamp oil from coconut milk, how to make soap. Nearby rivers and streams became bathtubs and washing machines. The Filipino women demonstrated how to beat dirt from clothes by pounding them against clean rocks. The method worked, but it broke down the fibres quickly. Almost every day the American women spent time mending or patching battered clothing. By the time of their rescue, the refugees were a ragtag bunch.

A major concern was contracting malaria. All the Americans slept under mosquito netting at night, and they brewed a bitter tea from the bark of the local dita tree, which a chemistry professor at Silliman University in Dumaguete had discovered helped to prevent malaria. Most Americans in the mountains also had a precious store of sulfanilamide tablets, a new and powerful antibiotic. In 1943, eight-year-old Dean Lindholm, the son of Presbyterian missionaries from Minnesota, had fallen deathly ill with dysentery; his life was saved because his parents had a few sulfanilamide tablets.

the Z Plan, it's unlikely that he would have run such a risk.) 'You have been our precious cargo,' Walker told his passengers. 'Your conduct aboard this ship has been magnificent.' The evacuees broke into loud applause.

The Australian patrol boat pulled alongside the *Crevalle*, and the evacuees climbed on board. As the patrol boat cast off its lines and Walker gave orders for the submarine to get underway, many were torn between watching the departure of the submarine that had rescued them and feasting their eyes on the first sight of Australia, where at last they would be safe.

# CHAPTER 20

# THE GREAT RAID
## The Rescue of the POWs of Cabanatuan

Captain Juan Pajota's plan had gone off perfectly. His men were in command of the bridge, and he had fanned them out along the banks of the Cabu River in either direction—it was the dry season on Luzon, the water was low, a child could wade across. At the first sound of rifle fire from the POW camp to their rear, Pajota's Filipino guerrillas opened fire on a Japanese battalion camped only 300 metres (984 feet) away.

Taken entirely by surprise, the Japanese stumbled out of their tents; recovering quickly, they charged the bridge. With their four machine guns Pajota's men cut down the enemy. The Japanese troops withdrew, reformed and charged again. Once again they were driven back, and once again they took heavy casualties. The guerrillas positioned along the creek bank killed those who tried to wade through the shallow water; a time-bomb that Pajota had planted under the bridge blasted a hole in the span that slowed the next charge. When two troop trucks rolled towards the bridge, Pajota's bazookamen

Half-starved and filthy, First Sergeant Orville E. Drummond was too exhausted to make it all the way onto his bunk after his gruelling time in the Cabanatuan prison camp and dramatic rescue by US Rangers and Filipino guerrillas.

The sky fills with smoke from anti-aircraft ordnance as the
aircraft carrier USS *Yorktown* takes a direct hit during the
Battle of Midway, June 1942.

fired—the trucks exploded in flames. Then they took aim at two tanks, scoring direct hits that crippled them both.

Pajota and his guerrillas battled the Japanese for an hour and a half. By then they had virtually wiped out the entire battalion without losing a single man of their own. Now Pajota gave fresh orders—the guerrillas were to act as rearguard for the US Army Rangers and the Allied POWs they had rescued from the camp, who they were moving as quickly as possible back to American lines at Guimba, 50 kilometres (31 miles) away.

## A flawless performance

By 1943 the war in the Pacific had begun to turn against the Empire of Japan. After years of easy conquests across Asia and the Pacific islands, Japan was experiencing the humiliation of defeat after defeat. Allied submarines were preying on Japanese merchant ships, causing shortages for the military as well as for the civilians back in Japan. At the Battle of Midway in June 1942, an American fleet commanded by Admiral Chester Nimitz had inflicted a crushing blow on the Japanese navy, sinking four aircraft carriers and a cruiser, destroying 332 aircraft, and taking the lives of approximately 3500 sailors and airmen.

Late in 1943, as American forces began to take back the Pacific, island by island, Lieutenant General Walter Krueger, commander of the Sixth Army, created a new elite force that would slip behind Japanese lines to gather enemy intelligence and rescue Allied prisoners of war. He called his elite squad the Alamo Scouts, after the 1836 battle in the Texas War of Independence, where 182 heroic defenders of the Alamo Mission held out against a Mexican army of 6000 men.

Krueger's teams of Alamo Scouts—each consisting of one officer and six enlisted men—were an overnight success: within nine months their daring clandestine missions and raids earned them nineteen Silver Stars, eighteen Bronze Stars and four Soldier's Medals. Incredibly, the Scouts never lost a man. Krueger was so impressed by their successes that he decided to incorporate them into a new outfit—the 6th Ranger Battalion—that would be able to tackle larger, more ambitious objectives. The man Krueger asked to take command and train the Rangers was Lieutenant Colonel Henry Mucci, a West Point graduate. A lean man with a prominent nose and a thin dark moustache that made him resemble the Hollywood actor Ronald Colman, Mucci was a born soldier, a natural athlete, and an expert in judo at a time when Asian martial arts were virtually unknown in the United States.

Mucci handpicked each Ranger. He knew the types of men he wanted—strong, beefy young fellows who had grown up on farms and ranches, who were accustomed to long days of physical labour and being outdoors in all weather. As tough and hardy as these farmers and ranchers might have been already, Mucci wanted them even tougher. He put his Rangers through a brutal course of training, taking them on long marches through the oppressively humid jungles of New Guinea, ordering them to find ways to cross treacherous, swift-flowing rivers, forcing them to climb steep mountains. He taught them how to fight hand to hand, revealed the secrets of jungle combat and night combat, and kept them at the shooting range until every man was a sharpshooter.

One of Mucci's Rangers, John Richardson, recalled, 'I wondered why he was putting us through so much, but before it was over, there was no question about it, I knew why. And once he got us trained and picked out, he loved us to death. And there wasn't anything too good for us.'

The new battalion first went into action on 17 October 1944—six days before a combined American and Australian force engaged the Japanese in battle for the Leyte Gulf in the Philippines. The Rangers came ashore on Dinagat, Guiuan and Homonhon—islands at the mouth of the Gulf—where they destroyed Japanese radio stations and cleared Japanese bunkers. They performed flawlessly.

## The 'Kill-All' policy

In January 1945, as the US Sixth Army drove into the heart of Luzon Island, General Krueger selected a new daring mission for the Rangers—to liberate Allied prisoners of war at the Cabanatuan POW camp. This would be the Rangers' most difficult, most dangerous mission. The camp lay deep in Japanese-held territory; the highways near the camp were used regularly by troops and tank battalions. It would be a risky operation, but Krueger felt he had no choice—there were more than 500 Allied POWs at Cabanatuan, and the general feared that with the Sixth Army closing in, their Japanese captors would very shortly murder them all.

Just a few months earlier, in August 1944, the Japanese War Ministry had adopted a 'Kill-All' policy regarding POWs, punishing the Allies while at the same time eliminating any witness who might later accuse Japanese forces of atrocities and war crimes. The order from the War Ministry read in part:

> *Whether they are destroyed individually or in groups, and whether it is accomplished by means of mass bombing, poisonous smoke, poisons, drowning, or decapitation, dispose of them as the situation dictates. It is the aim not to allow the escape of a single one, to annihilate them all, and not to leave any traces.*

In obedience to this policy, on 14 December 1944 Japanese guards at the camp on the Philippine island of Palawan had herded 150 American POWs into air-raid shelters, locked the doors, doused the shelters with bucket after bucket of fuel, touched them with a flaming torch and burned the helpless men alive.

News of the Palawan massacre reached the men at Cabanatuan in an unexpected way—by radio. Working over many weeks, the POWs had built their own radio, which they hid in a water canteen. Their method of construction was ingenious—and daring. According to POW James Hildebrand, the guards relied on the prisoners to keep their radios in working order. When they were ordered to repair a radio, the Americans would remove not just the non-working component, but also a part that was perfectly functional, and ask the Japanese to order replacements. They hid the salvaged working components. In this way, bit by bit, they assembled their own radio. This link to the outside world was invaluable as a morale booster, especially in 1944 as the Allies began to drive back the Japanese. But the report concerning the murder of American POWs at Palawan frightened the POWs at Cabanatuan. They knew from first-hand experience what the Japanese were capable of, and they saw no reason why they would be spared.

## 'We were in for deep trouble'

'A terrible silence settled over Bataan about noon on April 9,' remembered General Jonathan Wainwright. The general had assumed command of 11,000 American and Filipino troops on Corregidor after General Douglas MacArthur—under orders from President Franklin D. Roosevelt—evacuated with his family and staff to Australia (see chapter 16). Wainwright had no hope of rescue or of reinforcements, but he and his men were putting up a stiff resistance, so the news that General Edward King, commander on the nearby Bataan Peninsula, had surrendered came as a shock. There were 72,000 American and Filipino troops on Bataan; never in the history of the United States had such a large force surrendered to the enemy.

As the Japanese moved in, rounding up their prisoners for a march to a camp some 100 kilometres (62 miles) to the north, some Americans and Filipinos tried to escape inland where they hoped to join guerrilla bands. Richard Gordon of the 31st US Infantry Regiment made a run for it, but two days later he was captured by a Japanese patrol. They beat him, took all his personal possessions, then forced him at rifle point to join the tens of thousands heading for the camp. At the side of the road he saw his battalion commander, Major James Ivy. 'He had been tied to a tree and he was stripped to the waist and he was just covered with bayonet holes,' Gordon recalled. 'He was dead obviously. And he had bled profusely. He had been bayoneted by many, many bayonets. And that's when I knew we had some troubles on our hands. We were in for deep trouble.'

On the march, known in history as the Bataan Death March, the Japanese gave their prisoners no food, no water, no medicine for the wounded. Men who broke ranks to lap up water from puddles in ditches alongside the road were shot or stabbed to death with bayonets. Men who caught food tossed to them by Filipino farmers were killed, and so were the farmers. Men who staggered or collapsed from hunger, thirst and exhaustion were killed. The US Department of Veterans Affairs estimates that 650 American and 16,500 Filipino soldiers died on the Bataan Death March.

The prisoners' destination was Camp O'Donnell, an unfinished US Air Force facility. It was soon crammed with 9300 POWs, but had just two working water spigots that the Japanese guards would permit to flow for only a few hours each day. The lines were so long, the time that water was available so brief, that most men never reached the spigots. No exception was made even for prisoners in the camp hospital. In the first eight weeks of their captivity, 1500 American and 15,000 Filipino POWs died of starvation, thirst or disease, were executed for attempting to escape, or were killed at random.

When the 11,000 American and Filipino troops on Corregidor surrendered on 7 May, Camp O'Donnell could not hold all the prisoners; the Americans were transferred to Camp Cabanatuan, a former Philippines Army encampment, where conditions were no better than at Camp O'Donnell. In June of 1942, 503 Americans died at Cabanatuan; July's death toll rose to 786. By the end of World War II, 37 per cent of all POWs held in Japanese camps would die of mistreatment, torture, disease, starvation or execution. By contrast, the death rate in Nazi-run POW camps (as distinguished from concentration and slave labour camps) was 1.2 per cent.

## Just two local peasants

General Krueger gave Colonel Mucci a free hand to assemble a force for the liberation of Cabanatuan. Mucci selected eight officers and 120 Rangers, including two teams of experienced Alamo Scouts, men who had accomplished a similar mission only three months earlier at Maori in New Guinea. There the Scouts had struck a Japanese POW camp, freeing sixty-six Dutch and Javanese civilians and killing all the guards—without losing a single Scout. Mucci planned to repeat that success at Cabanatuan.

Mucci sent the two teams of Scouts to Guimba to rendezvous with Filipino guerrillas. From there the combined group would move to the outskirts of the Cabanatuan camp, where they would study the routines of the guards and assess the strength of the Japanese forces. However, here they encountered a problem. The ground around the camp was too open—there was no opportunity to get close enough for surveillance without being spotted by the guards.

Then Lieutenant Bill Nellist, commanding officer of one of the Scout teams, had an inspiration. On high ground beyond the camp he spotted an abandoned farmer's hut that might well provide a bird's-eye view of Cabanatuan. But there was still the question of how to get to it without attracting unwanted attention. Since the only people who could move freely outside the camp were the local Filipino population, Nellist decided to disguise himself as a farmer. He chose Rufo Vaquilar, a Filipino-American member of his team, to go with him. Wearing the rough clothes and straw hats of poor farmers, Nellist and Vaquilar walked up to the hut. If any guards did see them, they thought nothing of it—just two more local peasants.

The view from the hut was even better than Nellist had hoped—from this vantage point there was an unobstructed panorama of the entire camp and everyone moving in it. For two hours Nellist and Vaquilar made detailed notes of the layout, the location of the prisoners' barracks, the routine of the guards, and the best approaches for the raiders. They were just finishing when they heard something move outside the hut: out of the brush came three Scouts. Unable to resist the temptation, they had circled around the high ground and come up to the hut from the rear, crawling on their bellies the whole way. Nellist gave the three Scouts the notes and diagrams and ordered they be taken to Colonel Mucci at once.

## Water buffalo and P-61s

The man Mucci chose to lead the raid on the camp was Captain Robert Prince, a twenty-five-year-old graduate of Stanford University. Prince based his raid on three elements—surprise, speed and chaos. He wanted to get in, evacuate the prisoners, kill the guards and get out, all within thirty minutes. To achieve this he divided his forces. Half the Rangers would crash through the main gate, the other half would break in at the rear of the camp. The highway that ran in front of the camp would be secured by the guerrillas, with Captain Pajota commanding the bridge over the Cabu River, and Captain Eduardo Joson's guerrillas commanding the approach to the camp some 800 metres (2624 feet) down the road. Immediately before the raid, Joson's guerrillas were to cut the telephone lines leading to the camp.

The mission could not have been accomplished without Captain Pajota, his Filipino guerrillas and the local farmers. In temperament, Pajota was more like Mucci than Prince: both were charismatic, both were imaginative tacticians, and both were resourceful, enjoying the absolute confidence and loyalty of their men. For this raid, Pajota was indispensable. He knew every track through the jungle, he knew the mayor in every barrio, the chief man in every village, and he had an extensive network of ordinary Filipinos he could turn to for food, supplies and transportation.

It was Pajota's idea to borrow from the local farmers the large carts drawn by water buffalo to carry POWs too weak to walk. And while he was asking his friends for favours, he asked them to supply food and water for 650 men, too.

Pajota had a personal intelligence network that kept the Japanese under close surveillance. In his first meeting with Mucci on 29 January, the colonel had insisted that they raid the camp that evening. Pajota had replied, 'Sir, with all due respect, that is suicide,' explaining that the Japanese were planning to move a large body of troops and trucks that evening. Mucci scoffed, but his Alamo Scouts confirmed Pajota's report. Mucci swallowed his pride and rescheduled the raid for the following night.

As the Scouts and Rangers prepared for the raid, the guerrillas instructed the farmers in the areas outlying the camp to leash and muzzle their dogs—a sudden spate of barking might alert the Japanese that someone was coming. The guerrillas advised those farmers who lived really close to the camp to move deep into the jungle—but, they cautioned, there was to be no mass exodus, they must leave in small groups, only two or three families at a time, so as not to rouse suspicion.

Then Pajota made one final suggestion. He knew Mucci could call up air support. Why not have US aircraft fly low over the camp—no bombing, no strafing, just endless droning back and forth overhead? That would confuse the guards, and while they were distracted and trying to figure out whether they were under attack, the Rangers could move into position to break into the camp. Mucci loved the idea, and radioed to headquarters to request this unusual form of air cover.

It fell to Captain Prince to implement all these plans. In addition to coordinating the Scouts, the Rangers and the guerrillas, Prince had to ensure that the farmers had their water-buffalo carts in place and ready to roll, that the P-61 night fighter pilots would buzz the camp on schedule—and finally, he had to round up the POWs in the camp and get them all to safety, all the while battling the Japanese. And there was one final duty which Prince assigned to himself—at the last moment, he would run through the barracks to make certain that every single POW was out.

## 'Don't you want to be free?'

Night had fallen and James Hildebrand, the POWs' unofficial cobbler, was sitting in his shack repairing shoes when an explosion tore the roof off. He heard bursts of gunfire coming from every part of the camp, and overhead the drone of fighter planes. Hildebrand panicked. He was sure the Japanese had begun a Palawan-style massacre. Sprinting from his shack, he ran smack into the biggest man he had ever seen. 'Who the hell are you?' Hildebrand asked. But at once he knew the answer—this wasn't a Japanese massacre, it was an American rescue.

There was absolute pandemonium in the camp, with fusillades of small-arms fire coming from every direction and hand-grenades exploding inside Japanese pillboxes and beneath the watchtowers. The prisoners scattered, many of them trying to hide from what they believed was their execution. Bert Bank lay huddled on the ground, hoping no one would notice him, when a Ranger stood over him and said, 'Buddy, you're free. Up quick and get over to the gate!' But Bank, like many of his fellow prisoners, thought it was a Japanese trick, that once he stepped outside the gate he would be shot down, and he refused to move.

'What's wrong with you?' the Ranger asked. 'Don't you want to be free?'

In spite of the hellish noise all around him, from his prone position Bank thought he heard a twang in the Ranger's voice no Japanese could fake. 'Where you from, boy?' he asked.

'Oklahoma,' the Ranger replied.

'Oklahoma's good enough for me,' Banks said. Then, raising his pathetically thin arm he said, 'Say, give me a lift here.'

Throughout the camp the Rangers encountered prisoners who didn't believe they were being rescued, who became enraged when they were not permitted to go back to their barracks to collect their personal possessions, who seemed not to understand the order, 'Run to the main gate!' The POWs were feeble, pitifully thin, lice infested, some of them very ill, a few perhaps dying, and almost all were nearly naked, having stripped down for the night to their Japanese G-string-type underwear. Three years of abuse, of malnutrition, of repeated bouts of malaria and dysentery, had weakened their minds as well as their bodies; they simply could not fathom what was happening to them.

Many of the POWs were so feeble they could not move at the pace the Rangers demanded—the Rangers solved that problem by picking them up and carrying them cradled in their arms like children, or slung across their backs. For the sick they improvised stretchers. In spite of their lack of cooperation, in thirty minutes, exactly according to Captain Prince's plan, all the captives were out of Cabanatuan. All, that is, except one—a British civilian who'd lost his hearing was in the latrine

## The casualties of Cabanatuan

Captain Robert Prince and Lieutenant Colonel Henry Mucci brought out 512 POWs from Cabanatuan; most were American, but there were also a few British, Canadian, Dutch and Norwegian prisoners.

For the Rangers and the Filipinos, casualties were light: two Alamo Scouts were wounded, and twenty-one guerrillas. The Rangers' surgeon, Captain James Fisher, was wounded in the abdomen by mortar fire. He died at an American field hospital two days later. Corporal Roy Sweezy was struck twice in the back by friendly fire and died almost instantly.

One prisoner of Cabanatuan died during the raid. In the camp hospital Corporal James Herrick found a man curled in the foetal position on a bamboo mat. Herrick tried to persuade him to get up and run for the gate. 'No, no,' the dying man said, 'I'm a goner. Go save the others.' But Herrick wouldn't leave him behind. He lifted the man in his arms and headed for the gate. Before he reached it, the man died. Herrick left the body on the ground. The identity of this man remains unknown.

The Japanese guards suffered 523 killed and wounded.

After Cabanatuan: some of the weary but joyful 512 internees rescued from the prisoner of war camp in the spectacular and daring raid.

when the raid began, and did not emerge until the raid was over. The poor man was somewhat addled and thought nothing of it when he saw none of his fellow prisoners in the barracks. He remained in Cabanatuan for two days until he was found by a group of guerrillas and sent to an American field hospital.

Prince ran through each barracks—they were clear—and fired a single red flare, the signal to withdraw.

Down the road leading away from the camp were twelve Filipino farmers waiting beside their carts. The Rangers lifted the weakest POWs into the carts and the ragtag cavalcade set off for the safety of the American lines, 50 kilometres (31 miles) away. When they had moved about 1.6 kilometres (1 mile) from the camp, Prince fired a second flare, the signal to Captain Joson to pull back from his position on the highway.

The pace was slow—water buffalo do not move quickly, and many of the Rangers were carrying POWs who should really have been in the carts (that was the only error in planning the raid: everyone had underestimated the number of prisoners who would be too weak to walk).

About ten the next morning the sound of aircraft approaching the rear of the column was heard. 'Take cover!' one Ranger yelled. The men scattered as best they could, but as the Rangers prepared to fire, the planes abruptly pulled skyward and on their wings could be seen a single star. These were the P-61s that had buzzed the camp during the raid; the pilots were doing a flyover to welcome the prisoners to freedom.

The Rangers and the rescued POWs did not have to walk all the way—several kilometres further on they were met by a large convoy of trucks, ambulances and Red Cross vans, come to speed them to a field hospital where for the first time in three years the prisoners would receive medical care, eat nutritious food and sleep in clean, soft cots.

# CHAPTER 21

# THE HEADHUNTERS
### The Dayaks of Borneo Protect an American Flight Crew

With a horrific ripping sound an anti-aircraft shell from a Japanese ship in Brunei Bay struck the B-24 Liberator, badly damaging the flight deck and tearing holes the size of manhole covers in the waist of the plane. Shrapnel struck navigator Fred Brennan in the back of the head, killing him instantly. More shrapnel hit co-pilot Jerry Rosenthal on the left side of his head, shearing off his ear and leaving him mortally wounded. Pilot Tom Coberly was struck in the leg—the bone was shattered, and blood was pumping out like a geyser. Splinters of plexiglass from the nose-turret window were embedded in nose-gunner Eddy Haviland's eye. The uninjured members of the crew—bombardier Lieutenant Phil Corrin, radio operator Corporal Dan Illerich, tail-gunner Sergeant Francis Harrington, aerial photographer Elmer Philipps, and gunners Tom Capin and John Nelson—tended to the wounded while flight engineer Corporal Jim Knoch took over the controls. He could see smoke curling up from the No. 1 fuel tank, and the No. 2 tank had been punctured—fuel was

An armed native Dayak. Despite initial American
fears headhunting was uncommon by the 1940s.

spilling out rapidly. In the rear of the aircraft, Illerich was still trying to radio their base on Morotai in the Molucca Islands, but the transmitter was dead.

The plane was going down. Corrin and the other able-bodied crewmen strapped parachutes onto the wounded, then co-pilot Jerry Rosenthal gave the order to bail out. 'This is it, guys,' he shouted, 'I'm going. Hit the silk!'

One by one nine airmen jumped from the B-24, leaving the body of Fred Brennan lying on the deck. Co-pilot Rosenthal did not jump—when he shouted 'I'm going', he meant he knew he would not recover from his head wound, that he would go down with the plane. As the crew floated down into the dense jungle of northern Borneo, they saw the B-24 disappear over a mountain and almost immediately heard the roar of an explosion.

## 'Grin!'

The eleven young men of the wrecked US Army Air Force B-24 had been on Morotai Island barely a month. They belonged to the 23rd Bomb Squadron, nicknamed the 'Bomber Barons', part of the Jungle Air Force assigned to assist in driving the Japanese from the Philippines by cutting off their fuel supply. The crew had trained together at March Field outside Los Angeles in June 1944 and were all very young—at the age of twenty-two, Lieutenant Tom Coberly was the 'old man' of the group.

Japan had built its empire in the Pacific—the 'Greater East Asia Co-Prosperity Sphere'—to make the island nation politically secure and economically independent, particularly when it came to such essential resources as oil and rubber. In 1942 Japanese forces invaded Borneo to take control of its rich oilfields. Borneo did not disappoint—it delivered 40 per cent of Japan's fuel oil, 30 per cent of its heavy oil, and 25 per cent of its crude oil. The island's oilfields and refineries had become essential to Japan's war effort, and as the Allies began their campaign to retake the Pacific, island by island, cutting off Japan's access to Borneo oil became a priority for the Jungle Air Force.

On 16 November 1944, the day the crew bailed out, they were still rookies with limited combat experience and absolutely no experience of trying to survive in the jungle. Of the nine who parachuted into the unknown, the uninjured Corrin and Illerich were the only ones to land anywhere near each other. They teamed up and immediately headed for the wrecked plane, hoping to salvage some equipment.

They were both Californian boys, and while the jungle intimidated them they were fascinated by it, too—the trees that soared to a height of 30 metres (108 feet), the shafts of sunlight that penetrated the thick leafy canopy, the symphony of sounds of birds, animals and insects, most of which were camouflaged from their eyes. They were most worried about poisonous snakes, but soon learned there were other things to watch for—blood-sucking leeches, stinging ants that clung to vines, palm fronds as sharp as serrated knives. And then there was the stifling humidity—neither man had ever encountered anything like it; they felt as if they were trying to walk through a sponge.

They walked for hours to reach the crash site. The fuselage was still burning, and the remains of Fred Brennan and Jerry Rosenthal too hot to touch—they would not be able to bury them. The crash and the fire had destroyed almost everything except for two jungle survival kits and an inflatable life raft. The contents of the survival kits were meagre: some chocolate bars and little tins of cheese; a small first aid kit; a pocket knife; a collapsible machete; some mosquito repellent; water-purifying tablets; a few dollar bills and gold coins, and several rounds of .45 calibre ammunition. Both men were wearing Colt .45 automatic pistols, and Illerich also had a .32 semi-automatic. Corrin had a silk map of Borneo which would be useful if they could get to the coast; most of the interior was blank, indicating that vast portions of the island had not been charted.

During a stay at a base in New Guinea, Australian troops had told the Americans that if ever they were stranded in the jungle they should follow a waterway downstream— eventually it would lead them to a village. There had also been talk of headhunters and cannibals, but the Americans weren't sure about that—were the Australians being helpful or trying to spook them? But now they acted on the advice about finding a waterway and following it, and tried not to think about headhunters and cannibals.

When they found an abandoned hut beside a stream, the two airmen sat down to rest. A few moments later, a dozen men emerged slowly from a wall of bushes. They were dark-skinned, their lips and even their teeth were dyed black; they all wore loincloths with a machete hanging from a belt, and they carried spears and blowguns. The men were Dayaks. The two airmen got slowly to their feet. 'Grin,' Corrin said, and Illerich gave the strangers his biggest, toothiest smile. The Dayaks grinned back. When Corrin and Illerich dropped their sidearms, the Dayaks dropped their machetes and planted their spears and blowguns in the mud, then shook the Americans' hands.

Incredibly, one of the Dayaks, after examining their holsters, shouted, 'US! US!' With that, the party signed for Corrin and Illerich to follow them. Only a short distance away they reached a village where an excited group of Dayaks crowded around, chatting away happily in a language the Americans did not understand. The language didn't matter—it was clear to the two airmen that they were welcome. A man they took to be the chief appeared, and led them to a longhouse, a substantial structure about 12 metres (39 feet) in length, raised 2 metres (6½ feet) off the ground on sturdy poles, and roofed with thatch. The interior was spacious, with small hearth fires burning here and there, and beautiful woven mats covering the floor. Lined up on a high shelf was a long row of human skulls.

## Friends and allies

In 1944 in Borneo there were perhaps as many as 3 million Dayaks, divided into about 450 groups, many of which had their own language. Some Dayaks at this time had been converted to Islam, others had been converted to Christianity, but most still followed the animist religion of their ancestors. Almost all lived in communal longhouses like the one Corrin and Illerich visited, they hunted small game and birds with blowguns, and they still revered the custom of hunting their enemies and taking their heads.

Until the nineteenth century Dayak tribes waged frequent war against each other to take heads en masse. Change began to come after 1839, when James Brooke, a British trader and adventurer, arrived in the Sarawak province of Borneo and carved out an empire for himself. Brooke became known as the White Rajah, and one of his goals was the abolition of headhunting. He had some success, and over the next century other members of his family, who succeeded him as White Rajah, intensified the campaign. By the 1940s headhunting was limited to individual warriors who occasionally took the head of a particular enemy. Corrin and Illerich didn't know this, of course, so the rack of skulls made them extremely uneasy despite the warm welcome.

In general the Dayaks were pro-Allies and anti-Japanese. Following their usual practice, Japanese soldiers had treated any Dayak who crossed their path with great brutality. Later the American airmen would hear a story of a family of Christian Dayaks whose abducted teenage daughter had been installed in a brothel for officers. When her heartbroken parents called on the Japanese commander and requested that he release their child, he had taken the samurai sword hanging on the wall behind his desk and had slit their throats. This outrage and many others like it enraged the Dayaks; since the Americans were fighting the Japanese, the Dayaks regarded them as friends and allies.

## The art of the deal

The next morning Corrin and Illerich managed to communicate to their hosts that they wanted to return to the crash site—perhaps if other members of the crew had made it there, they might be able to pick up their trail. Following a breakfast of white rice, a small band of men led the two Americans back into the jungle. It was hard going: their combat boots could get no traction in the watery mud, and the jungle was infested with leeches that attached themselves to their legs and ankles, and even slithered up to their groins.

Before they reached the crash site, the Dayaks pointed to a well-constructed lean-to. Inside they found Eddy Haviland and Jim Knoch. Haviland, who had found himself hung up in a tree, now had a couple of broken ribs in addition to his eye injury. Knoch had landed in a tree, too, but he hadn't been hurt. Another group of Dayaks had found them, given them rice, and brought them to the lean-to; since Haviland found it difficult to walk, they had improvised a stretcher and carried him.

Despite Haviland's injuries, both he and Knoch joined the expedition. Still some distance from the downed plane they came upon the corpse of their pilot; his parachute unopened. It was a painful blow, and made the four survivors even more concerned about the fate of the other four crew members who had parachuted from the plane.

Reaching the B-24, the Americans poked through the wreckage again searching for anything that might be salvaged, but their efforts were fruitless. Their Dayak guides indicated that it was not safe to linger, that by now the Japanese would have learned of the crash, so they moved on. Their destination proved to be a large hut set in a rice field; here the Americans would be out of sight and safe. The Dayaks collected a pile of firewood, gave them rice and a cooking pot, and headed back to their village.

Without the Dayaks around, the young Americans felt nervous and vulnerable, and since none of the four knew how to cook rice, their first supper in the hut was wretched. They spent the next day debating where to go; they studied Corrin's silk map, finally deciding to try to reach the town of Kudat on the north coast where, it was said, Allied submarines cruised offshore looking for downed flight crews.

US landing craft unloads Australian troops on the south-east coast of Borneo.
Billowing black smoke from burning oil wells can be seen in the background.

The Headhunters

When the Dayaks returned with more food, Corrin tried the few words of Malay listed in his survival kit, hoping to get across the idea that they wanted to travel to Kudat by water. Once again they trekked into the forest, where the Dayaks uncovered a few dug-out canoes. After all that these friendly men had done for them, it struck the four Americans as unfair to ask the Dayaks to get them all the way to the coast for nothing, so they offered to hire their guides as paddlers. When it came to the art of the deal, however, the Americans were no match for these men, who haggled until they had virtually everything in the survival kits, including the collapsible machete.

## The feast

At a bend in the river the four Americans saw a handsome canoe paddled by several Dayaks and in the bow a man dressed in Western clothes who kept calling, 'Mister! Mister!' The airmen and their Dayak guides met the large canoe in the middle of the stream, where the man in the white shirt and cotton shorts introduced himself as William Makahanap, then ordered the Dayaks to paddle to the shore—they were going to the village of Long Kasurun of the Lun Dayeh tribe.

Makahanap could speak Dutch, but very little English; nonetheless, through gestures and Corrin's lists of Malay and Dutch vocabulary, the airmen learned that he was the Celebes-born District Officer for the area, a Christian who had once worked at a Dutch mission. As they sat in a longhouse struggling to make themselves understood, Makahanap ordered a meal—short ribs, boiled pork, fried rice and coffee—a feast for men who had been surviving on a few handfuls of plain rice. The conversation fell apart when Corrin pulled out his silk map of Borneo, and Makahanap brought out a paper map of the Dutch East Indies: they both pointed to towns on their maps, but neither could make out whether the other was saying 'That is where I want to go', or 'That is where I came from', or 'That is a place in Japanese hands and so should be avoided'. Eventually Corrin and Makahanap gave up; it was late, the Americans were tired, so Makahanap had them shown to a hut where they would spend the night.

While the men slept Makahanap met with the chiefs of Long Kasurun to discuss what to do with them. The debate lasted for hours as they weighed the risk of concealing the downed flyers. Ultimately their hatred for the Japanese overcame their anxiety, and they pledged to protect the Americans until they could get them to an Allied base.

## The kindness of strangers

Gunner John Nelson had been lucky, too, landing safely near a Dayak village. The first person he saw was a warrior who approached cautiously, spear at the ready. Nelson could not speak any foreign language, but he did remember a few words from his high school Spanish class, so he pointed to himself and called out 'Americano!' The warrior lowered his spear and walked over to greet the stranger. When he saw the hordes of leeches already covering Nelson's legs, the Dayak flipped them off with the blade of his machete, then wiped the bleeding wounds with moss. Together they walked to the village where the warrior's family welcomed Nelson, fed him and gave him a place to sleep in their longhouse. Three days later, a party of Dayaks entered the village bearing Sergeant Francis Harrington. He had made a very rough landing in which he was badly knocked about and lost almost all his equipment. When the Dayaks found him he had had nothing to eat in three days, and the river water he had drunk had given him diarrhoea. In the four days he took to recover, Harrington became part of the longhouse family along with Nelson.

About a week later a man dressed in Western clothes turned up in the village. He introduced himself as William Mongan, an assistant to American Protestant missionaries who had fled after the Japanese invaded Borneo. Like Makahanap he was Celebes-born. Mongan spoke some English, and he invited the Americans to stay with him and his family in a village called Long Nuat.

The Mongans lived in a Western-style house, and William's wife Maria had learned from the missionaries' wives how to make a few American dishes such as fried chicken. Nelson and Harrington did feel more at ease with the Mongans, and perhaps best of all they learned where they were—near the centre of the island, about as far as they could be from any coastal town.

## The Dayak grapevine

Gunner Tom Capin spent eight days alone in the jungle without food, and like Harrington drinking river water, which made him ill. When a band of Dayaks led by a warrior named Kibung found him, Capin was nearly dead from hunger and dehydration. They gave him some cooked rice, showed him how to suck the juice from a piece of sugarcane and led him to their village, where Kibung insisted that Capin would be his guest.

Capin remained with Kibung and his family for many weeks, long enough to learn some of the language, pick up some jungle-hunting and survival skills, and exchange his shredded flightsuit for a loincloth. He was an odd sight among the Dayaks: they were a little over 150 centimetres (5 feet) tall and dark of skin and hair; Capin was pale-skinned and red-haired and stood 195 centimetres (6½ feet) tall. But he tried to adapt to Dayak life, eating their food without complaint (including roasted grasshoppers), learning hunting skills, playing with the children. But this was not an idyll: the villagers were frightened of the Japanese, and Kibung told him that the Japanese knew an American plane had crashed in the jungle and were hunting for the flight crew.

Eventually Makahanap heard through the grapevine that these three airmen had been found—Nelson and Harrington, the two men living with the Mongan family, and Capin, living with Kibung's family in the village of Pa' Ogong. Photographer Elmer Philipps was still missing, and no one Makahanap spoke with knew anything about him. Philipps was never found.

## The limits of endurance

On 5 December, thirteen Japanese troops led by an officer named Takahashi and accompanied by a Malay translator arrived at Makahanap's house. They were searching for the survivors of the crash of the B-24—and they expected the Dayaks to help find them. As Makahanap's wife served dinner, Takahashi said, 'The Americans have escaped temporarily but surely they will be captured. I hope the Dayaks under your supervision will know what to do.' Makahanap nodded. His Dayaks indeed knew what to do—already they had moved Corrin, Illerich, Knoch and Haviland to a hut deep in the jungle.

In Pa' Ogong, Kibung also heard that Takahashi was searching for the Americans, so Capin now spent his daylight hours hiding in the jungle, rejoining the family only after dark. The Dayaks had taught him how to remain still for hours on end; previously he had used the skill only when he was hunting with them, but now he was the quarry.

On Christmas Day a runner brought word to Kibung that a Japanese patrol was nearby. Kibung found Capin in his hideout and together they fled further into the jungle. They had only just concealed themselves when the patrol passed within 6 metres (19½ feet) of them. The two men remained in hiding, absolutely silent, for several hours, before Kibung decided it was safe to go back to the longhouse.

## The flight crew after the war

Tom Capin longed to return to Borneo and repay Kibung and the other Dayaks for saving his life, but doctors told him his system had been so weakened by the tropical diseases he had suffered that exposing himself to infection again could be fatal. He remained with his family in Nebraska, where he became a licensed psychotherapist and was ordained a minister of the Methodist Church.

Phil Corrin returned to Los Angeles, enrolled in college, then went to work in the hotel management business. He wrote a memoir of his experiences in Borneo.

John Nelson worked in construction in Idaho, where he married and had a family. He also wrote a memoir of his months with the Dayaks.

Jim Knoch married and together he and his wife started a farm near Sacramento. On one occasion a local organisation invited him to speak about his experiences in Borneo, but he discovered when he finished the talk that most of the audience refused to believe his story.

Dan Illerich had a similar experience when he was asked to address a group of Boy Scouts and their families. One member of the audience wanted to know if his training as an Eagle Scout had kept him alive. 'No,' Illerich replied. In the jungle of Borneo he did not know what was safe to eat; if the Dayaks hadn't found him, he would have starved to death. This answer disappointed his audience.

Eddy Haviland became an attorney. He rarely talked about Borneo, but shortly before his death in 1994 he recorded his reminiscences on tape for his grandchildren.

Takahashi established headquarters in Makahanap's village for tracking down the Americans. It was an uneasy arrangement: the Japanese openly displayed their contempt for the Dayaks, the Dayaks were reluctant to put their families in danger by trying to fight with spears and blowguns men who had automatic weapons and hand-grenades. They tried to be patient with these unwelcome guests, but there was a great deal of aggravation to endure. As a sadistic form of amusement, the soldiers liked to force two Dayak men into a fistfight; the loser was flogged. Despite the Japanese presence, Makahanap still managed to get food and other supplies to the four Americans hidden in the jungle.

In mid-January 1945, a messenger arrived at Makahanap's longhouse with a letter for Takahashi, who by chance was not in the village at the time. The wily Makahanap did not read Japanese, but in the village were two Chinese traders who could read it a little.

Very carefully, one of the merchants steamed open the envelope, then the two men studied the text carefully until they got the gist of the message. The commander of the Japanese garrison at Tarakan had lost patience with Takahashi. It was obvious the Dayaks were playing the patrol for fools. Takahashi was to arrest Makahanap and all his family and bring them to Tarakan for punishment. Makahanap understood that this meant he, his wife and his children would be killed.

Makahanap thanked the traders and went to find the messenger. Despite Takahashi's absence, he told the messenger, he could pass on the information that Takahashi's men were closing in on the Americans; tell the Japanese in Tarakan that in a few more days the flight crew would be captured. As the messenger headed back to the garrison, Makahanap sent his own messenger inviting the headman of the village to a conference in his longhouse.

It was dark before the headman arrived. Sitting before the hearth in his longhouse, Makahanap detailed the outrages of the Japanese. They slapped and beat Dayak men and women for no reason; they showed no respect for the leading members of the village; they threatened to take hostages until the Americans were surrendered; they showed signs of wanting to rape the village women; and now they threatened the lives of Makahanap and his family. The headman agreed that they had reached the limit of their endurance.

The next morning the headman summoned his strongest warriors. As the Japanese patrol and their Malay translator were eating breakfast, the warriors attacked, beheading them all. The Japanese officers at the base camp never learned what happened to the patrol and the translator—it was as if they had vanished. Inexplicably, they never sent a second patrol to investigate.

It was with mixed feelings of shock and relief that the four airmen learned just how far the Dayaks were willing to go to protect them—and themselves—from the Japanese. But they were also beginning to realise that although the Dayaks would fight and kill to defend them, they could not get the Americans to any Allied base: it was too dangerous to travel to the coast of Borneo, which was almost entirely under Japanese control, and there was no place in the jungle where any Allied plane could land to pick them up. They were stranded.

Many weeks later, on 9 April 1945, another messenger came to Makahanap's village, with another letter. This one, amazingly, was for Phil Corrin. It was from a British reconnaissance officer, Major Thomas Harrisson, who commanded seven experienced Australian Special Operations agents, part of the Allies' drive into Borneo. Harrisson's mission was to arm Dayak guerrillas and coordinate their activities against the Japanese who, as the Australian, New Zealand and British troops seized the coast, had retreated into the interior of the island. But Harrisson was also charged, he wrote, 'to look for lost whites and help them get out in any way we can'. He was sending supplies via Dayak bearers, and he urged Corrin and his friends to travel to meet him at the village of Belawit on the Bawang Plain. Then he passed along some good news about the progress of the war: 'You Yanks have taken Iwo Jima and landed on another island 300 miles [483 kilometres] from Japan. Colossal raids on Tokyo. Negros taken. B-24 ships on Palawan. Jolo taken. In Europe, Montgomery and Patton over Rhine, Russians near Berlin.'

Laughing and crying at the same time, the Americans hugged each other, jumping up and down like happy schoolchildren. They had been found; they were going home. To celebrate, Makahanap killed a goat for dinner. Dayak runners carried the news to the other three airmen in hiding.

When the group some days later reached Belawit, a village on a high plateau in north-central Borneo, Major Harrisson greeted them with a round of Scotch whisky. The Bawang Plain was a large open area that over the following weeks Allied engineers fixed up as an airfield. It was also Harrisson's base for directing the Dayak guerrillas, who returned from their raids on the Japanese with fresh heads. These they impaled on spikes which they erected along the airstrip, to give the field spiritual power.

Harrisson worried that Japanese aircraft would try to blow out of the sky the rescue plane bearing the seven Americans, so he staggered their departure. Tom Capin was the first man out, then Jim Knoch. Six days later Phil Corrin and Francis Harrington departed, followed by Eddy Haviland the day after that, then John Nelson and Dan Illerich. All seven were suffering from parasite infestation and tropical diseases, so they spent their first weeks following their rescue in military hospitals. Then they were flown home to the United States. For them, the war was over.

# CHAPTER 22

# A TEXTBOOK OPERATION

## The Rescue of the Civilian Prisoners of Los Baños

O n an autumn day in 1944 Lieutenant Sadaaki Konishi, second in command at the Los Baños internment camp on the Philippine island of Luzon, informed a group of prisoners of his decision to allow them to remove from the guards' storehouse as many sacks of rice as would fit in the prisoners' kitchen. Before the war most of the men could have hefted the 45 kilogram (99 pound) sacks easily, but three years in Los Baños had left them weakened by repeated bouts of malaria, and emaciated by their meagre diet. Yet they went at the task eagerly, buoyed by the belief their families—Los Baños was a camp for civilians—would have full bellies for the first time in many, many months.

Konishi watched as the prisoners struggled in the blazing heat to carry the heavy sacks across the compound. After an hour, the prisoners' kitchen was packed solid; the men were exhausted, but content. Then Konishi announced he had changed his mind— they could not have the rice after all. And they must return all of it to the storehouse immediately.

American troops carrying a wounded soldier during the
battle to liberate the Philippines from the Japanese.

Lieutenant Konishi had discovered that food was an especially effective tool for tormenting the prisoners. Soon after this episode, he declared that the prisoners' kitchen gardens were not theirs to be used to supplement their diet, but belonged to the garrison. As the vegetables and fruit ripened, he confiscated the lot. Then he cut the salt ration, and took depraved satisfaction in watching prisoners suddenly collapse on the ground as vicious cramps from the lack of salt wracked their bodies.

Next he targeted the children. For as long as they had been interned at Los Baños every child had received one egg a day. Konishi eliminated the eggs, then cut the remainder of the children's rations by half.

Bananas, beans and camotes, a type of sweet potato, were readily available from the farms around Los Baños, but again and again Konishi cut the adults' rations, all but removing these vitamin-rich foods from their diet.

Carol Terry, one of the internees at Los Baños, recalled the morning a truck piled high with fresh vegetables pulled into the camp and the produce was dumped on the ground. Konishi declared that at four in the afternoon all prisoners would be free to gather as much of the vegetables as they desired. By then, of course, having sweltered for hours in the sun in humid 43°C (109°F) heat, the vegetables were a rotting mess thick with flies; nothing could be salvaged by the starving prisoners.

The prisoners speculated that Konishi had been driven insane by late-stage syphilis or severe alcoholism. What else could explain his cruel treatment of malnourished people, especially children? But Konishi was not mad—he was, as he described himself, 'the strongest white-race hater in the army'. With more than 2000 whites in his power, he had an easy outlet for his hatred.

## Striking examples of leniency

The Los Baños camp, located at a university agricultural campus 40 kilometres (25 miles) south-east of Manila and 3 kilometres (2 miles) from a lake called Laguna de Bay, had been established to take the overflow of Allied civilian prisoners from the camp at Santo Tomas University in Manila, which at one time held over 8000 inmates, far too many to house, feed and control. And so the Japanese authorities moved about 2100 prisoners to Los Baños. Aside from a dozen US Army nurses and a few servicemen, the inmates were almost entirely businessmen, schoolteachers and professors, Catholic clergy, and Protestant missionaries. Almost all were American apart from a couple of hundred Europeans and Australians.

The first officers to serve as commandants of the camp, Major Tanaka and his second in command, Major Urabe, were humane men who did not starve or mistreat the prisoners. Filipino farmers were allowed into the camp to sell fresh fruits and vegetables, eggs and meat to the inmates. Tanaka did not interfere with the delivery of relief packages via the Philippine Red Cross, nor would he permit the guards to ransack the packages looking for forbidden or subversive items. He also permitted committees of inmates to organise such routine duties as keeping the camp tidy, cleaning the barracks and other buildings, and running their own affairs. Perhaps the greatest relief of all was that Tanaka prevented the Japanese secret police, the Kempei Tai, from harassing the prisoners.

The most striking example of the leniency with which Tanaka administered Los Baños is the story of Martin Meadows. In December 1943 Martin turned thirteen, the age at which Jewish boys make their Bar Mitzvah. His father went to Tanaka with an extraordinary request: would the commandant permit the family to leave the camp for one day so Martin could perform the ceremony in the Manila synagogue? Tanaka gave passes to the boy and his father, but not to his mother—perhaps he was concerned that if he allowed the entire family to leave the camp they would not return. Nonetheless, the Meadows family was grateful to the major.

Commandants like Tanaka administered the camps on behalf of Japan's military, but no detailed rules were laid down for the treatment of the prisoners. If a commandant wished to be lenient or brutal, the military authorities did not care, so long as order was maintained and prisoners did not escape. The commandant of another internment camp at nearby Santo Tomas had in general treated the inmates kindly, but when two prisoners escaped the Kempei Tai were allowed to seize several men from the runaways' barracks and torture them for information.

Although Japan's representatives had signed the Third Geneva Convention of 1929, which called for the humane treatment of prisoners of war and internees, including adequate food and medical treatment, the Japanese parliament, the Diet, had never ratified the treaty. Consequently, commanders of prison camps had a free hand to treat POWs and internees as they saw fit.

The end of the war in the Philippines: cheering Filipinos greeting American forces as they push on to Manila.

In July 1944 Tanaka and Urabe were transferred from Los Baños and two new men took over—Major Iwanaka and Lieutenant Sadaaki Konishi. Iwanaka struck internees who met him as mentally confused, possibly senile, and it was soon obvious that he was commander in name only. Konishi took over the administration, transforming a camp where conditions had been tolerable into a nightmarish place where even children were not spared.

## Would Los Baños be next?

After lights-out at Los Baños on 12 February 1945—Abraham Lincoln's birthday—Freddy Zervoulakas, the nineteen-year-old son of a Greek father and a Filipino mother, crept underneath the barbed wire along the perimeter of the camp and escaped into the jungle. He kept running until he was found by Filipino guerrillas.

The prisoners had heard that General Douglas MacArthur had returned to the Philippines, and that US armed forces were driving back the Japanese and heading for Manila. Freddy asked if the guerrillas knew whether the Americans were planning to liberate the prison camps.

The answer was yes. In January MacArthur had expressed concern that the Japanese would massacre all their prisoners before they could be liberated by the Americans. Such a thing had happened on Palawan in December 1944, where guards herded 150 American POWs into underground bunkers, sealed the doors, then set the bunkers on fire, burning the defenceless men alive. To prevent a repeat of the tragedy, Army Rangers and Filipino guerrillas had already raided the camp at Cabanatuan, liberating more than 500 POWs (see chapter 20), and the 1st Cavalry had rescued over 3500 prisoners at Santo Tomas. Would Los Baños be freed next, the prisoners wanted to know.

The Americans had found that Filipino guerrillas were invaluable in any rescue mission. In the Manila area, however, the situation was complicated: there were at least four major guerrilla groups—the Hunters-ROTC (Reserve Officers Training Corps) Guerrillas, comprised of college students who had been cadets at the Philippine Military Academy at the time of the Japanese invasion; another outfit calling itself President Quezon's Own Guerrillas; Filipinos of Chinese descent who formed the Chinese Guerrillas of Luzon; and the Hukbalahaps, a group whose agenda included driving the Japanese from the Philippines and then bringing about a Marxist revolution. US Army Major Jay D. Vanderpool had the task of persuading these various groups to work together. He managed to form them into a new unit, the General Guerrilla Command of Luzon, and gave them their first assignment—the liberation of Los Baños.

When Freddy Zervoulakas crawled back under the barbed wire, he brought with him a copy of the letter Vanderpool had distributed to the guerrillas, ordering them to attack Los Baños and rescue the inmates. Freddy delivered the letter to the committee of prisoners who administered inmate affairs; the committee decided to do nothing, to wait for the liberators to come to them. Given Konishi's savagery, it would be most unwise to provoke him through any sign of open rebellion or act of sabotage.

## Doing the impossible

Dorothy Still Danner, a US Army nurse, had night duty in the camp hospital on 23 February. Like her fellow inmates she was hungry and demoralised. 'We were all feeling pretty low,' she recalled years later. But she had a newborn baby girl to tend, Lois Kathleen McCoy, whose mother was so undernourished she was unable to breastfeed. Danner was trying to get the infant to take the little powdered milk that remained in the prisoners' stores. At seven in the morning she heard the roar of aircraft flying low overhead. She rushed outside and looked up to see, from a height of only 150 metres (492 feet), a blizzard of paratroopers descending into the camp. Then came the crash of amtracs (amphibious vehicles) breaking through the fence at the rear of the compound. One drove directly to the hospital where a stunned Nurse Danner watched as American troops jumped out and ran towards her. 'Oh, we never saw anything so handsome in our lives,' she said. 'They looked so healthy and so lively.'

Six days before the raid Pete Miles, a civilian engineer, had imitated Freddy Zervoulakas, crawling under the barbed wire and running into the jungle. Like Freddy, Miles was lucky—guerrillas found him and at his request took him to the 11th Airborne Division headquarters at Paranaque. The 11th had been slugging it out with Japanese forces outside Manila, trying to destroy the Genko Line, a series of pillboxes that defended the south side of the capital. The 11th was commanded by Major General

Joseph Swing, who had been given two missions by MacArthur—break through the Genko Line, and rescue the prisoners at Los Baños. Destroying the Genko Line involved hard fighting, but reaching Los Baños seemed almost impossible—it was 40 kilometres (25 miles) behind enemy lines. None of the camps liberated thus far had been so deep in Japanese-occupied territory.

The plan for the raid was complicated, involving paratroopers and amtracs as well as a land attack. What the 11th needed was detailed information about the layout of the camp and the routines of the guards and the prisoners; that information arrived when the guerrillas brought Pete Miles into headquarters. Miles gave the officers in charge of the raid everything they needed to know. He also urged them to hurry—80 per cent of the prisoners suffered from at least one tropical disease, and several people died every day. Unlike Freddy Zervoulakas, Miles did not return to the camp, he remained with the soldiers and guerrillas who were planning the raid.

Thanks to Miles, the raid began to look feasible. The paratroopers would be the first inside the camp, dropping in at 7 am when the guards were performing callisthenics. Simultaneously, amtracs from across the bay would smash through the wire at the rear of the camp. The guerrillas would kill the sentries along the perimeter, and a combat team would attack the main gate while positioning themselves to intercept and destroy any Japanese reinforcements that might attempt to reach Los Baños.

The night before the raid, a reconnaissance platoon commanded by Lieutenant George Skau met the leaders of the guerrillas at the schoolhouse in the nearby barrio of Nanhaya. The guerrillas had brought along two men who knew the camp intimately—Ben Edwards, another escapee, and the intrepid Freddy Zervoulakas, who couldn't bear to wait idly to be rescued. Skau and the guerrilla commanders broke their men up into teams, and Edwards and Zervoulakas were each assigned to a team to help them find their way inside Los Baños. Now it was just a matter of getting in place and waiting until zero hour.

## A flawless military operation

Willie Jamieson and Herman Beard, two Protestant missionaries interned in Los Baños, had risen early to do some laundry before roll call. As he scrubbed away, Jamieson thought he heard the sound of motors, but he dismissed it as wishful thinking. Then the Reverend Beard shouted, 'Oh, Willie, look!' Glancing up, Jamieson saw the paratroopers floating down into the camp; he wasn't sure what surprised him more, the sight of his rescuers or his friend's excitement. 'It was the first time in three and a half years,' Jamieson recalled later, 'I had seen Herman show any measure of excitement.'

As the paratroopers landed, the guerrillas leaped up from the tall grass outside camp, cut through the barbed wire, and charged the Japanese guards who were performing their morning exercise routine, most of them unarmed, and taken completely by surprise. Some of the guerrillas targeted the guards in the watchtowers. Most joined forces with the paratroopers to defeat the garrison. Some of the guerrillas were armed with 45 centimetre (18 inch) bolo knives. Jamieson said later that the guerrillas so armed 'weren't just satisfied to kill the Japs, they cut them to pieces'. Within 45 minutes the battle was over, and every member of the Japanese garrison was either dead or in hiding; among those who had got away was Sadaaki Konishi.

The original plan called for the evacuation of the prisoners overland to Manila, but Major Henry Burgess, commander of the 1st Paratrooper Battalion, now aware that thousands of Japanese troops were in the area, feared they would never get through without heavy casualties. On the spot he altered the plan, ordering the fifty-four amtracs of the 672nd Amphibious Battalion to shuttle the rescued prisoners across Laguna de Bay to the town of Mamatid. The troops and guerrillas would cover them; once the civilians were safe, the amtracs would start ferrying the troops and the guerrillas to Mamatid.

Getting the prisoners organised for a quick getaway proved impossible. Severely stressed by sickness and malnutrition, most were now so dazed by the unexpected rescue that they wandered aimlessly round the camp, or returned to their barracks to pick through personal possessions. Major Burgess could not wait. He ordered his men to set fire to the barracks, and gently direct the newly liberated civilians to the rear of the camp where the amtracs were lined up.

It took most of the morning to set up the evacuation, but by noon the amtracs were moving back and forth across the lake at a steady pace, and the crowd waiting on the beach was thinning out. Burgess and his troops made several sweeps through the camp to make sure no one had been left behind.

It took two hours for an amtrac to make the journey across the lake to Mamatid. Several times Japanese troops fired on the vehicles, but no one was hurt. Finally, at three in the afternoon, the last amtrac left Los Baños.

The mission was a complete success. Two paratroopers and two guerrillas were killed during the raid, but not one of the camp's 2147 prisoners was killed or wounded. It was a flawless military operation, and the only rescue during World War II that involved the use of paratroopers.

On the sixtieth anniversary of the raid General Colin Powell, at the time Chairman of the US Joint Chiefs of Staff, paid special tribute to the 11th Airborne Division: 'I doubt that any airborne unit in the world will ever be able to rival the Los Baños prison raid. It is the textbook airborne operation for all ages and all armies.'

## Retaliation

Lieutenant Sadaaki Konishi had evaded the rescue forces, and a few days later he returned with a large Japanese force. They went house to house in every barrio in the Los Baños neighbourhood, dragging entire families from their homes and tying them to the stilts that supported the houses. Then they set the houses on fire.

The first Americans to discover this atrocity were members of the 11th Airborne, among them the men who had liberated Los Baños. Major Burgess estimated that Konishi was responsible for the murder of 1500 Filipino men, women and children.

Konishi did not escape from the Philippines; he was captured by American troops; at first his captors did not realise who he was, but eventually they discovered his true identity. For his brutality to the civilian prisoners at Los Baños, and for the massacre of the Filipino villagers outside the camp, he was put on trial for war crimes, convicted and sentenced to death by hanging.

Japanese leaders stand for sentencing for war crimes by the International Military Tribunal of the Far East in Tokyo in 1948. Seven were sentenced to death by hanging, sixteen to life imprisonment.

# Bibliography

## Books

Ambrose, Stephen E. *Band of Brothers: E Company, 506th Regiment, 101st Airborne, from Normandy to Hitler's Eagle's Nest*. Simon & Schuster, 1992.

Aubrac, Lucie, *Outwitting the Gestapo*, translated by Konrad Bieber with the assistance of Betsy Wing. University of Nebraska Press, 1993.

Carse, Robert. *Dunkirk 1940*. Prentice-Hall, 1970.

Churchill, Winston S. *Blood, Sweat, and Tears*. G.P. Putnam's Sons, 1941.

Cogan, Frances B. *Captured: The Japanese Internment of American Civilians in the Philippines, 1941–1945*. University of Georgia Press, 2000.

Crowe, David M. *Oskar Schindler: The Untold Story of His Life, Wartime Activities, and the True Story Behind the List*. Westview Press, 2004.

Dalin, David G. *The Myth of Hitler's Pope: How Pope Pius XII Rescued Jews from the Nazis*. Regnery Publishing, 2005.

Deaglio, Enrico. *The Banality of Goodness: The Story of Giorgio Perlasca*, translated by Gregory Conti. University of Notre Dame Press, 1998.

D'Este, Carol. *Patton: A Genius for War*. Harper Perennial, 1996

Donovan, Robert J. *PT 109: John F. Kennedy in WWII*. McGraw-Hill, 2001.

Duus, Masayo Umezawa. *Unlikely Liberators: The Men of the 100th and 442nd*, translated by Peter Duus. University of Hawaii Press, 1987.

Eby, Cecil D. *Hungary at War: Civilians and Soldiers in World War II*. Pennsylvania State University Press, 1998.

Eisner, Peter. *The Freedom Line*. William Morrow, 2004.

Endelman, Todd M. *The Jews of Britain, 1656 to 2000*. University of California Press, 2000.

Farago, Ladislas. *Patton: Ordeal and Triumph*. Westholme Publishing, 1964.

Frischauer, Willi and Jackson, Robert. *The Altmark Affair*. Macmillan, 1955.

Fralon, José-Alain. *A Good Man in Evil Times: The Story of Aristides de Sousa Mendes, the Unknown Hero who Saved Countless Lives in World War II*, translated by Peter Graham. Carroll & Graf, 2001.

Freeman, Gregory A. *The Forgotten 500: The Untold Story of the Men Who Risked All for the Greatest Rescue Mission of World War II*. NAL Caliber, 2007.

*German Crimes in Poland, Volume 1*, compiled by the Central Commission for the Investigation of German Crimes in Poland, Warsaw, 1946.

Glines, Carroll V. *The Doolittle Raid: America's Daring First Strike Against Japan*. Orion Books, 1988.

Goldberger, Leo. *The Rescue of the Danish Jews: Moral Courage under Stress*. New York University Press, 1987.

Gordon, Bertram M. (ed.) *Historical Dictionary of World War II France: The Occupation, Vichy, and the Resistance, 1938–1946*. Greenwood Press, 1998.

Harris, Mark Jonathan and Oppenheimer, Deborah. *Into the Arms of Strangers: Stories of the Kindertransport*. Bloomsbury, 2000.

Hawkins, Ian. (ed.) *B-17s Over Berlin: Personal Stories from the 95th Bomb Group*. Brassey's, 1995.

Heimann, Judith M. *The Airmen and the Headhunters: A True Story of Lost Soldiers, Heroic Tribesmen and the Unlikeliest Rescue of World War II*. Harcourt, 2007.

Karonczay, Karoly. *Refugees in Hungary Shelter from the Storm during World War II*, translated by Eva Barcza-Bessenyey. Matthias Corvinus Publishing, 1999.

Kershaw, Alex. *The Longest Winter: The Battle of the Bulge and the Epic Story of WWII's Most Decorated Platoon*. Da Capo Press, 2005.

Lapide, Pinchas E. *The Last Three Popes and the Jews*. Souvenir Press, 1967.

Lawson, Red W., edited by Robert Considine. *Thirty Seconds Over Tokyo*. Random House, 1943.

Levine, Hillel. *In Search of Sugihara: The Elusive Japanese Diplomat who Risked his Life to Rescue 10,000 Jews from the Holocaust*. The Free Press, 1996.

Lightoller, Charles Herbert. *Titanic and Other Ships*. Nicholson & Watson, 1935.

Manchester, William. *American Caesar: Douglas MacArthur 1880–1964*. Little, Brown, 1978.

May, Ernst R. *Strange Victory: Hitler's Conquest of France*. Hill & Wang, 2000.

Nelson, Craig. *The First Heroes: The Extraordinary Story of the Doolittle Raid—America's First World War II Victory*. Penguin Books, 2002.

O'Brien, Michael. *John F. Kennedy: A Biography*. Macmillan, 2006.

Rosenfeld, Harvey. *Raoul Wallenberg: Angel of Rescue*. Prometheus Books, 1982.

Saari, Peggy and Saari, Aaron Maurice (eds). *The Holocaust and World War II Almanac*. Gale Group, 2001.

Sarfatti, Michele. *The Jews in Mussolini's Italy: From Equality to Persecution*, translated by John and Anne C. Tedeschi. University of Wisconsin Press, 2006.

Schoenbrun, David. *Soldiers of the Night: The Story of the French Resistance*. E.P. Dutton, 1980.

Sebag-Montefiore, Hugh. *Dunkirk: Fight to the Last Man*. Viking, 2006.

Sides, Hampton. *Ghost Soldiers: The Forgotten Epic Story of World War II's Most Dramatic Mission*. Doubleday, 2001.

Smith, George W. *MacArthur's Escape: John 'Wild Man' Bulkeley and the Rescue of an American Hero*. Zenith Press, 2005.

Smith, Steven Trent. *The Rescue: A True Story of Courage and Survival*. John Wiley, 2003.

Stille, Alexander. *Benevolence and Betrayal: Five Italian Jewish Families under Fascism*. Penguin Books, 1991.

Tucker, Spencer C. and Roberts, Priscilla Mary (eds). *Encyclopedia of World War II: A Political, Social and Military History*, 5 volumes. ABC-Clio, 2005.

Yahil, Leni. *The Rescue of Danish Jewry: Test of a Democracy*, translated by Morris Gradel. The Jewish Publication Society of America, 1969.

## Articles

Bradsher, Greg. 'The "Z Plan" story: Japan's 1944 naval battle strategy drifts into U.S. hands', *Prologue Magazine*, Fall 2005.

Danner, Dorothy Still. 'Dorothy Still Danner: reminiscences of a nurse POW', *Navy Medicine*, May–June 1992.

'The Eagle of Yugoslavia', *Time*, 25 May 1942.

Gluekstein, Fred. 'General George S. Patton and the Lipizzaners', *Army*, June 2006.

Harder, Ben. 'Has Ballard found JFK's PT-109?' *National Geographic News*, 29 May 2002.

Kaszeta, Daniel J. 'Lithuanian resistance to foreign occupation 1940-1952', *Lituanus: Lithuanian Quarterly Journal of Arts and Sciences*, Volume 34, No. 3, Fall 1988.

King, Michael J. 'Leavenworth Papers: Rangers: selected combat operations in World War II', *Combat Studies Institute*, June 1985.

McGowan, Sam. 'Liberating Los Baños', HistoryNet.com.

Newman, Aubrey. 'The miracle of the children: an address for the Second National Holocaust Memorial Day, 27th January 2002', University of Leicester.

Steinhouse, Herbert. 'The real Oskar Schindler', *Saturday Night*, April 1994.

Wheeler, Shin. 'Old men remember', *The Bulletin*, 19 October 2000.

## Web Sites

The Association of Dunkirk Little Ships: www.adls.org.uk

The American Experience: Bataan Rescue: www.pbs.org

The Comete Line: home.clara.net/clinchy/neeball.htm

The Doolittle Raid: www.doolittleraider.com

The Doolittle Tokyo Raiders: www.doolittletokyoraiders.com

Go For Broke Educational Center: www.goforbroke.org

Halsey-Doolittle Raid, April 1942:
www.ibiblio.org/hyperwar/AAF/rep/Doolittle/Report.html

The International Raoul Wallenberg Foundation:
www.raoulwallenberg.net/?en/wallenberg

Lieutenant John F. Kennedy, USN: www.history.navy.mil/faqs/faq60-2.htm
The Kindertransport Association: www.kindertransport.org
Aristides de Sousa Mendes:
    www.jewishvirtuallibrary.org/jsource/biography/Mendes.html
Giorgio Perlasca: www.giorgioperlasca.it/inglese/intro.html
PT Boats, Inc.: www.ptboats.org
Sara Salkahazi: www.salkahazisara.com/index_en.html
The World Famous Lipizzaner Stallions: www.lipizzaner.com

## Acknowledgments

Writing a book is often considered a solitary occupation. In fact, every writer needs a small army of allies, and I have been very fortunate in mine. My first word of thanks goes to my long-time friend Joseph Cummins, who recommended me to Murdoch Books. My publisher, Diana Hill, and the editors at Murdoch Books are among the very finest I have ever worked with—smart, imaginative, helpful, and in every way professional. And I will always be grateful to the staff members of the libraries at the University of Connecticut and Fairfield University, and the Connecticut state library system.

## Image credits

Corbis: front cover, pp. 8–9, p. 13, p. 35, p. 41, p. 45, p. 55, pp. 58–59, p. 62, p. 74, pp. 78–79, p. 85, pp. 90–91, p. 101, p. 103, pp. 112–113, p. 115, p. 132, p. 135, p. 141, p. 146, p. 153, p. 157, p. 165, p. 167, pp. 170–171, p. 173, p. 179, p. 189, p. 191, pp. 196–197, pp. 202–203, pp. 210–211, p. 222, p. 235, p. 249, p. 253, p. 258, p. 273, p. 274, p. 284, p. 287, pp. 292–293

Getty Images: back cover, p. 11, pp. 16–17, p. 25, pp. 30–31, p. 39, pp. 42–43, pp. 52–53, p. 123, p. 129, p. 192, p. 205, p. 207, p. 219, p. 233, p. 245, p. 279, p. 301, p. 304, p. 309

photolibrary.com: p. 71

United States Holocaust Memorial Museum: p. 217
'The views or opinions expressed in this book, and the context in which the images are used, do not necessarily reflect the views or policy of, nor imply approval or endorsement by, the United Stated Holocaust Memorial Museum.'

United States Navy: p. 261

# Index

Published in 2009 by Pier 9, an imprint of Murdoch Books Pty Limited

Murdoch Books Australia
Pier 8/9
23 Hickson Road
Millers Point NSW 2000
Phone: +61 (0) 2 8220 2000
Fax: +61 (0) 2 8220 2558
www.murdochbooks.com.au

Murdoch Books UK Limited
Erico House, 6th Floor
93–99 Upper Richmond Road
Putney, London SW15 2TG
Phone: +44 (0) 20 8785 5995
Fax: +44 (0) 20 8785 5985
www.murdochbooks.co.uk

Publisher: Diana Hill
Editor: Anne Savage
Designer: Katy Wall
Photo researcher: Amanda McKittrick

National Library of Australia Cataloguing-in-Publication Data

Author:          Craughwell, Thomas J., 1956–
Title:           Great Rescues of World War II / Thomas Craughwell.
ISBN:            9781741964523 (pbk.)
Notes:           Includes index.
                 Bibliography.
Subjects:        World War, 1939–1945—Search and rescue operations.
                 World War, 1939–1945—Jews—rescue.
Dewey Number: 940.531835

A catalogue record for this book is available from the British Library.

Printed by 1010 Printing International Limited in 2009. PRINTED IN CHINA.